One Quarter of Humanity

One Quarter of Humanity

Malthusian Mythology and
Chinese Realities, 1700–2000

JAMES Z. LEE AND WANG FENG

HARVARD UNIVERSITY PRESS
Cambridge, Massachusetts, and London, England

First Harvard University Press paperback edition, 2001

Library of Congress Cataloging-in-Publication Data

Lee, James Z., 1952–
    One quarter of humanity : Malthusian mythology and Chinese realities,
  1700–2000 / James Z. Lee and Wang Feng.
      p. cm.
    Includes bibliographical references.
    ISBN 0-674-63908-1 (cloth)
    ISBN 0-674-00709-3 (pbk.)
    1. Demography—China.   2. Marriage—China.   3. Birth control—China.
  4. Infanticide—China.   5. China—Population.   I. Wang Feng.   II. Title.
  HB3578.L44   1999
  304.6'0951—dc21   99-11863

To Sandy and Haiou

After the desire for food, the most powerful and general of our desires is the passion between the sexes, taken in an enlarged sense. Of the happiness spread over human love by this passion, very few are unconscious. Virtuous love, exalted by friendship, seems to be that sort of mixture of sensual and intellectual enjoyment, particularly suited to the nature of man, and most powerfully calculated to awaken the sympathies of the soul, and produce the most exquisite gratifications. Perhaps there is scarcely a man who has once experienced the genuine delight of virtuous love, however great his intellectual pleasures may have been, who does not look back to that period, as the sunny spot in his whole life, where his imagination loves to bask, which he recollects and contemplates with the fondest regard, and which he would most wish to live over again.

—THOMAS R. MALTHUS, *AN ESSAY ON THE PRINCIPLE OF POPULATION* (1803)

Acknowledgments

We wrote this book in three cities—Pasadena, Irvine, and Beijing—over two and a half years. The work that went into it, however, is the product of ten years of collaboration, both at Caltech and over great distances.

In this book we have borrowed liberally from our collaborative publications with Cameron Campbell and others and have drawn upon the insights of other scholars, to whom we want to express gratitude here. First and foremost is our colleague and friend Cameron Campbell, whose intellectual companionship and editorial assistance resulted in many contributions to these pages. In addition we owe thanks to Li Bozhong for helping us to revise a 1996 conference paper that appears as Chapter 3 here.

Many other friends assisted in other ways. Cai Yong helped produce the map. Tommy Bengtsson, Guo Zhigang, Andy Hinde, Hao Hongsheng, Jan Oldervoll, Roger Schofield, Gunnar Thorvaldsen, Hanne Willert, and Xie Zhenming provided vital information in a timely fashion, while Gu Baochang, Tamara Hareven, and Wu Chengming supplied important bibliographic help. Mark Elliott, Hill Gates, Ramon Myers, William Rowe, Charles Tilly, Susan Watkins, and Arthur Wolf read an early draft and gave useful advice; George Alter, Tommy Bengtsson, Mark Elvin, Charlotte Furth, François Godement, Susan

Greenhalgh, Morgan Kousser, William Lavely, Li Bozhong, John McNeill, Kenneth Pomeranz, David Reher, Roger Schofield, John Shepherd, Dorothy Solinger, Judith Treas, Noriko Tsuya, R. Bin Wong, E. A. Wrigley, and Zhao Zhongwei also wrote extensive comments on both substance and style. Several anonymous readers who reviewed the manuscript gave careful advice that helped us to improve the book in important ways, as did our editors Michael Aronson and Ann Hawthorne.

We also thank the five institutions and their staffs that housed us during this period: the California Institute of Technology, the University of California at Irvine, the Chinese Center for Advanced Science and Technology in Beijing, the East-West Center in Honolulu, and the University of Hawaii. Caltech in particular made crucial financial and other contributions by inviting Wang Feng to teach for four quarters. We are grateful to our colleagues, Provosts Barclay Kamb and Steven Koonin, and division chairs David Grether and John Ledyard for arranging these visits.

Finally, we thank our families and friends, who have sustained us throughout. Andrea, Andrew, and Max: thanks is not enough.

Contents

Illustrations

Figures

Map

Tables

One Quarter of Humanity

PART I

Mythologies

CHAPTER 1

Introduction

A history of the early migrations and settlements of mankind, with the motives which prompted them, would illustrate in a striking manner the constant tendency in the human race to increase beyond the means of subsistence.

MALTHUS, *AN ESSAY ON THE PRINCIPLE OF POPULATION* (1826)

Malthusian Legacy

During the last 300 years world population has increased tenfold. In 1700 world population was less than 700 million; today it stands at over 6 billion. This dramatic increase is the result of a gradual decline in mortality and an increase in fertility that began in the late eighteenth century. In consequence, world population doubled to 1.25 billion by 1850, to 2.5 billion by 1950, and to 5 billion by 1985. While population growth rates have recently begun to decline throughout much of the world because of a sharp reduction in fertility, our population is expected to double again, to 11–12 billion, before we stabilize in the year 2200.[1]

Population has been a central focus of social theory since the eighteenth century. All the classic economists—particularly Adam Smith, David Ricardo, and Robert Malthus—were preoccupied with the relationship between population and social welfare. Their writings have greatly influenced our thinking on the processes and consequences of demographic change. Even with the transformation of modern economic growth in the late twentieth century, the Malthusian concern that population growth imposes constraints on economic growth and social well-being has persisted. Economic concerns have moreover expanded into ecological anxiety.[2] While we now believe economic constraints to be increasingly elastic, we also regard environmental constraints as increasingly inelastic.[3]

The Malthusian legacy is just as strong in our understanding of population control. In his famous essays on population, Malthus identified two general types of checks.[4] Either population growth was controlled by restricting nuptiality, which Malthus termed the preventive check and identified with the modern Western world; or population grew uncontrollably until increasing poverty led to rises in mortality, which Malthus termed the positive check and associated with the nonmodern Western world and the non-Western world. For Malthus, family planning required a uniquely modern Western ability to calculate consciously the costs and benefits of having children and to decide to delay or curtail marriage. While the rise of contraceptive and abortive technology has enabled us to control fertility, replacing the previous preventive check, our understanding of population mechanisms in the premodern world is still fundamentally Malthusian.

Modern science and technology, however, have fundamentally changed the nature of population dynamics. Worldwide, fertility and mortality have recently declined with the discoveries and dissemination of modern medicine and public health measures. This sequence of an initial decline in mortality, followed by a rise in population and an eventual decline in fertility, is often conceptualized as the "demographic transition." Few changes in population behavior have been as universal or have had as profound an effect on individuals as the rise in life expectancy in recent centuries on the one hand, and the decline in childbearing in this century on the other hand. At the same time, few demographic processes have had as global an impact as the population explosion.

The speed of such technological diffusion, if not technological innovation, appears to be fundamentally linked to cultural constructs and social formation. This linkage is especially strong with regard to reproductive technology. Family planning is associated with our increased ability to calculate consciously the costs and benefits of having children and to decide deliberately to control reproduction. Similarly, the development and dissemination of medical technology require a new sense of control over ourselves and the natural world.

Moreover, the rise of such consciousness appears to be connected to the spread of individual decision making associated with the rise of small families, the increase in literacy, the emergence and diffusion of Western individualism, and the growing penetration of market economies. Scholars such as John Hajnal (1965, 1982) and Alan Macfarlane

(1978, 1986, 1987) have suggested that the European origins of the demographic transition, the European roots of individualism, and even the European development of nineteenth-century capitalism are intertwined and embedded in a European family and demographic culture that encouraged such revolutionary social and economic changes. By identifying and linking demographic systems both more explicitly and more systematically to social, economic, and cultural systems than Malthus did himself, these and other contemporary social theorists have elevated the level of Malthusian discourse and have amplified the theoretical implications of Malthusian formulations (Goody 1996).

In such a conception, non-Western patriarchy, social formation, and economic processes are all subsumed in a universal binary other that by its very nature is antimodern. China, in particular, is singled out as the personification of this "other"—partly as a consequence of its size, partly as a consequence of its better-documented history. Malthus specifically identified China as the prime example of a society dominated by the positive check and virtually devoid of any preventive check.[5] Similarly, Hajnal (1982) and Roger Schofield (1989) have proposed that if the Western family system stood at one extreme of the social spectrum, China, together with India, occupied the other.[6]

This conflation and confusion originate at least partially from a paucity of empirical knowledge about Chinese society and population. Even two decades ago there were virtually no demographers of China and few available data. China was at once the largest and the least known of any historical or contemporary human population.[7] As a result, while research on Western population history has confirmed Malthus' observations of Western, particularly English, population behavior,[8] the absence of similar studies of Chinese population history has facilitated the perpetuation of the binary opposition elaborated by Malthus.[9] Superficial observations by eighteenth-century European travelers have become time-honored truths; Malthusian hypotheses have become accepted theories.

All this, however, is beginning to change. Recent censuses and sample surveys have illuminated the demographic history of the twentieth century.[10] Similarly, new data and methods have begun to illuminate the demographic history of the eighteenth and nineteenth centuries.[11] Preliminary research has reconstructed the population history of virtually all the 1.7 billion Chinese alive since 1950 and 0.5 million of the 3 billion Chinese alive in the eighteenth, nineteenth, and early twentieth centuries.[12] Although this research is only beginning to uncover regional variations in Chinese population behavior, the broad contrasts with both Western and Malthusian population behavior are already apparent.

As a result, we can better appreciate the significance of China's historical and contemporary populations. The third-largest country in the world in terms of area, China is the largest in terms of population.[13] There are currently 1.2 billion Chinese, one-fifth of world population. This share was even larger in the past.[14] Figure 1.1 compares Chinese and world population figures over the past two millennia, virtually the entire period for which we have recorded demographic data. For most of that time, one of every three to four human beings has been Chinese.

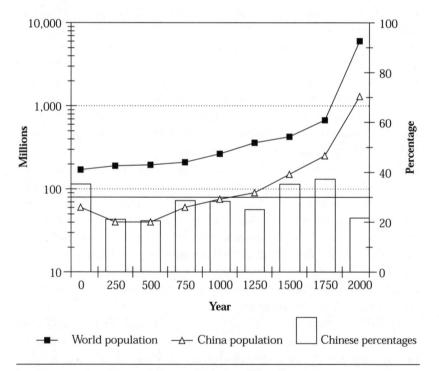

Figure 1.1. China and world population, 0–2000 A.D.
Sources: Durand (1974), McEvedy and Jones (1978), Biraben (1979), Zhao Wenlin and Xie (1988).

In this book we summarize our current understanding of Chinese demography and construct a stylized model of Chinese demographic behavior that confronts the "ideal" model first proposed by Malthus and elaborated by others on the basis of European, especially English, population behavior. By revising the current understanding of Chinese society and economy over the last three centuries, Chinese demographic behavior not only provides an alternative demographic model to the Malthusian model of preventive and positive checks; it also reveals that many differences in population behavior between East and West are a product of regional and historical differences in social organization rather than of different population checks.[15]

Chinese Realities

The Chinese Demographic System

Four distinctive aspects of Chinese historical population behavior that persist today qualify the Malthusian understanding of comparative population behavior in general and of China's in particular. Together they characterize what we call the Chinese demographic system.[16]

Mortality is the first such legacy. Whereas Malthus thought that "famines were the most powerful and frequent of all the positive checks to the Chinese population" (1826/1986, 109), recent historical studies suggest that female infanticide may have been more important in late imperial China (Lavely and Wong 1998).[17] In some Chinese populations, families regularly practiced infanticide to regulate the number and sex of their children, with recorded rates for some years as high as 40 percent of female births.[18] Even boys were vulnerable to such practices. By contrast, infanticide has been largely unknown in Western society—at least since the seventeenth century.[19] Although infanticide declined spectacularly in China during the early twentieth century, sex ratios continue to be biased toward males, implying the continued practice of infanticide and neglect, though at several orders of magnitude lower than in the past. As a result, the average number of female children surviving to adulthood was much lower than in the West (Lee and Campbell 1997, 62, 67).

Excess female infant and child mortality produced the second distinctive feature of the Chinese demographic system: a gender-unbalanced marriage market. Females married universally and early; males married later or not at all. The shortage of marriageable females was exacerbated by the practice of polygyny and the discouragement of female remarriage. But whereas marriage in the West has always been restricted for both sexes, marriage in China, at least among females, has always been universal.[20] In the nineteenth century, for example, while less than 60 percent of females aged 15–50 in Western Europe were currently married (Coale and Treadway 1986), close to 90 percent of their Chinese counterparts were so married. Even in the twentieth century, with marriage increasingly common in Europe, at least 5 to 10 percent of all women are unmarried by age 45. In China the corresponding share of spinsters is virtually zero.[21]

Persistently high nuptiality, however, did not inflate Chinese fertility, because of the third distinctive aspect of the Chinese demographic system, the low level of fertility within marriage.[22] While Western married women in the absence of contraception had on average a total marital fertility rate (TMFR)—the number of children a married woman would bear in her life time if she experienced at each age the fertility rates of a given year—of 7.5 to 9,[23] Chinese married women had a TMFR of 6 or less. This low marital fertility is one of the most distinctive features of the Chinese demographic system. Contrary to the perception of Malthus and his contemporaries that Chinese fertility was relatively high, overall fertility was probably not much higher than in Europe, while marital fertility was significantly lower.[24]

When fertility declined, it declined later and faster in China than in the West. As late as 1970, the Chinese total fertility rate (TFR)—the number of children any woman would bear in her lifetime if she experienced at each age the fertility rates of a given year—was still almost 6. By 1995, however, the Chinese TFR was around 2. Although fertility in both China and the West has fallen to or below replacement level—2.1 children per couple—the Chinese decline took less than a quarter of a century, while the Western decline took more than half a century.[25] Chinese marital fertility, in other words, not only was much lower than Western marital fertility; it also declined far faster.

Finally, despite the strong Chinese preoccupation with lineage perpetuation and a social welfare system that relied on family and kin, because of low fertility and low survival rates, Chinese parents frequently had to resort to fictive kinship to replace biological productivity.[26] Whereas adoption was virtually nonexistent in the early modern West and only 1 in every 100 or 1,000 children in the West is adopted today (Goody 1983), as many as 1 in every 10 to 100 children in

China are brought up by nonbiological parents. Unlike Western adoption, which in most cases involves infants or very young children, many adoptions in China involve adolescents, and some involve adults. Virtually all such older adoptees are male; some are daughters' husbands. By contrast, many younger adoptees are female and include sons' wives (A. Wolf and Huang 1980).

Thus the Chinese demographic system was characterized by a multiplicity of choices that balanced romance with arranged marriage, marital passion with marital restraint, and parental love with the decision to kill or give away children, and the adoption of other children. In contrast to the Malthusian paradigm, human agency in China was not restricted to nuptiality. Moreover, it was exercised largely at the collective rather than individual level. Chinese individuals constantly adjusted their demographic behavior according to collective circumstances to maximize collective utility. The distinctive features of Chinese demographic behavior were, in particular, consequences of two salient features of China's historical legacy: patrilineal ancestor worship and bureaucratic state autocracy.

The Chinese Demographic Transition

These and other distinctive features and traditions produced a different demographic transition process in China from that in the West. In the West the transition process was largely discontinuous; in China the process has been largely continuous. Moreover, while the transition in the West came about largely through an extension of individual agency from nuptiality to fertility and mortality behavior, the Chinese demographic transition reflects the expansion of the collective decision-making process from the family to the state.[27]

The main process in the decline of Western fertility was a shift from delayed marriage to birth control within marriage.[28] For Westerners, the idea of controlling birth within marriage was largely new and required the bold adoption of novel techniques and novel thinking. Technological innovations introduced new methods of contraception. At the same time, cultural diffusion popularized the idea that family planning was both desirable and achievable. Individuals now could marry earlier and limit their fertility within marriage.

In contrast, the demographic transition in China was the product of several behavioral changes stemming from a long tradition of demographic planning. For Chinese, planning demographic events has always been an important part of life. Controlling childbearing and child survival is not a new concept. Therefore, transitions did not require new thinking either to restrict reproduction or to reduce morbidity and mortality, just new institutional programs and new technology. Whereas Chinese parents in the past curtailed their fertility or killed their children in response to the dictates of household economy, today they reduce their fertility largely in response to the perceived needs and strong dictates of the national economy, and increasingly to maximize their family welfare.

While the Western transition is tied to the rise of individualistic demographic behavior at the turn of the twentieth century, Chinese demographic decision making on the eve of the twenty-first century continues to be largely a collective enterprise. In the West, it was mostly individuals who seized upon new contraceptive technology and new ideas of marital birth control to maximize their own interests. Individuals have the right to make demographic decisions and also are ultimately responsible for the consequences of their actions.[29]

In China, demographic decisions are never individual. Decisions require careful considerations of collective needs at both ends of the social spectrum: the family and the state. Marriage, for instance, is not a personal arrangement between two individuals. Rather, it is an institution through which family and kinship ties are formed, maintained, and expanded. Similarly, infanticide is not a result of lack of parental love, but a sacrifice to benefit the whole family. The same collective logic applies to behavior such as childbearing and adoption. Rational decision making in this context is a process of negotiation that takes into full account hierarchical prerogatives and collective interests. What matter are not just individual preferences, but the person's gender, birth order, and relation to the household head within the family, and occupation, residence type, and political status in the society.

Ironically, what most distinguishes such a collective process from individual decision making is the enormous cost borne by the individual. At no stage of an individual's life can he or she behave so as to maximize personal interests at the expense of others. Until recent decades, marriage was arranged by parents and elders; marital life was monitored and controlled by other people. There was little room for personal romance or sexual indulgence. Perhaps most painfully for a society in which the parental relationship is the primary social relationship, many parents were forced to kill or acquiesce in killing their own children. While Chinese can now choose their own spouses, they still cannot choose the number of their children. Moreover, if they live in cities or work for state enterprises, they can have only one child. The Chinese population system, in other words, seems to deny individuals what would be considered fundamental human rights in the West.

The most conspicuous example of the collective nature of Chinese demographic decision making is the state family planning program implemented during the past two decades. In the name of the common collective good, the Chinese government has reimposed a series of far-reaching economic and political constraints on individual demographic behavior. The populace has responded with surprising efficacy, if not enthusiasm. Current reductions in Chinese fertility have already reduced world population growth by 250 million. By 2030, when China's population is predicted to plateau at 1.6 billion, its size will be at least 1 billion smaller than it would have been in the absence of this fertility decline.[30]

Not surprisingly, as fertility has declined in recent decades to an extremely low level, sex-selective abortion has risen. To some extent, infanticide and adoption, which had declined or even disappeared, have also returned, but with contemporary trappings.

Organization

The distinctiveness of the Chinese demographic system and the collective nature of Chinese demographic processes are the subjects of this book. Chapter 2 completes our presentation of background material, surveying the classic Malthusian paradigm of population growth and subsequent social theories and misunderstandings of contemporary and historical population behavior and of Chinese population dynamics in particular.

In Part II we turn to the realities of Chinese population behavior. In Chapter 3 we challenge the myth that China was overpopulated and show that the Chinese standard of living at the time of Malthus was not only comparable to the West's; it even rose, if not monotonically or uniformly, in recent centuries, and not just in recent decades.

In Chapters 4, 5, and 6 we overturn the Malthusian myth of Chinese population processes. In so doing we demonstrate that Chinese population behavior differed fundamentally from the existing understanding of comparative population dynamics. Whereas Malthus regarded famine as the major form of positive check in China, we highlight in Chapter 4 the role of deliberate mortality through sex-selective infanticide and neglect. Whereas Malthus regarded marriage in China as universal and early, we show in Chapter 5 that although this pattern held for females, marriage was neither early nor universal for males. Whereas Malthus emphasized only one form of deliberate preventive check, delayed marriage and premarital sexual restraint, which he called "moral restraint," we establish in Chapter 6 that in China sexual restraint within marriage, which we call "marital restraint," was also important.[31] Malthus characterized Chinese population growth as a product of the positive check; we demonstrate that the preventive check was more important.

In Part III we conclude with an overall assessment of the Chinese demographic system, including adoption, in Chapter 7 and a discussion of the social and political origins and implications of such behavior in Chapters 8 and 9. In contrast to the European demographic system, which involved only one form of voluntary control over population growth—marriage—the Chinese demographic system was characterized by multiple forms of control. Chinese could vary their age at marriage and marriage type, control their fertility within marriage, and regulate the survivorship of their births according to a wide variety of demographic, social, and economic circumstances. Indeed, through several forms of adoption they could even overcome the limits inherent in human biology. In consequence, Chinese demographic behavior early on exhibits a form of rationality rivaling that of post-transition populations.

These demographic checks and institutions derived from long-standing social, cultural, and political traditions. In contrast with the Malthusian stress on individual restraint and private property, Chinese demographic behavior was the product of collective responsibility and public institutions. To the extent that individuals sought to maximize their opportunities, they did so within an opportunity structure defined to a large degree by collective institutions, interests, and ideologies.[32] Although such circumstances existed in Europe, and even England, as well (Gillis 1985), the contrast with China is striking.

Our book fundamentally qualifies our understanding of population processes in the past and present and in so doing proposes an alternative to the Malthusian model. China, despite its size in Malthus' time—300 million—was able to grow fourfold, to 1.2 billion today. At the same time, despite, or perhaps because of, the persistence of Chinese culture and institutions, China has achieved among the lowest fertility and mortality of any large population. This apparent anomaly—unpredicted growth and unexpected decline—challenges a major strand of Western social theory persisting today.

Ever since the appearance of the first edition of *An Essay on the Principle of Population* in 1798, the Malthusian model of positive and preventive checks has remained predominant in the intellectual discourse of demography. While our increasing scientific and technological productivity has proved his pessimistic predictions about world population and living standards to be incorrect, the Malthusian focus on the potentially precarious balance between population and resources remains a central preoccupation (Overbeek 1974). Moreover, Malthus' empirical and theoretical work on the social and economic implications of population behavior continues to impress successive generations of social scientists. Not only did he create a multidisciplinary standard for much subsequent demographic research,[33] but recent empirical work has indeed confirmed that the broad outlines of his theory were correct for Western Europe, and especially England, before the nineteenth century. Two centuries after the publication of Malthus' famous essay, it therefore seems especially appropriate to review the Malthusian paradigm and to see to what extent he and his intellectual successors have been correct with regard to the Chinese reality.

CHAPTER 2

Malthusian Myths

... in every age, and in every state, in which man has existed, or does now exist, the increase of population is necessarily limited by the means of subsistence: Population invariably increases when the means of subsistence increase, unless prevented by powerful and obvious checks.

MALTHUS, *AN ESSAY ON THE PRINCIPLE OF POPULATION* (1798)

The checks to population, which are constantly operating with more or less force in every society, and keep down the number to the level of the means of subsistence, may be classed under two general heads; the preventive, and the positive checks.

MALTHUS, *AN ESSAY ON THE PRINCIPLE OF POPULATION* (1803)

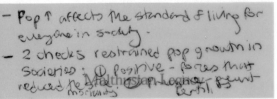

The Malthusian paradigm has two sides. First, Malthus believed that population growth was inherently bounded by resource constraints. His basic premises, which he widely popularized, were that population growth is food based, and that population policy is vital for social well-being.[1] Malthus was therefore responsible for a fundamental shift from a previous policy of population increase to our contemporary policies of population control. Previously, policymakers had believed that the more people there were, the stronger a state would be. After Malthus they worried that the larger the population was, the lower the standard of living would be.

Second, Malthus proposed that in every society two types of check restrain population growth. In the first edition of his *Essay on the Principle of Population,* he emphasized the role of the positive check to reduce population size. This included all those forces that shorten the duration of human life and can therefore be classified under the general category of mortality. In his second and subsequent editions,

Malthus elaborated on the role of the preventive check to limit population size. This included all those customs and institutions that prevent the birth of children and can therefore be classified under the general category of fertility. While Malthus recognized the wide variation in mortality causes, he associated the operation of the positive check ultimately with subsistence economies and subsistence crises (1798/1992, 42–43; 1826/1986, 314–315). Similarly, while Malthus recognized that the preventive check could include variations in fertility, he believed that the preventive check operated largely through delayed marriage since he assumed that "the passion between the sexes" was more or less the same in every age and every society.[2]

Malthus classified human society into two sorts: Western and non-Western. After an exhaustive twenty-five-chapter review in the second and subsequent editions of his *Essay* of the interplay of population checks in past and present times,[3] Malthus concluded that Western societies, by which he meant modern Europe,[4] were characterized by the preventive check. Non-Western and nonmodern Western societies were dominated by the positive check.[5]

In the West, in other words, individual rationality had forged a social economic demographic system that produced prosperity. Marriage was tied largely to economic conditions. Increases in wages gave rise to subsequent increases in marriage, while increases in fertility led to subsequent decreases in wages. Individuals rationally changed their marriage behavior on the basis of economic conditions and economic expectations. Such preventive checks avoided overpopulation and kept living standards high. The result was not only a relatively homeostatic demographic regime, but also a more prosperous economy.

The absence of such a preventive check reduced all other societies to more or less subsistence levels. In some societies, human inventiveness was simply so primitive and the land so barren that civilization simply never developed.[6] In other, more advanced societies, either markets or property rights were too underdeveloped or tyranny was too developed for capital to accumulate and the standards of living to rise.[7] Even in major polities and economies where this was not true, the excessive encouragements to marriage doomed the population to live at the bare subsistence level.[8] Just as the presence of the preventive check in the modern West guarded and guaranteed prosperity, its absence in the non-modern West and the non-West predicted poverty.

As a result, China, one of the richest of human societies, was also one of the poorest.[9] Despite the advantages of natural geography, native industry, and a patriarchal state that raised agricultural production and agricultural productivity to prodigious levels, the prevalence of universal and early marriage reduced most people to a level of subsistence, forcing the poor to live in a state of abject poverty.[10] This trend was exacerbated by a custom of partible inheritance that doomed even the rich after a few generations.[11]

Population, in other words, drove Chinese inexorably downward to poverty and worse. Chinese living standards were characterized by low wages and poor nutrition.[12] Extreme misery encouraged the common practice of infanticide, which in turn further encouraged marriage.[13] While Malthus acknowledged that this increased poverty was not associated with frequent epidemics, he thought that famine, despite an imperial welfare system, was common.[14] Malthus concluded that Chinese population processes were overwhelmingly dominated by the positive rather than the preventive check.[15] Indeed, he saw famines as "the most powerful of all the positive checks to the Chinese population" (1826/1986, 109).

Malthus, in other words, was one of the first social theorists to compare modern Western society to non-Western and non-modern Western societies and to link the gap in affluence to specific population processes.[16] His conclusion, that Western affluence was a product of delayed marriage, which in turn was a product of Western individualism and Western rationality, has had a powerful influence not only on Western social theorists but also on the Chinese themselves. Over the past two centuries, as world population has increased along with the gap between affluence and poverty, many scholars have extended and embellished the Malthusian paradigm. In the West, this elaboration has become an important strand of economic liberalism and cultural particularism. In China, it has become the basis of important state policy and is currently part of state ideology.

Western Myths

A number of well-known Western, particularly English, social theorists have expounded on the historical origins and social implications of the Malthusian paradigm to explain not only Western population processes but also Western acquisitiveness, Western social mobility, and even Western individualism.

Demographers, in particular, seized on the importance of individual choice as one of the most important preconditions for the demographic transition. This idea, of course, is derived from Malthus' formulation of the preventive check.[17] Just as individuals have both the freedom and the capability to make decisions on marriage, they use this responsibility rationally, fully aware of the costs and consequences of their actions and can weigh the costs and benefits against other opportunities. The extension of this calculus to the birth of children lies at the heart of the fertility decline. This formulation is true not only of Gary Becker's 1960 theoretical economic model of fertility analysis, but also of the most current theoretical and analytical models of fertility behavior in developing countries (Bulatao and Lee 1983).[18] The ideology of "individual decision making" has therefore dominated Western academic explanations of the determinants of fertility decline.[19]

Reacting partially against this demographic concern with individualism, some anthropologists have suggested that such decision making also required the adaption of Western social structure and social behavior. Specifically, they have pointed out that in many developing countries, parents are reluctant to curtail their fertility because of the upward flow of income from children to parents. According to this formulation, developed by John Caldwell (1976), parents begin to restrict their fertility only when the flow of wealth switches direction, downward from parents to children—a social revolution often associated with the replacement of large, multiple-family households by nuclear families.[20]

Indeed, according to the more elaborate formulation by John Hajnal, the delayed-marriage system, identified by Malthus as the preventive check, was part of a Western family system characterized by life-cycle service, delayed marriage, and independent household formation or succession upon marriage. In two landmark articles, Hajnal (1965, 1982) demonstrated that delayed marriage was characteristic of much of Western Europe and a product of the Western family system. He further contrasted this Western system, characterized by life-cycle service, delayed marriage, and independent residence, with a non-Western system characterized by familial labor, early and universal marriage, and virilocal, often joint residence. If the Western system was characteristic particularly of England, the non-Western system was characteristic particularly of India and China.[21]

Other social scientists, inspired at least partly by Hajnal's formulation, have traced the Western family system as far back as the twelfth century, and therefore suggest that the Malthusian paradigm both facilitated the subsequent rise of Western commercialism and Western capitalism and reinforced the development of "ego-centric," individualistic decision making, which lies at the heart of Western society and Western mores. According to this logic, propounded most frequently by Alan Macfarlane (1978, 1986, 1987), the one hard-and-fast rule of the "Malthusian revolution" was that a newly married couple had to be independent at the time of marriage.[22] The main purpose of marriage was to satisfy the psychological, sexual, and social needs of the individuals concerned. Children were a consequence rather than a reason for marriage. Marriage was therefore based on compromise between economic necessities on one hand and psychological and biological pressures on the other. Above all, the fact that marriage was a choice and ultimately about individual satisfaction meant that the decision to marry was one of costs and benefits weighed against other opportunities. Malthus, according to Macfarlane, consciously advocated a marital and family system that was the natural corollary of what today is called market capitalism. Where capitalism flourishes, so does delayed marriage and the culture of individual choice (1986, 322–323).

This last idea has become so influential that some policymakers recently have even reversed this neo-Malthusian equation and propounded a view that the market economy is necessary for individualistic demographic decision making. Not surprisingly, this approach has been particularly popular in the United States (Finkle 1985). Reversing its stand on population control in the first World Population Conference, held in 1974 in Bucharest, the United States vigorously promoted the idea that the "market economy is the best contraceptive" at the 1984 World Population Conference in Mexico City. This argument, that a "free" market system would simultaneously promote both economic growth and the culture of individual decision making, has persisted and is now predominant.[23] Only under such an economic system do individuals assume the responsibility of reproduction and take into consideration the costs and benefits of childbearing.

Chinese Myths

Just as Western scholars developed a variety of neo-Malthusian myths based on the original Malthusian paradigm, so Chinese scholars have perpetuated the Malthusian myth of China as a land of famine and poverty. The monumental work on Chinese population history from 1400 to 1950 by Ho Ping-ti illustrates the extent of Malthus' influence. While Ho made numerous important contributions to our understanding of the numbers and circumstances of the Chinese population increase from 80 million around 1400 to 530 million around 1950, he also believed that China was in a Malthusian trap that began to close by the early nineteenth century.[24] Although it is now commonly accepted that the timing and even the processes of such overpopulation varied by region, our understanding of this "national" pattern has endured for almost half a century.

China scholars have long been fascinated by the Malthusian implications of this sustained rise in population from about the sixteenth century. Indeed, nearly all attempts to understand the macroeconomic processes of the recent Chinese past are conditioned by the rise in population.[25] The general agreement is that population processes played a decisive role in both expanding and restraining Chinese economic development.[26] On the one hand, rising population and population density initially led to intensified production, heightened commercialization, and greater urbanization in the eighteenth century. On the other hand, sustained population growth eventually culminated in the inevitable decline of per capita production and subsequent emiseration in the nineteenth and twentieth centuries. The process was Boserupian on the upswing, Malthusian on the downswing (Boserup 1965/1996; R. Lee 1987).

Many scholars have sought to explain further the specific processes of Chinese impoverishment. According to their depiction of these processes, the Malthusian scissors had two blades: excessive fertility due to universal marriage and a primordial desire for many children, especially sons;[27] and low wages due to the consequent oversupply of labor.[28] The result was what some have termed "quantitative growth with technological stagnation" (Elvin 1973; Chao 1986), and what others have called "growth without development" (P. Huang 1990). Simply put, excess labor stunted the development of labor-saving technology, which formed the basis of modern economic growth in the West.[29] Agricultural involution and declining per capita productivity followed. As the Malthusian scissors closed, rising impoverishment and mortality ensued.

Moreover, these scholars generally assume that the positive check, mortality, was solely responsible for keeping population and resources in balance in China over the long as well as the short term. The logic is essentially the same as in Malthus: not only did the allocation of resources within the extended family system protect age at marriage against the effects of short-term fluctuations; it also shielded the age at marriage against the effects of secular trends of increasing pressure on resources.[30] Similarly, the primordial desire for large families that allegedly prevented couples from delaying births in response to short-term fluctuations also prevented them from reducing family size in response to a long-term worsening in economic circumstances. Thus as population pressure increased, only mortality could fluctuate, and it did so with disastrous consequences,[31] the most commonly cited example of which is the perceived Malthusian crisis in China from the late eighteenth through the late nineteenth centuries.[32]

The Malthusian interpretation of Chinese history, however, has only recently become popular in contemporary China. Although some Chinese observers voiced Malthusian concerns as early as the beginning of the nineteenth century, these concerns were largely dismissed, especially in view of China's sustained growth.[33] It was not until the 1960s that the government encouraged family planning in urban China;[34] and it was not until the late 1970s that a forceful government population control policy was formulated and enforced. The primary motivation under Mao Zedong and his immediate successor, Hua Guofeng, was the doubling of population since 1950 from 500 million to almost 1 billion and the prospect of future doublings in the absence of family planning. This program was reinforced under Deng Xiaoping by an overriding desire to raise per capita living standards as rapidly as possible to levels commensurate with those of other world powers.

Current Chinese goals to limit population to 1.2 or 1.3 billion by the year 2000 are derived from an explicit policy target to quadruple Chinese living standards to $800 per capita by 2000.[35] The result was the creation and implementation of one of the most draconian family planning policies in world history.[36] While this program has been highly successful in lowering fertility, it has also justified various extreme measures of birth planning on grounds of the need to raise China's economic development and living standards. The escalation of such pressing Malthusian concerns has made population control, along with economic reform, one of the two most important formal state policies. Whereas previously families adjusted their own demographic behavior to economic realities in spite of natalist government policies,[37] the current government enforces family planning in spite of some individual family resistance.[38]

China's leaders, in other words, launched the largest family planning program in the twentieth century on the basis of little more than nineteenth-century social theory. Government policy seems to have virtually embraced the original Malthusian paradigm without full consideration of its consequences. China's poverty is believed to be largely the product of Chinese overpopulation. This explanation has been accepted in the absence of any serious social scientific research. Despite the subsequent development of population studies in China and the vast increase in our understanding of Chinese population processes, Malthusian or neo-Malthusian theory continues to provide virtually the sole justification and motivation for China's unprecedented family planning program.

Given this background, China's fertility decline seems very much the product of autocratic state policy, not of individual rational decision making. As a result of both the existence of such a policy and the absence of Western individualism, China's demographic transition has been viewed largely as an outcome of government intervention, a coercive family planning program devoid of individual initiative and rationality and violating individual human rights (Aird 1990). At the same time, while the recent rise of economic growth is attributed to an intrusion of global economy with attendant technology transfer and capital flow, the credit for the success of the Chinese family planning program is largely given to the autocratic legacy of the Chinese state. Within China, any hesitation in controlling birth has been labeled "feudalistic," antimodern, and nonrational. The Chinese demographic transition, in other words, has been largely treated as anomalous and unreplicable.

Such attitudes perhaps explain why the popular press continues to warn of the Malthusian consequences of China's large population. Despite rapid economic advances and rapid fertility decline in recent decades, China continues to be considered a potential Malthusian bomb. Lester Brown (1995) is only the most recent to warn of the perils of China's overpopulation.[39] His new twist, however, is not the perils of Chinese poverty, but the dangers of Chinese prosperity. Brown warns that if China follows the same patterns of increasing food demands and decreasing cultivated acreage as its Asian neighbors, Japan, Korea, and Taiwan, China by the year 2030 will face a grain shortage of 369 million tons, which is nearly double current world grain exports (ibid., 97). The increase in the Chinese standard of living, according to this formulation, could result in an unthinkable worldwide food shortage, causing poverty if not in China, then elsewhere in the world. While these claims on examination seem erroneous and overblown,[40] they have reawakened interest in the Malthusian paradigm and fear of Chinese overpopulation.

So have the increasingly strident Malthusian claims of environmentalists who warn that China may soon lack adequate energy, land, water, and even air. China, if only because of its large territory and population, is already responsible for much of world pollution and environmental depletion. This, of course, is far from true at the per capita level, where Western, especially American, pollution levels and environmental depletion rates are easily an order of magnitude, sometimes several orders of magnitude, higher (Press and Siever 1994). Nevertheless, China's growing economy, hand in hand with rising per capita pollution, seems to guarantee further extensive environmental deterioration, destruction, and degradation, transforming the "good earth" into the "bad earth" (Smil 1984, 1993).

Despite the rapid rise in Chinese affluence and the rapid increase in our knowledge of China, past and present, the Malthusian mythology of Chinese population persists and even flourishes. Common knowledge of the rise in Chinese living standards and the decline in Chinese fertility can consequently coexist with common impressions of Chinese poverty and overpopulation without any apparent contradiction. Partly because of distance, partly because knowledge of Chinese demography and economy is only recent, popular understanding of Chinese population—both the interrelationships between its population and economy, and the underlying demographic mentalities and mechanisms—has not differed much from the writings of Malthus.

This persistence and elaboration of Western myths on China is true, of course, not just for population, but for a wide variety of other Chinese behaviors as well. The same paradox predominates. While empirical knowledge of China has increased greatly in recent years, so has our mythology of China. Fomented by an unfortunate combination of media sensationalism, political opportunism, and popular ignorance, and encouraged by an ethnocentric legacy, the mythology of China as the "other" predominates and overwhelms rational thought.[41] The result has been dogma and demagoguery on both sides of the Pacific.

In Part II we summarize the past and present realities of Chinese population behavior, focusing on four distinctive characteristics: high sex-differential mortality, high sex-differential nuptiality, low marital fertility, and high rates of adoption. We begin, however, with perhaps the most persistent of all Chinese population myths, the myth that China was only a subsistence economy, a land of famine and poverty.

PART II

Realities

CHAPTER 3

Subsistence

"In some countries, population appears to have been forced; that is, the people have been habituated by degrees to live upon almost the smallest possible quantity of food. There must have been periods in such countries when population increased permanently, without an increase in the means of substance. China seems to answer to this description. If the accounts we have of it are to be trusted, the lower classes of people are in the habit of living almost upon the smallest possible quantity of food and are glad to get rid of any putrid offals that European laborers would rather starve than eat . . . A nation in this state must necessarily be subject to famines.

MALTHUS, *AN ESSAY ON THE PRINCIPLE OF POPULATION* (1798)

Malthusian Legacy

For centuries, European travelers to China have remarked on the poverty and populousness of Chinese society (Lach and Van Kley 1993).[1] It is therefore not surprising that early Western economists, including Malthus, linked these phenomena.[2] By Malthusian standards, eighteenth-century China was perhaps the best-documented model of overpopulation and poverty. Population density, as measured by population per cultivated acreage, was among the highest of any large national population.[3] Per capita consumption of energy and food appears to have been among the lowest of any major national population.[4] In consequence, the average stature of a Chinese male was appreciably lower than that of a European peasant in the same period.[5]

And yet China's population, despite such low living standards, ironically began a sustained process of almost exponential growth beginning in the early eighteenth century. Figure 3.1 outlines the stylized contours of this population increase. We can distinguish three rough stages: a rapid rise from 160 million in 1700 to 350 million in 1800, a slower increase to almost 600 million in 1950, followed by a sharp acceleration to over 1.2 billion today. Moreover, despite recent state efforts to restrict nuptiality and fertility, the number of Chinese will continue to increase, though at a slower rate, until the middle of the next century. By then the population will be at least 1.6 billion. In consequence, contemporary China faces a variety of economic, ecological, and social constraints.

While many China scholars have long been fascinated by the Malthusian implications of these population increases, there is no agreement on their consequences, or even their criteria, location, and timing. Malthus himself emphasized the demographic consequences, the rise in mortality as population growth caused per capita output to fall below subsistence levels.[6] More recently, others have focused on larger economic processes; some seek to determine when population

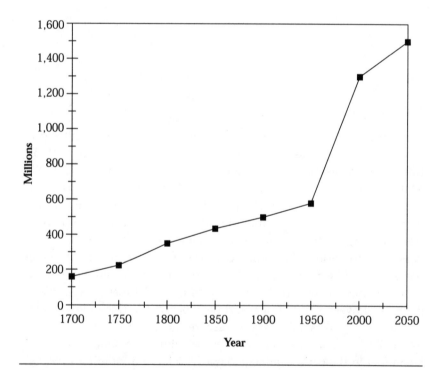

Figure 3.1. China's population explosion, 1700–2050 A.D.
Sources: Ho (1959), Durand (1974), Schran (1978), and Zhao Wenlin and Xie (1988).

exceeded an optimum determined by China's resources and technology,[7] others to identify when the marginal productivity of labor approached zero—in other words, when rural employment turned into underemployment.[8]

Such confusion over the Malthusian implications of China's population growth has been exacerbated by a lack of geographical specificity, as well as a paucity of empirical quantitative studies on both the contemporary and late imperial Chinese economy.[9] It is safe to say that just as China was both one of the largest and one of the least understood of any populations, it was also one of the largest and least understood of any economies.

The change during the last two decades has been remarkable.[10] New data and new methods have begun to illuminate the economic history as well as the population history of late imperial and contemporary China. The results here too challenge common knowledge. We now believe that throughout this period food production was well above the subsistence level. Indeed, as we shall see later in this chapter, the Chinese economy even grew on a per capita basis in the eighteenth century in such regions as Jiangnan, and in the twentieth century nationwide. This growth was due in part to a process at the macro level (described in Chapter 7) whereby population growth spurred technological innovation and subsequent economic growth. It was also due to a micro-level feedback loop in which families changed their population behavior and regulated their size and composition according to changing economic circumstances. In other words, the Malthusian assumption that population growth inevitably leads to diminishing returns is incorrect even in late imperial China.

Chinese Realities

Three different indices—per capita food production, per capita food consumption, and life expectancy—puncture the myth of China as a land of Malthusian poverty and famine.

Food Production
Despite the sixfold increase in population from the eighteenth through twentieth centuries, recent economic studies have documented a variety of advances in economic production with the rise of commercialization in the eighteenth century, urbanization in the nineteenth cen-

tury, and industrialization in the twentieth century. Increases in per capita productivity and consumption, slow and uneven to begin with, have recently accelerated considerably.

Per capita grain production, the single most important measure of Malthusian pressure in an agrarian society, did not decrease during the last 300 years.[11] Rather, for much of this period, despite a decrease in cultivated land, per capita grain production remained constant and even increased in some areas, if sometimes only slowly and not always uniformly throughout the country (Perkins 1969; Chao et al. 1995).[12] During the twentieth century, for which we have better national level estimates, output per capita exhibits a steady upward trend. According to Figure 3.2, per capita grain production grew moderately under the collective farming system and has increased substantially since the late 1970s. Per capita grain output rose from 260 kilograms per per-

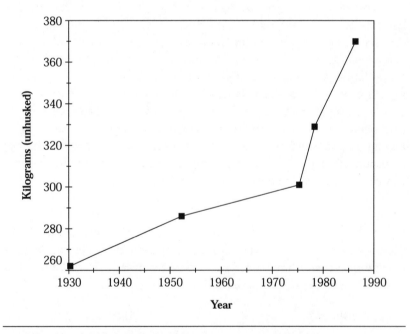

Figure 3.2. Per capita grain production, China, 1930–1986
Sources: 1930: estimate for 1929–1933, Buck (1966); 1952: Buck (1966); 1975: estimate for 1970–1978, Rawski (1979); 1978, 1986: Walker (1988).

son per year in the 1920s, to 300 in the mid-1970s, to 370 by the late 1980s, and to 390 by 1990.

So did labor productivity. Although this upward progress was by no means uniform, economic growth was evident, particularly in such areas as the Lower Yangzi and the northeast. In western Songjiang, which is especially well documented, annual net output per farm worker increased by 30 percent from the sixteenth through eighteenth centuries, from 18.8 *shi* to 24.5 *shi*.[13] Li Bozhong (1998) has estimated that for the entire Lower Yangzi in the same period, average yield per *mu* (one-sixth of an English acre) increased by 47 percent and annual net production per worker by 52 percent.[14] This increase in farming labor productivity was accompanied by a shift in female labor to sericulture and rural industry. By the late 1970s, per capita grain output in the provinces of the Lower Yangzi and the northeast was still well above the national average.[15]

Such increases in productivity became nationwide by the mid-twentieth century. Even during the period of China's most rapid population growth (from the mid-1950s to the mid-1970s), rural labor productivity increased from 232 *yuan* per person-year to 255 *yuan* per person-year (Rawski 1979).[16] Such an increase in rural labor productivity, albeit moderate, was a spectacular achievement given the massive increase in rural labor force during this period. By 1975 rural laborers had increased by 100 million, to a level 40 percent higher than in the mid-1950s. Nevertheless, labor productivity in rural areas has accelerated since the late 1970s at an even more explosive rate. In per capita terms, the average rate of growth in the value of agricultural output during the last two decades is more than ten times higher than in the period 1957–1978.[17]

By contrast, such hilly areas as the northwest (Shaanbei, Gansu) and the southwest (Guizhou, Yunnan) experienced declining per capita productivity in the late nineteenth and the twentieth centuries because of ecological deterioration (Yan and Wang 1992). Excessive hillside farming and improper terracing resulted in large scale deforestation and soil erosion. Consequently, by the late 1970s per capita grain output in these provinces was 15–30 percent below the national average. The best years of agricultural production in China's recent history, from the late 1970s through the mid-1980s, did not improve the status of these provinces. By 1986 per capita grain output there had slid to 14–40 percent below the national average. Per capita grain output did not improve at all in Gansu Province, and in Guizhou and Yunnan Provinces it declined.[18]

Food Consumption

Overall, however, gains in food production paid off in improved nutrition. Nutritional and anthropometric measures from specific populations suggest improvements in the standard of living date back at least to the turn of the century and in some regions of China perhaps even earlier. Anthropometric indices reveal a gradual increase in physical well-being in the early twentieth century.[19] Numerous studies of historical and contemporary populations around the world have established the link between nutrition and stature. The average values of the height of young adults reflect, perhaps better than any other single index, a population's nutritional status and living standards (Fogel 1986; Floud, Wachter, and Gregory 1990; Kolmos 1994; Steckel 1997).

Nevertheless, while Chinese by European standards have been short, this was a consequence of diet composition as well as caloric intake. Chinese at least since the twelfth century have eaten chiefly vegetables and grains rather than meat and dairy products, providing a mix of fats, proteins, and other nutrients very different from those consumed in Europe (Anderson 1988). As a result, even though per capita nutrient availability was in the low 2,000 kcalories in the early twentieth century and substantially higher in some regions (Pan 1997), heights lagged behind European standards for the same level of caloric intake. However, as per capita nutrient availability increased substantially during the second half of the twentieth century to 2,326 in 1956, 2,500 by the end of the 1970s, and the high 2,000s by the 1990s, so did stature (Piazza 1986; Brown 1995).[20]

In consequence, Chinese stature has increased markedly during the last 75 years. While national surveys of human stature became available only in the 1950s, anthropometric analyses of specific populations strongly suggest that nutritional standards began to rise in the early twentieth century. Figure 3.3 summarizes the available data. Analysis of several thousand members of the Beijing imperial guard indicates that male stature of the general population was no more than 163 centimeters around 1900,[21] approximately the same value as those deduced for urban Chinese by the first attempt to survey Chinese stature nationwide in the 1920s.[22] By the 1980s male stature had risen to 171 centimeters. In less than three-quarters of a century, in other words, male stature rose by more than 8 centimeters. This appears to have occurred in two stages. During the first half of the twentieth century, in both mainland and island China, stature increased from 0.5 to 1 centimeter a decade depending on sex and place of residence.[23] After 1949 the rate of increase increased to 1 to 1.4 centimeters a decade, equal to that of Japan and European countries during their period of most rapid anthropometric improvement (Piazza 1986).[24] While national-level data for rural China are still lacking for earlier periods, thus preventing comparison over time, available information for selected rural locales has shown even faster growth in rural areas than in cities.[25]

Of course changes in stature reflect changes in morbidity as well as changes in nutrition. Not only has nutrient availability increased sub-

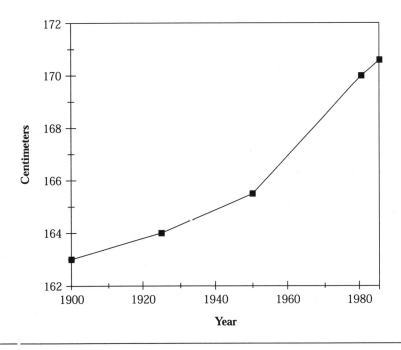

Figure 3.3. Male mean stature, China, 1900–1985
Source: A. Chen and Lee (1996).

stantially and steadily despite sustained population growth; there has also been a marked improvement in health, directly related to disease control and prevention. Nevertheless, these changes in stature corroborate improvements in the overall standard of living.

Moreover, there is some evidence that in some regions of China these improvements in nutrition began well before the twentieth century. While most Chinese historians assume that nutritional levels were low, indeed minimal, during the late imperial period, their conclusion seems unsubstantiated by the historical record. Recent research has discovered that instead the people in the most densely populated regions generally had better diets than those in less populated regions (Luo 1989). Scattered records of the ordinary diet of farm workers in late imperial Lower Yangzi, the most densely populated region in China, show that they were fed at a level probably higher than in any other region in China.

This standard of living appears to have improved substantially from earlier times. Comparison of late imperial agricultural handbooks that recorded rural wage compensation and diet indicates that from the seventeenth century on, Chinese in the lower Yangzi and elsewhere ate more fish, meat, and tofu; drank more tea and wine; and consumed more sugar than ever before (Fang 1996).[26] Whereas an ordinary farm laborer in the sixteenth century was provided with meat 10 days a month during the busy season, this allotment increased to 15 days a month in the seventeenth century and to 20 in the nineteenth.[27] The quality and quantity of meat also improved. On meat days, daily farm workers, for example, were fed only small portions of so-called humble meat—preserved meat, dried fish, and animal intestines—in the seventeenth century, but ate large quantities of pork in the nineteenth.[28] While the portions of pork were smaller for yearlong farm workers, they were provided with fish on nonmeat days as well.[29] The quantity and quality of alcoholic beverages similarly increased.[30] Thus for some farm workers, by the mid-nineteenth century even ordinary days had become days of meat and wine. This was true for ordinary peasants as well.[31]

Nor were these improvements in the standard of living restricted to diet. Ken Pomeranz (forthcoming) has recently estimated that per capita consumption of cloth, furniture, and perhaps even energy was comparable in eighteenth-century China and Europe.[32] The common assumption, that population increases led to impoverishment and even starvation, does not therefore seem to apply to China, nor especially to the Lower Yangzi.[33] China's population not only increased despite constant Malthusian pressure; it did so (as we shall see in the next section) without increases in mortality and famine. And it did so without any apparent decline in per capita productivity. Indeed, there is clear evidence of improvement in the quality of life, even before the economic advances of the late twentieth century. In these senses, then China, in particular its most populous region, the Lower Yangzi, does not seem overpopulated.

Life Expectancy

Nor does China as a whole appear to have experienced high death rates and frequent famine. Previously, the common wisdom was that Chinese population was controlled largely by mortality: war, pestilence, famine, and infanticide. Chinese population, in other words, oscillated around an equilibrium, driven by changes in positive, not preventive, checks. Improvements in the standard of living lead to increased population size; as population outgrows the means of subsistence, the standard of living falls. The positive and to a lesser extent preventive checks are brought into play, and the growth rate declines. Mortality, what Malthus termed the positive check, held Chinese population growth in check.[34]

This emphasis on the role of the positive check in China encouraged many initial efforts in Chinese historical demography to focus on mortality despite the inherent limitations of the genealogical sources used in analyses (Harrell 1985; Liu Ts'ui-jung 1985; Lee, Anthony, and Suen 1988).[35] According to these and later studies, mortality in most eighteenth century Chinese populations was broadly similar to mortality in Western Europe.[36] Life expectancy at birth ranged from the late twenties to the early thirties depending on sex, class, and residential environment. Males lived longer than females (Lee, Anthony, and Suen 1988; Lee and Campbell 1997). Elites lived longer than commoners (Telford 1990a, 1990b). Rural residents generally lived longer than urban residents regardless of class (Lee, Campbell, and Wang 1993).

Even though Chinese population growth during the nineteenth and early twentieth centuries should have, according to Malthusian predictions, led to high death rates and frequent famine, mortality rates do not appear to have increased during this period.[37] Life expectancy among the imperial lineage, undoubtedly the best-recorded Chinese population, for example, shows no sign of decrease even though its members grew steadily worse off through the nineteenth century (Lee, Campbell, and Wang 1993; Lee, Wang, and Campbell 1994).[38] This pattern applied to commoners as well (Lee and Campbell 1997). Instead, there are clear indications of the beginnings of a sustained decline in mortality, at least in selected urban and rural populations beginning in the early twentieth century. In Beijing, for example, Cameron Campbell (1997) has documented an improvement in life expectancy of more than ten years for both sexes at age five, a decline he ascribes largely to voluntary public health measures initiated in the 1910s and 1920s. Similar health measures have been described in Tianjin and other cities (Benedict 1993; Rogaski 1996) and were soon followed by national public health policies whose effectiveness has only recently been appreciated (Yip 1995).

While spectacular mortality spikes did interrupt this mortality decline, these crises hardly restrained long-term population growth. Famines were relatively few and had a very limited impact.[39] Moreover, Chinese famines and associated population loss appear to have been the products of political and organizational problems, not excess population per se. Perhaps the most salient case is that of the 1958–1961 Great Leap famine, possibly the worst ever in human history, with as many as 30 million estimated premature deaths and 30 million postponed births (Ashton et al. 1984). That famine, though exacerbated by unusual and severe adverse natural conditions, was primarily the result of a series of human errors associated with the Great Leap Forward, which unrealistically accelerated rural communalization and industrial development (D. L. Yang 1996). Lack of communication and political concerns led to such foolish decisions as to export grain in 1960, when the famine had already reached its height.[40] Earlier famines seem to have been the products of similar confusion and ignorance.[41] Politics, not population, pushed China beyond the brink of subsistence (Bernstein 1984).

By the mid-twentieth century, Chinese mortality began to decline at a rate unmatched elsewhere in the world by any large population. Infant mortality fell from 200 per 1,000 in 1950 to less than 50 per 1,000 today. Life tables constructed from the three censuses show that life expectancy for males rose from 42.2 years in 1953–1964 to 61.6 in 1964–1982, implying a rate of improvement of 1.5 years of life expectancy per year since 1949. By 1980 life expectancy was 69 years. High levels of government investment in public health produced this rapid progress (Jamison et al. 1984). Recent data suggest that mortality has continued to decline, if much more slowly, during the last ten years, especially in such remote provinces as Gansu and Guizhou.[42]

Overall there is no evidence of increases in mortality or in the frequency and intensity of mortality crises during the last 300 years. To the contrary, mortality remained roughly stable or even decreased as population increased. Malthus' expectations, in spite of his powerful arguments, were never met. Despite a sustained population increase from 225 million in 1750 to almost 600 million in 1950 and to over 1.2 billion today, the threat of overpopulation appears to have been a myth.

Population and Economy

This escape from overpopulation was due to two demographic-economic processes: first, a causal process at the societal level, whereby population growth induced technological innovation and subsequent economic growth (Boserup 1965/1966); and second, a feedback loop at the individual family level, whereby changing economic circumstances induced people to change their population behavior and consequently regulated their fertility and, to a lesser extent, their mortality. The first process of technological innovation and rising labor productivity has been described in detail by many scholars (Ho 1955; Tang 1986; Guo Wentao 1988; Li Bozhong 1998). The second process of premodern population control, which is less well understood, we shall examine in detail in Chapters 4–7.[43]

Agricultural Expansion

For many years the common explanation for the rise of population during the late imperial period was broadening of the food base through new crops and new cropping patterns. Ho Ping-ti (1955, 1959, 1978), in particular, emphasized that the dissemination of new food crops from America and from elsewhere in Asia enabled Chinese to increase not only agricultural yields but also agricultural acreage, particularly in the mountainous western and southwestern frontier and in the many mountainous regions of the interior. As a result, the southwest, for example, which accounted for less than 5 percent of

China's population in the mid-eighteenth century, accounted for over 15 percent by the early twentieth century.[44]

Later work by Japanese and American scholars shifted the emphasis to other forms of technological innovation and reversed the causal sequence. Agricultural expansion was the product, not the cause, of population pressure.[45] Elvin (1973), in particular, building on the work of largely Japanese scholarship, identified how increases in population lead to increases in productivity—specifically from single to multiple cropping, from dry to wet farming, from limited to extensive application of fertilizer, and from limited to intensive labor investment. His work, however, was based largely on national figures and therefore lacked the detail necessary to document the process of causation.

Recently, in a series of publications focusing on the Lower Yangzi, the best-documented region of late imperial China, Shiba Yoshinobu (1991) and Li Bozhong (1998) have documented in great detail a pattern of economic growth whereby per capita productivity and per capita consumption rose at least in this region.[46] They conclude that many traditional technologies did not become widespread until the late eighteenth and early nineteenth centuries.[47] Moreover, as the rational use of resources improved, the value of labor output also increased. On the one hand, Lower Yangzi farmers increased the rational use of available resources—cultivated land, water surface, human labor, and animal labor. On the other hand, they also raised the intensity of production, that is, they increased the amount of labor and capital invested in a given area and time to raise production. The two processes proceeded hand in hand. Thus the spread of double-cropping paddy and winter dry-field cropping, multiple cropping of cotton and paddy with winter dry-field crops, and intercropping in mulberry orchards increased both the number of work days per year and the market for human and animal labor. At the same time, farmers also increased investment in cash crops, changing planting schemes and shifting land to more intensive crops. Increasing levels of fertilization were particularly important. Indeed, fertilizer inputs rose even faster than labor inputs. These changes occurred alongside the expansion of rural industrialization and commercialization in the Lower Yangzi. Expanding domestic and international markets provided Lower Yangzi peasants with an opportunity to profit through comparative advantage and increasing division of labor, shifting millions of peasants, mainly women, from rural farm labor to the higher returns of rural industry. For all these reasons, total productivity in the Lower Yangzi increased greatly during the eighteenth and nineteenth centuries.

Labor Intensification

Agricultural expansion, in other words, was accompanied by a parallel process of labor intensification. This transformation, which superficially resembles what Akira Hayami (1977) has called the "industrious revolution" in Japan, appears, however, to have been driven largely by increased economic opportunity in the eighteenth and nineteenth centuries and by ideological demands in the late twentieth century rather than by demographic pressure.[48] We identify two separate processes differentiated by time, gender, and motivation.

On one hand, men worked longer hours per day and more days per year. In late imperial China, Lower Yangzi male farmers worked in the field all year around, whereas northern China's harsh winters had enforced a long period of idleness for farmers. Nevertheless, by the third quarter of the twentieth century, not only were all adult males in rural China employed, but the average number of days worked per year had increased by over 50 percent, from 160 to 250 (Rawski 1979, 115).[49] The increase in rural labor input was due mostly to the increased labor demands of more-intensive cultivation, represented by increased multiple cropping and increased sown area, at least until the mid-1970s.[50] Other major sources of rural labor demand were land preparation and rural construction, which expanded substantially under the collective farming system.

On the other hand, women increasingly joined the main labor force, working first in subsidiary nonagrarian economic activities in the eighteenth and nineteenth centuries and in subsidiary agrarian activities in the twentieth century. By the end of the late imperial period, female participation in farming and especially in cotton and silk handicraft production was already high in such areas as the Lower Yangzi, but was much lower in other areas such as northern China.[51] Beginning in the 1950s, however, female participation in the labor force markedly increased nationwide. State policies mandated that women work in the fields and be paid as much as men for the same work. Consequently, female participation in agricultural production in some areas literally doubled the rural labor force in just a few years.

Despite the tremendous rise in labor supply, per capita output does not appear to have declined.[52] On the contrary, it increased, as did a variety of measures of living standards. In the Lower Yangzi, for example, real wages in farming rose sharply in cash and moderately in kind. One study even claims that whereas it had required as many as four to five adult laborers in the early seventeenth century to earn enough to support even one additional adult, by the mid-eighteenth century just one or two workers could make enough to support an additional person (Wei 1983, 483–442, 490, 496–499). This increase in income and in living standards is reflected by changes in ordinary clothing as well as in diet. Again according to Fang (1996), while many peasants still wore hemp and ramie in the seventeenth century, almost everyone wore cotton and even silk by the mid-nineteenth century.[53] The most conspicuous examples of increased consumption of luxury goods were alcohol, opium, and tobacco.[54]

In the Lower Yangzi, at least, population growth, such as it was, occurred without any long-term decrease in consumption and income.[55] While the secular increase in production, nutrition, and well-being was nationwide only in the twentieth century, some regions, such as the Lower Yangzi, experienced a similar process at least in the eighteenth century. The Malthusian pressures that existed throughout Chinese history never led to a Malthusian mortality crisis. This major achievement should not have occurred in the demographic system that Malthus described for China, one in which productive capacity had reached its limits, fertility was unregulated, and death was the only way to bring population back into line with resources.

The avoidance of Malthusian crisis was not only a product of economic growth at the macro level; it was also facilitated by constant demographic adjustments at the micro level, which we describe in Chapters 4–6. Chinese demographic behavior spanned multiple methods of population control that allowed them to adjust actively their mortality, their nuptiality, and their fertility. The Chinese demographic system, in other words, enabled them to create a feedback loop between population and economic growth. As a result, they could adjust their population behavior according to their social and economic circumstances. Unlike peasants elsewhere, Chinese peasants produced and kept children only when it was to their advantage. In China population therefore grew largely in response to increased opportunities. Consequently Chinese could check or release population growth without an increase in the positive check, at least at the exogenous, macro level described by Malthus.

Chinese population behavior constitutes a demographic regime, which we describe in Chapter 7, as an alternative to the Malthusian paradigm. Combined, these demographic mechanisms—controlled marital fertility, infanticide, and male celibacy—served as a powerful component of a feedback loop between economy and population. On the one hand, demographic behavior was highly contingent upon economic circumstances. On the other hand, such a system with multiple means of population control also enabled the Chinese population to grow over a long period without the prolonged famine and mortality crises predicted by Malthus.

CHAPTER 4

Mortality

> The positive checks to population are extremely various and include every
> cause, whether arising from vice or misery, which in any degree
> contributes to shorten the natural duration of human life . . . all
> unwholesome occupations, severe labour and exposure to the seasons,
> extreme poverty, bad nursing of children, great towns, excesses of all
> kinds, the whole train of common diseases and epidemics, wars,
> pestilence, plague, and famine.
>
> MALTHUS, *AN ESSAY ON THE PRINCIPLE OF POPULATION* (1803)

Malthusian Legacy

For Malthus, mortality, which he called the positive check, was the
original check on population growth. In contrast to the preventive
check, which operated through moral restraint, the positive check operated through a mixture of what Malthus termed "misery," which
was a force of nature, and "vice," which was man-made. Whereas
moral restraint was purely volitional, the extension of rational decision making, vice was voluntary only to a degree, and misery was
totally involuntary.

While famine may have been the "ultimate" positive check, Malthus
also acknowledged numerous intermediate checks on population
growth.[1] Many were mainly involuntary, but some proceeded from
volitional vice. Foremost among the vices was infanticide. According
to Malthus, infanticide was typical of many non-Western and non-
modern Western societies, including the ancient Greek and Roman
world, South America, the Pacific Islands, Australasia, South Asia,
and East Asia, particularly China. Infanticide prevented population
growth directly by reducing population size, and indirectly, when sex
selective, by reducing the number of females.[2] While such behavior
varied by class, it was not only common among the poor, but in some

societies also practiced by the rich.[3] In these societies, infanticide alone could control population growth. Malthus accordingly described a population cycle oscillating between depopulation when infanticide was "prevalent," and repopulation when such "habits" changed.[4] Where such intermediate checks did not exist, or when they were inadequate, the principal residual checks were war in more "savage societies," and famine in more sophisticated states.[5]

After infanticide came the misery of disease. Here too, Malthus' understanding of such positive checks was quite complex. While he was particularly sensitive to the links between disease and poverty, he distinguished between those caused by poor nutrition and those caused by poor sanitation and hygiene.[6] He was particularly interested in such specific diseases as smallpox and, to a lesser extent, plague.[7] Moreover, he was fully aware of the demographic and social differences in mortality such as those associated with age, class, and residence.[8] Residence in particular seemed especially important. Indeed, Malthus attributed much of the improvement in mortality in modern Europe to improved urban sanitation (1803/1992, 43; 1826/1986, 315).

Nevertheless, despite Malthus' sophisticated analysis of mortality as a combination of involuntary misery and proactive vice, the subsequent study of mortality, and in particular the mortality transition, has been far less complex. Inspired by his original proposition that population growth is fundamentally limited by the availability of food, research on mortality initially focused almost exclusively on the etiology, frequency, and consequences of mortality crises, in particular those associated with famine.[9] While much of this work paradoxically centered on Europe,[10] there has also been important work on the history of famine and famine relief elsewhere, especially in South and East Asia.[11] Together, these researches have qualified and verified two of Malthus' earlier generalizations. First, "true famine" was less frequent than Malthus thought. Second, even when famines and natural catastrophes struck, much as Malthus suspected, they had only a minor impact on population growth (1803/1992, 35; 1826/1986, 307). Put in Malthusian language, "sickly seasons, epidemics, pestilence, and plague" could be more important than famine (1798/1992, 43; 1826/1986, 251).

More recent research on the mortality transition has consequently been devoted largely to the human conquest of disease. We now recognize that this occurred in three stages: a diminution in mortality crises in the eighteenth century; improvements in public health and associated mortality decline at the turn of the twentieth century; and the more universal decline in mortality, linked to the discovery and use of modern medicine, in the late twentieth century. Our current understanding is that the recent decline in mortality was driven largely by the dissemination of specific efforts against disease.[12] Most important, recent research has documented that the secular decline in modern mortality beginning in the late nineteenth century is due largely to the rise of public health institutions, first in specific cities and then nationwide.[13]

Although these mortality studies have greatly advanced our understanding of the mortality decline, one unintended consequence has been to reduce the complicated Malthusian description of mortality to an increasingly simplistic, exogenous, largely biological and medical phenomenon.[14] While demographers recognize the differential impact on mortality of age, class, environment, and gender, they also tend to view mortality as a largely exogenous force, somewhat akin to that of Malthusian misery, whose only differentiating principle is largely biological.[15] Only recently have modern demographers become increasingly aware of the need to focus more on individual rather than aggregate response to mortality. While techniques for such analysis are well developed,[16] results of these analyses in historical demography are only just beginning to appear.[17]

Despite Malthus' own careful attention to mortality in the past and in non-Western societies in particular, the powerful importance of the mortality decline and the global demographic transition has reoriented historical demography to relatively recent history, especially Western history. As a result, mortality studies tend to view the past through an increasingly contemporary, ethnocentric, and especially technical lens. Preoccupied by their desire to produce refined measures of mortality, demographers pay less and less attention to the role of mortality in the past and the function of mortality as a positive check in the demographic system.[18]

Chinese Realities

Health Culture and Mortality Control

In China the distinctive impact of mortality on population was not through famines or epidemics, but through individual proactive interventions. Famines of course occurred. So apparently did epidemics.[19] But these crises appear to have had less severe mortality consequences than elsewhere. Successive historic Chinese states developed a variety of institutions to combat poor harvests, including an empirewide system of granaries that annually redistributed up to 5 percent of the national grain supply during the eighteenth and nineteenth centuries (Will and Wong, with Lee 1991).

Numerous individual efforts supplemented these large-scale collective enterprises. This culture of mortality control through individual agency, which has existed for millennia, produced a pattern of mortality that was highly differentiated by age, class, gender, and residential group. On one hand, educated or wealthy Chinese families with access to knowledge of preventive techniques and the means to make use of them could prolong the life of favored members by paying particular attention to personal hygiene and diet. On the other hand, Chinese could take life by resorting to infanticide especially of their daughters.

As a result of a long and self-conscious medical tradition devoted to preserving health and life, morbidity and mortality in late imperial China were subject to proactive human intervention. Indeed, the current term for public health, *weisheng,* originally referred to individual practices of health maintenance involving a regimen of diet, breathing techniques, and exercise.[20] Most important, perhaps, was a dietary culture that emphasized personal sanitation by drinking boiled water or tea, avoiding uncooked foods, bathing whenever possible, and using soap.[21]

A rising appreciation of children and childhood in the seventeenth and eighteenth centuries led to the development and spread of a pediatric culture devoted to infant and child health care. According to recent work by Hsiung Ping-chen (1995a, 1995b), the late imperial period saw a marked increase in the quality of child care, reflected in the publication and contents of numerous pediatric handbooks. These texts advocated long breastfeeding by the biological mother, attention to maternal nutrition, and slow weaning only when the child had begun to walk sometime during the second year of life, and only gradually progressing from soft, plain, easily digestible foods to more nutritious meats.

New techniques to combat smallpox may also have contributed substantially to a decline in child mortality during the late eighteenth century. Perhaps the most important of such improvements was the gradual dissemination, recently reconstructed by Angela Leung (1987) and Du Jiaji (1994), of primitive methods of inoculation against small-pox, which had been the major cause of death among young children. As early as 1687 the Kangxi emperor established a pediatric clinic for the imperial lineage and made smallpox inoculation mandatory for all lineage children after their first birthday. Although his efforts encountered initial resistance, presumably because some inoculated children subsequently died, repeated government appeals for greater compliance led to the spread of pre-Jennerian inoculation. By the early eighteenth century, Kangxi's successors extended mandatory inoculation to include all Manchu children, so that by midcentury more than half of the registered population of Beijing were regularly inoculated through state clinics.

The result was a steady secular decline in child mortality. This is documented most clearly among the imperial nobility, who also had easy access to these new techniques. Figure 4.1 shows the decline in the probability of dying among the 33,000 boys and girls aged one to

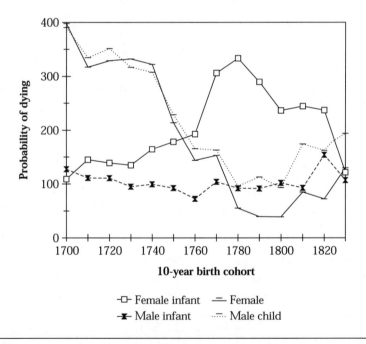

Figure 4.1. Infant and child mortality, ages 0–4, Beijing, 1700–1830
Source: Lee, Wang, and Campbell (1994).

four born to lineage parents from 1700 to 1830. Child mortality declined from 400 per 1,000 to 100 and below. In consequence, male life expectancy at birth nearly doubled, from the low twenties to the high thirties. Life expectancy at age 1 doubled from the mid-twenties to 40. Female life expectancy made approximately similar gains after the first month of life. The proportion of people who survived childhood accordingly increased substantially. Whereas only half of all children born during the first quarter of the eighteenth century survived past age 10, two-thirds of all girls and three-quarters of all boys born during the last quarter of the eighteenth century lived through adolescence. The decline in child mortality due to such medical intervention was so large that it even overrode the effects of the other long-standing tradition of mortality intervention, that is, a rise in female infanticide and differential neglect over roughly the same period.

Infanticide

The long-standing practice of infanticide enabled parents to terminate the survivorship of their children more easily than they could prolong it (B. Lee 1981; Lee and Campbell 1997). The origins of this practice can be traced back to the first millennium.[22] It existed among the poor as well as the rich, and was practiced on females as well as on males, though on the latter to a much smaller degree. In some areas, such as the Lower Yangzi, the Middle Yangzi, and southeastern China, as many as half of all newborns were sometimes killed by their families.[23] In other areas, such as Taiwan, infanticide appears to have been uncommon.[24] Such an active use of mortality meant that survivorship was determined as much by endogenous decision making as by exogenous "misery." Chinese mortality patterns were consequently highly differentiated not just by biology but also by choice.

Most prominent and prevalent among these choices was a primordial prejudice against daughters. Son preference dates back to the origins of ancestral worship in the second and third millennia B.C. and was reinforced by a patrilineal and patrilocal familial system, supported by the imperial and especially late imperial state, which systematically discriminated against daughters (Bray 1997). Only sons could sacrifice to the family spirits. Only sons could carry the family name. Only sons, with rare exceptions, could inherit the family patrimony (Bernhardt 1995). Not only did patrilocal marriage customs require daughters to marry out, but also hypergamous marriage patterns required upper-class families to provide a dowry to accompany them. Daughters, therefore, were not only culturally considered inferior; they were also perceived by most families as a net economic and emotional loss.[25]

Chinese mortality patterns were thus highly differentiated by sex. Figures 4.2 and 4.3 compare infant and child mortality in three European populations and the one Chinese historical population for which we have adequate data, the Qing imperial lineage. The contrast is striking. While European males and females died more or less in equal numbers during the first year of life, Chinese females died in far larger numbers than Chinese males. Although these differences varied by time and place, they were largest among female neonates, whose death rate was as much as four times higher than that of males (Lee, Wang, and Campbell 1994). At the same time, while a highly differentiated

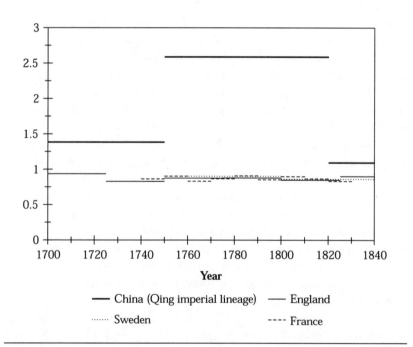

Figure 4.2. Ratios of female to male infant mortality ($_1q_0$), four countries, 1700–1840

Sources: China: Lee, Wang, and Campbell (1994); England: Wrigley et al. (1997); Sweden: Statistika Centralbyran (1969); France: Blayo (1975).

pattern by gender continued among Chinese children aged one to four, the direction in this age group was reversed, with almost half as many female as male deaths. Evidently those Chinese families who decided to use infanticide to limit the number of their children, especially daughters, also used newly available methods of pediatric care to preserve the health of their remaining children, again especially their daughters.

This pattern existed at both ends of the social spectrum. In a study of infant and child mortality among 33,000 members of the Qing lineage born between 1700 and 1830, we discovered that one-tenth of all female children were probably killed during the first few days of life (Lee, Wang, and Campbell 1994). Figure 4.4 compares female perinatal, neonatal, and infant mortality by decadal birth cohort during this period. As imperial emoluments and subsidies were gradually reduced during the late eighteenth century (Lee and Guo 1994, 116–

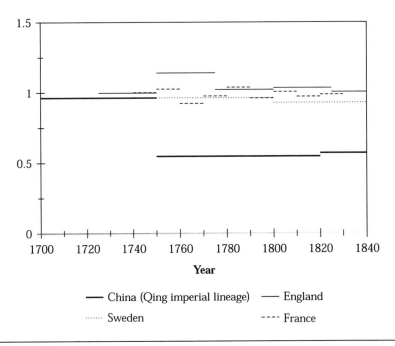

Figure 4.3. Ratios of female to male child mortality ($_4q_1$), four countries, 1700–1840
Sources: See Figure 4.2.

133), the proportion of neonatal deaths for certain decades increased sixfold, from 50 to 300 per 1,000. At the same time, the proportion of infant deaths during the first month increased from 30 to well over 90 percent.

Such an unnatural concentration of female infant mortality in the very early months, combined with unnaturally high rates of sex-selective mortality, indicates that members of the imperial lineage practiced female infanticide. Indeed, where precise death dates (year, month, and day) are available (for 15,249 sons but only 5,949 daughters), death rates during the first day of life are *ten* times higher for females (72 per 1,000) than for males (7.5 per 1,000).[26] Given an overall probability of dying during the first month of life of 45 for males and 160 for females, we can deduce that as many as one-tenth of all daughters born into the imperial lineage during the 130 years under consideration were victims of infanticide.

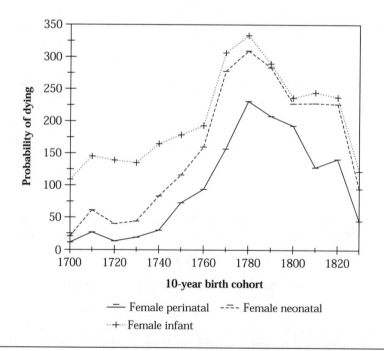

Figure 4.4. Female perinatal, neonatal, and infant mortality, Beijing, 1700–1830
Source: Lee, Wang, and Campbell (1994).

Infanticide rates were even higher among some commoners. In a study of mortality among 12,000 northeastern peasants born between 1774 and 1873, relying on indirect methods, Lee and Campbell (1997) have estimated that between one-fifth and one-quarter of all females died from deliberate infanticide. Peasants used female infanticide to respond to short-term changes in economic conditions. Increases in grain prices and declines in food availability clearly provoked increases in male mortality, which was largely registered, and in female infant mortality, which was unregistered. As a result, male mortality exhibited strong positive correlations with grain price increases while fertility, especially female fertility, exhibited strong negative correlations with grain price increases, with correlation coefficients in the range of 0.44 to 0.68, depending on the type of grain (Lee, Campbell, and Tan 1992). While infanticide may not have been equally popular throughout China, these findings have been replicated for several other rural populations as well (Campbell and Lee 1996).

Moreover, among these commoners female mortality was much higher in childhood as well. In rural Liaoning, girls aged one to five experienced 20 percent greater mortality than boys, a probability of dying of 316 per 1,000 versus 266 per 1,000 (Lee and Campbell 1997, 64). While the reasons for such excess female mortality are unclear, studies of contemporary South Asia have attributed excess female mortality in childhood there to discrimination against daughters in the allocation of nutrition and health care.[27] This may have been the case in northeastern China as well. Ethnographic accounts from the early twentieth century, for example, document that in this region females often ate only after all males finished, including servants and farm hands.[28]

The Chinese Transition

Such a proactive tradition of mortality control helps explain the speed and the unusual pattern of China's unprecedented mortality decline in the twentieth century. Because individual Chinese were predisposed to use new curative and preventive techniques as soon as they were available, the same health policies were more effective in China than elsewhere.[29] Whereas China's per capita gross national product is still among the lowest in the world, Chinese life expectancy is among the highest. As a result, while the average Chinese person receives less than one-tenth the income of a resident in any of the advanced industrialized societies, he or she lives nearly as long as the average American.[30]

On one hand, mortality began to decline from the very beginning of the twentieth century with the adoption of public health measures in selected populations. The proactive culture of mortality prevention facilitated the early adoption of public health measures at least in specific cities. In Beijing, public health efforts from 1910 through the 1930s had a significant effect in reducing mortality, facilitating an increase between the nineteenth and the mid-twentieth century in life expectancy at age five for both sexes by more than 10 years (Campbell 1997 and forthcoming). Similar public health efforts were carried out in Tianjin and other Chinese cities (Benedict 1993; Rogaski 1996). These and other urban public health programs fundamentally changed the residential pattern of mortality. Whereas mortality in cities used to be higher than in the countryside, this pattern was reversed in some cities no later than the 1920s. In Beijing, for example, a male reaching the age of five could expect to live 14 years longer than his counterpart in the countryside. A female reaching age five could expect to live 10 years longer than her rural counterparts.[31]

This health transition accelerated rapidly in the 1950s with the development of a national "patriotic" public health program *(aiguo gonggong weisheng yundong)*. Such a program was made possible not only because it relied on a well-organized bureaucracy that was able to reach down to the rural village level, but also because Chinese public health programs emphasized simple, preventive measures rather than costly medical treatment and cure facilities (Salaff 1973; Jamison et al. 1984). This long tradition of proactive prevention in China undoubtedly facilitated the acceptance and efficacy of a prevention-oriented program.[32]

On the other hand, a secular decline in infanticide, starting in the late imperial period, drastically reduced infant mortality, especially in females.[33] This rapid reduction in infanticide explains much of the decline in Chinese infant mortality, which fell from over 200 per 1,000 to less than 50 per 1,000 nationally, and to less than 10 in cities. With the rise of modern censuses this decline in infant mortality can be seen at a national level. Moreover, the disappearance of excess female deaths, reflected in such materials and summarized in Figure 4.5, documents the rapid decline in female infanticide and neglect at least from the mid-1930s onward.

By the early twentieth century, excess male births had already fallen from the 20–40 percent levels recorded in specific eighteenth- and nineteenth-century populations to 10 percent nationwide. The ratio of males to 100 females declined further from 114 in 1936 to 109 in 1949 and to 107 in 1960. Correspondingly, the estimated proportion of excess female deaths also declined from over 15 percent before 1940 to below 5 percent by 1950 and to 2 percent in the 1970s (Coale and Banister 1994, 464). It is unclear to what degree this decline in female infanticide and neglect is a product of changing economic and political circumstances, or the result of an apparent attitudinal shift that can be traced back to the rise of child-centered values in the late imperial period.[34]

This decline in sex-selective mortality, combined with the merger of proactive individual and collective health measures, boosted life expectancy. Tables 4.1 and 4.2 summarize the rise in life expectancy for

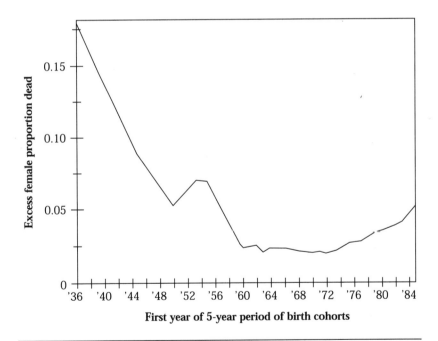

Figure 4.5. Excess female deaths, China, 1936–1984
Source: Adapted from Coale and Banister (1994) on the basis of the 1953, 1964, 1982, and 1990

Table 4.1 Male life expectancy at selected ages, China, selected periods and populations

Period	Location	Life expectancy at age 0	Life expectancy at age 10	Life expectancy at age 20
1300–1880	Anhui	31	38.9	32.4
1644–1739	Beijing	27.2	36.9	29.9
1740–1839	Beijing	33.6	37.2	29.5
1792–1867	Liaoning	35.9[a]	43.2	36.4
1840–1899	Beijing	34.7	37.8	32.2
1906	Taiwan	27.7	33.5	—
1921	Taiwan	34.5	40.8	—
1929–1931[b]	China	34.9	47	40.7
1929–1931[c]	China	24.6	34.2	30.1
1929–1933	Beijing	40.9	52.7	44.7
1936–1940	Taiwan	41.1	45.6	—
1953–1964	China	42.2	44.3	36.1
1964–1982	China	61.6	57.2	48
1973–1975	China	63.6	59.9	50.5
1981	China	66.2	60.4	50.9
1989–1990	China	68.4	61.1	51.5

Sources: Anhui 1300–1880: Telford (1990b); Beijing 1644–1899: Lee, Campbell, and Wang (1993); Liaoning 1792–1867: Lee and Campbell (1997); Taiwan: Barclay (1954); China 1929–1931[b]: Notestein and Chiao (1937); China 1929–1931[c]: Barclay et al. (1976); Beijing 1929–1933: Campbell (forthcoming); China 1953–1964 and 1964–1982: Coale (1984); China 1973–1975, 1981, and 1989–1990: Huang Rongqing and Liu (1995).

a. Life expectancy at 1 *sui*, which is approximately at 6 months of life. Actual life expectancy at birth was accordingly several years lower.

specific age groups by gender from 1644 to 1990 in a variety of historical and contemporary populations. For both sexes, mortality appears to have been relatively stable over the long term historically, with a life expectancy at birth in the high twenties for females and the mid-thirties for males. This pattern changed abruptly in the early to

Table 4.2 Female life expectancy at selected ages, China, selected periods
and populations

Period	Location	Life expectancy at age 0	Life expectancy at age 10	Life expectancy at age 20
1300–1880	Anhui	26	35	33.5
1644–1739	Beijing	24.6	34.8	30.7
1792–1867[a]	Liaoning	29	36.5	33.6
1906	Taiwan	29	27.2	—
1921	Taiwan	38.6	46.4	—
1929–1931[b]	China	34.6	46	40.1
1929–1931[c]	China	23.7	33.9	29.3
1929–1933	Beijing	35.1	45.3	33.8
1936–1940	Taiwan	45.7	50.8	—
1953–1964	China	45.6	49.7	41.2
1973–1975	China	66.3	62.4	53
1964–1982	China	63.2	59.6	50.4
1981	China	69.1	63.3	53.8
1989–1990	China	71.9	65	55.4

Sources: See Table 4.1.
a. Life expectancy at 1 *sui,* which is approximately at 6 months of life. Actual life expectancy at birth was accordingly several years lower.

mid-twentieth century with the introduction of public health. Life tables constructed from three censuses (1953, 1964, 1982) document a rise in life expectancy nationally for males from 42.2 in 1953 1964 to 61.6 in 1964–1982 and for females from 45.6 to 63.2 (Coale 1984, 67). By 1980, life expectancy for both sexes was 68 years, implying a rate of improvement of 1.5 years of life expectancy per year since 1949, a rate unmatched by any comparably sized population (Banister and Preston 1981, 107–108; Banister 1987).[35]

Some of this advancement in life expectancy was a product of a decline in sex-selective neglect along with the virtual disappearance of infanticide. It is hard, however, to decompose the relative contributions of the rise of public health and the fall in infanticide and neglect,

since they occurred more or less simultaneously. Table 4.3 summarizes
the reduction in the probability of dying for specific age groups between 1929–1931 and 1973–1975. While the early data for the older
(40 plus) age groups seem suspect, we can see that young adult (20–
29) mortality declined by 10–40 percent and middle-aged adult (30–
39) mortality by no more than 15 percent, compared to a decline in
infant and child mortality of 60–75 percent.[36] The rapid decline in
infant and child mortality, driven by the abandonment of infanticide
and child neglect, accounts for a very substantial portion of the rise in
Chinese life expectancy.

China has now completed the epidemiological transition. The primary causes of death today—cancers, cerebrovascular and heart diseases—parallel those of advanced economies, which have completed
such a transition from infectious to degenerative diseases (Rong and Li
1986). Further advances in life expectancy, which presumably require
a shift toward curative medicine, have come more slowly and at a
much higher cost. From 1980 to 1990 life expectancy at birth for both
sexes advanced only two years, from 68 to 70. Although the squeeze
of the Malthusian trap was never tight, the rise in economic productivity guarantees that China will be free of famine in the future, barring
political fiasco.

Table 4.3 Age-specific mortality rates, 1929–1931 and 1973–1975

Age group	Female			Male		
	1929–1931	1973–1975	% reduction	1929–1931	1973–1975	% reduction
0	154.90	42.79	72.38	161.50	48.93	69.70
1–4	104.90	36.26	65.43	100.90	35.43	64.89
5–9	27.50	10.51	61.78	29.50	11.47	61.12
10–14	7.60	4.23	43.16	8.10	5.04	37.78
20–24	11.60	7.26	37.41	8.30	7.38	11.08
30–34	11.90	10.37	12.86	9.20	9.94	−8.04

Sources: 1929–1931: Notestein and Chiao (1937); 1973–1975: Huang Rongqing and Liu
(1995, 19).

Note: We exclude comparisons at higher age groups because of unusually low adult mortality in
the 1929–1931 data, probably due to suspect data. According to Barclay et al. (1976), female infant
and child mortality was also very likely to be underrecorded. The real magnitude of infant mortality
reduction may therefore be larger than that reported here.

Nevertheless, sex-differentiated mortality has persisted throughout the twentieth century, particularly in some poor areas where neonatal and infant female excess mortality is reported to be several times the national average (Lavely, Mason, and Li 1996). At the national level, however, differential mortality is primarily child mortality. The best documented example is a study of excess female child mortality between 1965 and 1987 derived from the 1988 Two-per-Thousand fertility survey (Choe, Hao, and Wang 1995). Contrary to the generally observed mortality pattern among children aged one to four where male mortality is 10 percent higher than female mortality, in China female child mortality during this period exceeded expected male mortality by 10 percent.[37] This difference in mortality was particularly acute among later births, where there was 15 percent excess mortality, and especially rural births and later births who have older sisters and brothers, where there was 25 percent excess mortality. In other words, a girl born in the countryside whose parents already have children of both sexes would have 50 percent greater mortality than if she had been a boy (Choe, Hao, and Wang 1995, 61).

These differences in sex-selective behavior have grown even sharper in the last 10 years as sex-selective abortion has become widely available. For births recorded for 1977–1981 the reported male-to-female ratio was 108. By 1985–1989 the ratio had risen to 113 and by 1990–1994 to around 115.[38] The ratios at higher parities were even more skewed, rising from 108 in 1977–1981 to 123 in 1985 to 1989 (Gu and Roy 1995). These numbers imply that by 1985 as many as 500,000 girls were "missing" each year from the number of registered births. While many are apparently unregistered births and/or unreported adoptions, excess female infant deaths are still estimated to be 45,000 per year (Johansson, Zhao, and Nygren 1991).[39] This recent rise in the sex ratio reflects the revival of proactive traditions of mortality control common to China and elsewhere in East Asia.

Collective and Individual Strategies

The combination of infanticide and medical intervention provided Chinese parents with two powerful methods of shortening and prolonging life. Many parents in the past simply used infanticide to limit the number of children.[40] Others, guided by preferences for the number and composition of their children, used infanticide to remove their least-wanted children, and preferential feeding and health care to enhance the survival chances of the most wanted.[41] As a result, mortality patterns in China differ greatly according to a variety of circumstances such as birth order and gender of the child and the social status of the parents. While there has been little study of the circumstances surrounding contemporary parental decision making to abandon or kill their children,[42] historical studies have suggested that this was a highly rational decision based on social and economic resources as well as the number and sex of existing and anticipated children.

The Qing nobility are a particularly well-documented example.[43] Low nobles, in some periods, were twice as likely to kill their female infants as high nobles. They were also far more likely to protect their female children vigorously. As a result, daughters born to low nobles were much more likely to die as infants than daughters born to high nobles, but if they survived were far less likely to die as children. Thus daughters born to monogamous low nobles were 2.36 times more likely to die in the first month of life than daughters born to high nobles in polygamous marriages, 2.85 times more likely if their parents were polygamous. Conversely, if the daughter of a low noble survived to her first birthday, her chances of dying before age five were only one-fifth the chances of a daughter of a high noble.

While data preclude similarly direct calculations of neonatal mortality among commoners, calculations of registered births by gender indicate similarly conscious planning. The sex ratio of registered births differed greatly by birth order and completed family size. Table 4.4 presents sex ratios of registered births for approximately 1,000 completed marriages in rural Liaoning from 1792 to 1840. The ratio of male to female births increased with the number of children already born, but decreased with completed family size. Thus, in single-child families there were 576 boys for every 100 girls. For families with two children ever born, there were 211 boys per 100 girls at the first birth and 450 boys to 100 girls at the second birth. For families with three children ever born, the ratio was 156 boys to 100 girls at first birth, 194 boys to 100 girls at second birth, and 324 boys for every 100 girls at the last birth. This highly unnatural pattern continues through all other completed family sizes. Such behavior suggests that parents were relatively unconcerned about the sex of their first few children but thereafter allowed additional children to survive only if they were male. The closer a girl's birth order was to a couple's completed family size, the less likely her parents were to allow her to survive to registration.[44]

Table 4.4 Male-to-female ratio by birth order and completed family size,
Liaoning, 1792–1840

Birth order	Completed family size					
	1	2	3	4	5 or more	Total
1	576	211	156	158	88	188
2	—	450	294	229	139	265
3	—	—	324	278	149	240
4	—	—	—	422	138	223
5 or more	—	—	—	—	162	162
Total	576	290	240	246	138	214
Number	115	328	428	401	599	1871

Source: Lee and Campbell (1997, 96).
Note: This calculation includes only children born to the 883 completed first
marriages beginning before 1840. Births after 1840 are included in the completed
family size but not in the computations of sex ratios because of the decline in female
registration after 1840. Inclusion would show even more lopsided sex ratios in later
parities.

This pattern was especially clear for "elite" parents. It was often
those at the top who were more ruthless in determining the sex composition of their children. In rural Liaoning, for example, while household heads and heads' sons may have had more children than other
relatives, they had proportionally fewer daughters. Figure 4.6 contrasts the number of girls and boys born to each male family member
in the eighteenth and early nineteenth centuries. The sex ratio of surviving children born to household heads was twice as lopsided as
children born to those at the bottom of the multiple-household hierarchy—nephews once or twice removed. The closer people were to the
line of succession, the larger the proportion of sons. The further away
from the head, the larger the proportion of daughters. Brother's son is
a particularly conspicuous example, with slightly more girls even in
absolute terms than the household head. Presumably in expectation of
their need to transmit headship, household heads and their sons were
under far greater pressure than other married men to produce male
heirs. By contrast, nephews who were unlikely ever to achieve headship found it more advantageous to have daughters. Sexual differentials in infant and child mortality, in other words, were basic boundary
conditions for the hypergamous marriage market.

Indeed, the prevalence of female infanticide among lower Qing imperial nobles was also a consequence of this marriage market. While low-status daughters earned bride price, high-status daughters cost dowry: the higher the social position, the larger the dowry. As a result some Qing nobles were almost as likely as high Qing peasants to kill their daughters.[45] This was especially true from the late eighteenth century onward, when such dowries became especially burdensome.[46] As we shall see in the next chapter, marriage requirements explain many family planning decisions.

Infanticide, in other words, was a product of rational decision mak-

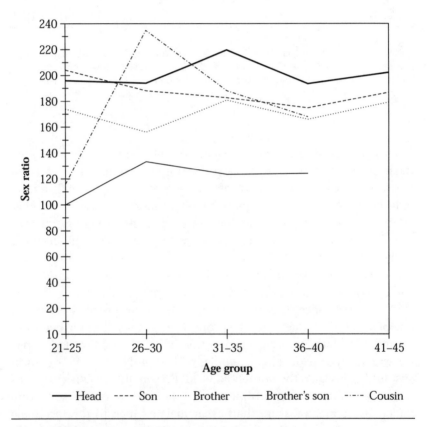

Figure 4.6. Male-to-female ratios of children already born, by family relationship, Liaoning, 1792–1840
Source: Lee and Campbell (1997).

ing embedded in a peculiar cultural attitude toward life. Chinese peasants may not have thought of killing their children as murder. Traditionally, the Chinese did not consider children during the first year of life as fully "human" (Furth 1987; Hsiung 1995b). Indeed, a well-known and oft-cited prescript claimed that infants were just young animals.[47] "Life" rather began sometime after two *sui,* that is, from around the sixth month of life.[48] Chinese peasants and elite alike therefore probably conceptualized infanticide as a form of "postnatal abortion."[49] While such behavior has long been ruled illegal, it has not been considered immoral.[50]

That is not, however, true today. While infanticide is now both illegal and widely considered immoral, abortion in China is both legal and encouraged.[51] It is therefore hardly surprising that Chinese take advantage of the recent dissemination of ultrasound technology to control not only the number but also the sex composition of their children. Abortion has become as common as in the United States.

Children are a lifelong responsibility in China. Parents not only have to raise them to adulthood; they may also have to provide for them their entire lives. Daughters may move out when they marry. Sons live with you until you die. Parents not only have to find their children a suitable spouse; they also have to pay the dowry or bride price associated with their status as well as expenses associated with their marriage, their careers, their children, and their lives.

While parents may hope that their children will succeed and support them in their old age, there are no guarantees. Having children means taking risks. In the past, half of all children would die before adolescence or adulthood, and one child out of five would be physically handicapped.[52]

As a result, parents had to calculate carefully whether the risks associated with childbearing were economically sensible or even desirable. Daughters, in particular, were expensive—especially for the wealthy or elite, who were required to produce a dowry. Even sons were neither a sure nor a slight investment. Most sons required not only brides and a bride price but often other investments as well. Sons were therefore only potential productive assets. Given the demands and risks of childbearing, many parents may have decided that the risks outweighed the rewards. This is especially true in contemporary China as fertility has declined from six to less than two children per couple and as the investment required per child has increased an order of magnitude. The result is the sex selective mortality patterns typical of the Chinese demographic behavior: "fertility" with Chinese characteristics.

Low female survivorship also had a profound effect on marriage markets (discussed in Chapter 5) and, to a lesser extent, on population growth rates (discussed in Chapter 7).[53] Given that marriage was virtually universal for females regardless of economic class, female infanticide effectively reduced the number of first marriages by some 10 percent or more at the national level throughout the late imperial period, averting at the very least several hundred million births during these two centuries and lowering China's total population around 1900 from 600 to 500 million.

CHAPTER 5

Marriage

The Chinese acknowledge two ends in marriage. The first is that of perpetuating the sacrifices in the temple of their fathers; and the second the multiplication of the species. . . . a father feels some sort of dishonor, and is not easy in his mind, if he does not marry off all his children. . . . These extraordinary encouragements given to marriage have caused the immense produce of the country to be divided into very small shares, and have, consequently, rendered China more populous, in proportion to its means of subsistence, than any other country in the world . . . the encouragement to marriage has not only been an addition of so much pure misery in itself, but has completely interrupted the happiness which the rest might have enjoyed.

MALTHUS, *AN ESSAY ON THE PRINCIPLE OF POPULATION* (1826)

Malthusian Legacy

For Malthus, delayed marriage, which he called the preventive check, was the preferred check on population growth. In contrast to the positive check, which operated through vice or misery, the preventive check operated largely through "moral restraint," which was an individual decision to forgo marriage until one could support a family. This not only encouraged savings and discouraged poverty; by restricting population growth, it kept the price of labor high and assured general prosperity.[1]

Malthus recognized that the preventive check did not always operate through moral restraint. In some societies, the impediment of bride price prevented some women from marrying.[2] In other societies, women might marry, but low fertility associated with either polygamy or promiscuity prevented population growth.[3] He observed, however, that only societies which practiced moral restraint were able to preserve high living standards. He was therefore the first social theorist to link societal well-being to late marriage, and he ardently advocated the preservation of such a custom.[4] While Malthus recognized that the biological pressure to marry was strongest among the young, he suggested that more mature love was also better love.[5]

Here again, despite Malthus' awareness of variant forms of marriage and a marriage market differentiated by gender and class, the study of nuptiality, especially in the past, continues to focus on the effectiveness of the preventive check through delayed marriage.[6] Subsequent demographic studies of marriage have focused largely on techniques and calculations of marital status and marriage age.[7] With the exception of recent research on divorce and remarriage, there has been little attention paid to sex differentials in the marriage market and its implications for a demographic system.[8]

As a result, in China, where marriage is supposedly universal and early, marriage is far less studied by demographers than mortality. This Malthusian preconception of Chinese marriage persists today. On the one hand, because of a primordial and political preference for children, young people are assumed to marry early. On the other hand, because of the pervasive and protean nature of the Chinese family, they are supposed to be able to do so virtually regardless of economic circumstances. In contrast with the classic Western European family system, where individuals had to inherit or establish independent means to marry (Hajnal 1982; Macfarlane 1986), Chinese couples could draw on the resources of the multiple-family household (Tawney 1932; Chao 1986).[9] Whereas high infant and child mortality may have curtailed population growth, nuptiality has long been perceived as the most powerful engine propelling Chinese population growth, and depressing Chinese living standards.

Chinese Realities

Excess female infant and child mortality, however, has had fundamental consequences-for marriage markets, marriage institutions, and marriage practices in late imperial and contemporary China. The shortage of women, exacerbated by the practice of polygyny and the discouragement of female remarriage, prevented a significant proportion of Chinese males in the past, and some even today, from ever marrying. As a result, marriage markets differed greatly by gender.

They were also highly hypergamous—at least for females. Almost all grooms or their families had to provide a bride price to secure a marriage. Far fewer brides or their families had to supply a dowry except to confer special status on their married daughters, or to compensate for unusually low or high family status.[10] Because females married hypergamously, bride price was more important toward the bottom of the social ladder. At the same time, dowry was essential among the social elite.

The Chinese accordingly developed a wide variety of marital strategies, including such variant forms of marriage as levirate and little daughter-in-law. In addition, because of low fertility and the preoccupation with patrilineal descent, they developed a variety of uxorilocal marriage types. In China, as in the West, a multiplicity of marriage types had existed in the far past. But whereas Western marriage was characterized by the rapid predominance of monogamous marriage in the Christian era (Goody 1983), marriage in China remained highly variegated.

Major Marriage

In the most common and most approved form of Chinese marriage, termed major marriage, a female marries and moves in with a male spouse and his family.[11] Major marriages account for the vast majority of marriages today. While we have no marital statistics for China as a whole in the past, the proportion of major marriages among historical populations varied from a scant to an overwhelming majority. However, the female and male patterns of major marriage were almost symmetrically opposite.

Female major marriage. In China, females have always married universally and early, while males have married later or not at all. Female marriage therefore fits the Malthusian model of Chinese marriage, in contrast to female marriage in Western Europe, which occurred late or not at all. Figure 5.1 contrasts the proportion of never-married females by age group in several European and Chinese largely early nineteenth century European and Chinese populations. By age 20–24 most Chinese females were already married, while the vast majority of European females were still single. By age 30–34, virtually no Chinese females remained single, whereas 30 percent of their Western counterparts were still spinsters.

This Chinese female marriage pattern is further confirmed by an analysis of mean age at first marriage in several periods and populations. Table 5.1 summarizes the findings. Until as recently as the

1960s, the mean age at first marriage stayed within a narrow band, between ages 16 and 19. The only exception, age 21 among daughters of the imperial lineage, is very likely due to the hypergamous female marriage market (Lee, Wang, and Ruan in press). In China, as else-where, virtually no one wanted to marry a princess. Yet despite such prejudices Chinese females in the late imperial period married in greater numbers than Western females regardless of social back-ground, and they did so 5 to 10 years earlier.

Since the 1950s, however, this gap has begun to narrow, with age at marriage rising in China (Wang and Tuma 1993). In 1950, despite a legal female marriage age of 18, the mean female marriage age was slightly over 17, rising slowly thereafter to almost 20 in 1970, and shooting up to 23 in 1979.[12] This sudden latter rise reflected a govern-ment family planning policy, implemented in 1973, that advocated

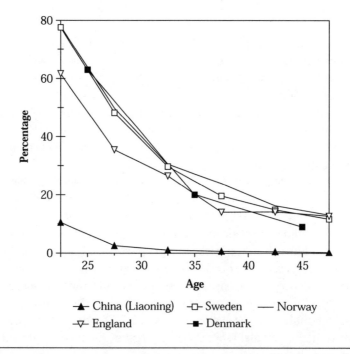

Figure 5.1. Share of never-married females, by age, selected countries, ca. 1800
Sources: China (Liaoning): Lee and Campbell (1997); Sweden: Hofsten and Lundstrom (1976); Norway: Statistisk Sentralbyra (1980); England: Hinde (1985); Denmark: Statens Statistiske Bureau (1905).

Table 5.1 Female mean age at first marriage, China, selected periods and
populations

Period	Location	Mean age	Number
1550–1850[a]	Zhejiang	17.6/19.1	1,994/1,078
1640–1900	Beijing	20.7	12,942
1774–1840[b]	Liaoning	18.3	812
1929–1931	Northern China	17.2	841
1929–1931	Southern China	18.7	919
1950–1954	China	17.5	46,233
1960–1964	China	19.1	46,233
1970	China	19.7	46,233
1982[c]	China	22.4	2,677,408
1990[c]	China	22.1	327,855,996
1995[c]	China	22.6	3,625,859

Sources: Zhejiang: Harrell and Pullum (1995, 146), from two different lineages;
Beijing: Lee, Wang, and Ruan (in press); Liaoning: Lee and Campbell (1997); northern
and southern China: Notestein and Chiao (1937); China 1950–1970: Wang and Yang
(1996); China 1982, 1990, 1995: SSB (1987, 1993, 1997), calculated from raw data
from the censuses and the One-per-Hundred survey.

a. With the exception of the Beijing nobility, which recorded dates of birth and
marriage for females, most historical genealogical sources did not record information
on either daughters who married out or daughters-in-law who married in. The
calculations by Harrell and Pullum are therefore based on indirect estimates, by
subtracting an estimated first birth interval of 4.6–4.7 years from age at first birth.

b. Marriage age obtained by subtracting 1.5 from 19.78 *sui*.

c. Singulate mean age at marriage.

later marriage. Female marriage ages have not increased further, remaining at a level comparable to the mean first marriage age among
Western females.[13]

The proportion of unmarried females has remained the same
throughout the last three centuries. Table 5.2 compares the percentage
of females never married by age 30 in the periods and major populations for which data are available. In spite of the substantial increase
in marriage age, the proportion never marrying by age 30 has hardly
changed, exhibiting a pattern of "stalled convergence."[14] While 15
percent of Western females continue to remain unmarried at age 40,

Table 5.2 Females never married by age 30, China, selected periods and populations

Period	Location	%	Number
1640–1700	Beijing	4.0	1,664
1741–1760	Beijing	4.0	2,215
1774–1873[a]	Liaoning	1.0	3,014
1801–1820	Beijing	4.0	2,753
1929–1931[a]	Northern China	0.0	19,801
1929–1931[a]	Southern China	0.1	22,637
1900–1925	China	2.2	7,215
1945–1949	China	1.1	5,877
1955–1959	China	1.2	8,018
1982	China	1.0	84,281
1990	China	1.0	6,923,442
1995	China	1.2	124,877

Sources: Beijing: Lee, Wang, and Ruan (in press); Liaoning: Lee and Campbell (1997, 85); northern and southern China: Notestein and Chiao (1937, 378); 1900–1959 birth cohorts: Wang and Tuma (1993); China 1982, 1990, 1995: SSB (1987, 1993, 1997), calculated from raw data from the censuses and the One-per-Hundred survey.

Note: 1900–1925, 1945–1949, and 1955–1959 are birth cohorts.

a. Women aged 30–34.

only 1 percent of Chinese females are unmarried at age 30. In other words, the majority of Chinese women are postponing, but not forgoing, married life.

As the mean age at first marriage has risen, the age pattern of marriage has become more compressed within a narrower age range, rather than simply shifting to a later age (Wang and Tuma 1993). Evidently the pressure and importance of marriage are still perceived by Chinese females or their families as strongly today as in the past. This is true even in urban settings, where female marriage age has risen significantly. In 1990, for example, only 2.3 percent of urban women aged 30 were single, in contrast to 15 percent of their counterparts in the West (Hofsten and Lundstrom 1976; Wang and Tuma 1993).

Male major marriage. An attitudinal survey conducted in 1991 of urban residents in Baoding, Hebei, found that four-fifths of ever-married women and six-sevenths of ever-married men still believed that a woman must marry to live a full and happy life.[15] Thus Chinese men believe in the institution of marriage at least as deeply as Chinese women, and more than men in other Asian societies.[16] However, while women have been able to marry easily and early, the scarcity of females and the cost of marrying has prevented many men from ever marrying. Figure 5.2 contrasts the proportion of married males by age in several early nineteenth century European and Chinese populations. While Chinese men married slightly earlier, some 20 percent of all men in all societies were still unmarried by age 30. Even by age 40–45, in both China and the West between 10 and 15 percent of males were still bachelors. Male marriage clearly did not fit the Malthusian model of Chinese marriage. In fact Chinese males were no more likely than Western males ever to marry.[17] But whereas male bachelorhood in

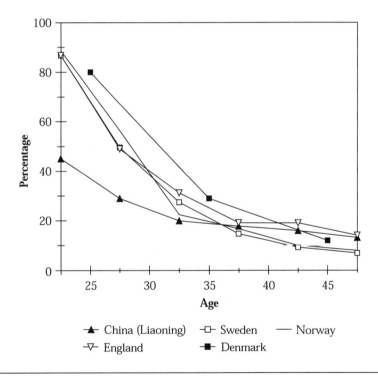

Figure 5.2. Share of never-married males, by age, selected countries, ca. 1800. *Sources:* See. Figure 5.1.

China was due primarily to what demographers call "marriage squeeze," the unavailability of females, male bachelorhood in Europe was due to marriage avoidance.

Indeed, male bachelorhood seems to be a universal phenomenon in China regardless of time and place. Table 5.3 compares the share of never-married males by age 30 and 40 in selected periods and popula-

Table 5.3 Males never married, China, selected periods and populations

Period	Location	% never married		
		By age 30	By age 40	Number
1640–1900	Beijing	13	7	1,103
1700–1724[a]	Anhui	8.2	—	1,040
1750–1774[a]	Anhui	16.1	—	1,949
1774–1873[b]	Liaoning	20.4	16	3,547
1800–1819[a]	Anhui	12.6	—	2,353
1820–1839[a]	Anhui	14.1	—	2,567
1929–1931[b]	Northern China	11.5	7.9	21,560
1929–1931[b]	Southern China	7.7	3.9	24,874
1900–1925[c]	China	13.7	6.8	6,538
1945–1949[c]	China	12.7	6.7	6,295
1955–1959[c]	China	9.8	—	8,661
1982	China	10.7	6.3	88,869
1990	China	8.3	5.3	7,159,677
1995	China	7.7	4.7	125,367

Sources: Beijing: Lee and Wang (in press); Anhui: Telford (1994, 936); Liaoning: Lee and Campbell (1997); northern and southern China: Notestein and Chiao (1937); 1900–1959 birth cohorts: Wang and Tuma (1993); China 1982, 1990, 1995: SSB (1987, 1993, 1997), calculated from raw data from the censuses and the One-per-Hundred survey.

Note: 1900–1925, 1945–1949, and 1955–1959 are birth cohorts.

Note: Genealogical records notoriously underrecorded bachelors, as they have no surviving progeny and are therefore far less likely to be remembered centuries later at the time of compilation.

a. Proportion unmarried over age 20.

b. Ages 30–34 and 40–44.

c. Ages 30–35.

tions. From the seventeenth through the late nineteenth centuries 10–20 percent of all men were unmarried. The sole exceptions were the Qing imperial nobility, and even they had a bachelor rate as high as 13 percent. This phenomenon of male celibacy continues today. In 1995, at age 30, when virtually all women were married, close to 8 percent of Chinese men were still single. Even by age 40, about 5 percent of Chinese men had never been married (SSB 1997, 412).

Nevertheless, with the decline in female infanticide since the late nineteenth century, the rate at which males married increased greatly. According to Table 5.3, by the early twentieth century the proportion of never-married males at age 30 had fallen by about half, from 20 to 10 percent. A large-scale survey conducted in 1929–1931 reported that fewer than 12 percent of males aged 30–34 in northern China and fewer than 8 percent in southern China were single (Barclay et al. 1976).[18] An even larger retrospective survey conducted in 1988 similarly found that only 14 percent of men born in 1900–1925 were still single by age 30, and only 7 percent had not married by age 40 (Wang and Tuma 1993). While the proportion of unmarried men has continued to decline in the late twentieth century, and could decline even further in the twenty-first, this trend of rising male marriage is over a century old.

Although the proportions of married men were similar in China and in the West, Chinese men historically married earlier. Table 5.4 summarizes mean age at marriage in the major available periods and populations. From the sixteenth through nineteenth centuries, Chinese men on average married around age 21. Western males married at age 26 or older depending on their nationality. This gap, however, narrowed during the second half of the twentieth century as male age at marriage, like female age at marriage, rose steadily. By 1996 the male mean age at marriage in China was 25, approximately the same as in the West. In contrast with the "stalled convergence" of Chinese females, Chinese and Western males now marry in equal proportions and at similar ages.

However, while the mean age of marriage for males may have been only a little higher than female age at marriage, the variance was far greater. As a result, the age patterns of first marriage differ drastically between females and males. Figure 5.3 shows the traditional age patterns of marriage for females and males born in 1900–1925. For females the rate of first marriage rises steadily after age 15 and reaches its highest value around age 20, dropping precipitously thereafter. For

Table 5.4 Male mean age at first marriage, China, selected periods and populations

Period	Location	Mean age	Number
1520–1661[a]	Anhui	21–22	8,295
1550–1850[b]	Zhejiang	20.9/22.4	1,994/1,078
1700–1900	Beijing	20.9	918
1774–1840[c]	Liaoning	20.8	1,790
1929–1931	Northern China	20.3	743
1929–1931	Southern China	20.7	857
1900–1925	China	22.2	6,538
1945–1949	China	23.6	6,295
1982[d]	China	25.2	2,883,147
1990[d]	China	23.4	350,973,807
1995[d]	China	24.4	3,701,787

Sources: Anhui: Telford (1992); Zhejiang: Harrell and Pullum (1995); Beijing: Lee, Wang, and Ruan (in press); Liaoning: Lee and Campbell (1997); northern and southern China: Notestein and Chiao (1937); 1900–1925 and 1945–1949 birth cohorts: Wang and Tuma (1993); China 1982, 1990, 1995: SSB (1987, 1993, 1997), calculated from raw data from the censuses and the One-per-Hundred survey.

Note: 1900–1925 and 1945–1949 are birth cohorts defined by time of birth, not marriage, and include only those married by age 35.

a. Marriage age inferred from father's age at birth of first son, minus 5 years.

b. Marriage age inferred from father's age at birth of first son, minus 4.6 or 4.7 years from age at first birth, with corrections for marriage type.

c. Estimated by subtracting 1.5 from the 22.3 *sui* recorded.

d. Singulate mean age at marriage.

males the pattern is totally different. The rate rises to a high level (but only a third of the female's) around age 20, then remains at about the same level for at least the next ten years, from age 20 to over age 30.

This contrast between female and male age at marriage is heightened by cultural restrictions on female remarriage. Table 5.5 again summarizes the available information for China. As in the West, remarriage was more common for males than females. Moreover, the proportions in China were more or less the same as in Europe. In the West, roughly one-third of all widowers and perhaps one-fifth of all widows in the past remarried.[19] Among the peasant populations of

Liaoning, the proportions ever remarried were one-third of widowers and one-tenth of widows. While these differences appear even greater among elite populations, this may be a result of biased reporting.[20]

This prohibition against female remarriage has persisted through-out the twentieth century. Even in early twentieth-century Taiwan, where widow remarriage was more common than in other Chinese populations, most widows did not remarry (A. Wolf 1981).[21] More recently on the Chinese mainland, remarriage has accounted for no more than 2 percent of all female marriages. Overall, remarriage is still markedly less frequent than in the West, where remarriages have ac-counted for one-fifth of all marriages in the past, and nearly half of all marriages today.[22]

Moreover, the desire of both bachelors and widowers for young

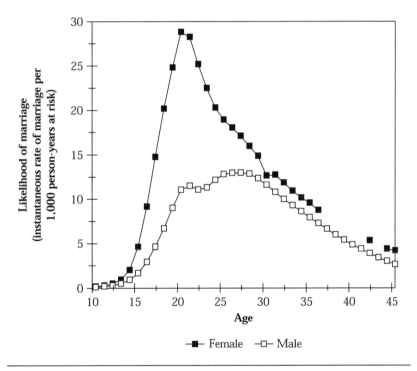

Figure 5.3. Age patterns of female and male marriage, China, birth cohort 1900–1925
Source: Wang and Tuma (1993).

Table 5.5 Remarriages, China, selected periods and populations

Period	Location	Male		Female	
		%	No.	%	No.
1700–1724	Anhui	12.5	816	—	—
1750	Jiangsu	11.4	664	—	—
1750	Guangdong	24.6	781	—	—
1750–1774	Anhui	13.3	1,298	—	—
1750–1790[a]	Beijing[a]	41.6	3,628	—	—
1792–1867[b]	Liaoning	27.8	97	12.2	41
1800	Hunan	14.3	925	—	—
1800–1819	Anhui	21.6	1,708	—	—
1840–1880	Anhui	21.0	1,335	—	—
1906–1945[c]	Taiwan	—	—	5.0	38,941
1980[d]	China	3.0	—	3.0	7,166,528
1990[d]	China	4.1	—	4.1	9,486,869

Sources: Anhui: Telford (1994); 1750 Jiangsu, Guangdong, Hunan: Liu Ts'ui-jung (1995b); Beijing: Lee, Wang, and Ruan (in press); Liaoning: Lee and Campbell (1997); Taiwan: A. Wolf (1981); China 1980, 1990: Feng Fanghui (1996).

Note: Because no historical sources except Liaoning differentiate between polygynous and monogamous marriages, some of the remarriages are additional wives of polygynous husbands.

a. Based on Qing nobles and includes polygynous marriages.
b. Men and women widowed at 26–30 *sui* who remarried within the next 3 years.
c. Sample size refers to woman-years.
d. Figures refer to total remarriages for both sexes.

brides produced several variations in the age difference between spouses. Most couples married at approximately the same age, but some men who remarried were far older than their wives, and a few others were much younger than their wives. For older men seeking remarriage, the preference for a bride in her late teens or early twenties took priority over any concern about the age difference. Similarly, for very young men seeking first marriage, the desire to find a bride overrode any concern about her age. As a result, the marriage market constraint faced by both widowers and bachelors was not the number of unmarried women of their own age, but rather the number of never-married women in early adulthood.

   Such a trimodal male marriage age pattern is illustrated by an analysis of 1,790 first marriages from rural Liaoning. While husbands on average were 1.8 years older than their wives, there was a wide range of spousal age differences, determined not by the bride's age at marriage but by the groom's. Apparently men or their families were interested only in young brides who were already adults. Consequently, there were virtually no marriages between children or adolescents. The popular image of the Chinese child bride was simply not valid for this Liaoning population. All except one of the 77 males who married by age 14 *sui* had wives who were older than they; three-quarters of these were four or more years older than the husbands. Most of the 1,300 or so males marrying in their mid-teens to mid-twenties, as expected, married wives who were the same age or younger, although the proportion of older wives was still considerable. The 400 males marrying later took substantially younger wives.[23]

Variant Institutions

While Malthus' assumption of universal marriage in China must be qualified, his description of the strong Chinese desire for marriage is fundamentally correct. So is his depiction of their motivation. Chinese wanted to marry to perpetuate their lineage and to support their old age. While the desire for marriage and children is on some level universal, it is particularly acute in Chinese society. The desire for biological perpetuation has been traced back to the prevalence of ancestor worship in the third millennium B.C. (Ho 1975, 322–327). Numerous texts as early as the first millennium B.C. articulated the need for marriage and children. The famous saying of Mencius, that of all unfilial deeds none is more serious than the failure to produce male descendants, is perhaps the most direct statement of this belief.[24]

   As a result, the Chinese developed a variety of marriage forms that are only beginning to be studied. Anthropologists commonly distinguish two other categories of Chinese marriage besides major marriage: little-daughter-in-law marriage, in which the woman moved in with the man's family at infancy and married only years later; and uxorilocal marriage, in which the man married and then moved in with the woman and her family.[25] In addition, recent studies have identified the practice of polygyny among the elite and levirate among the poor.

   Polygyny. Polygyny, the marriage of one man to more than one wife, in China was largely an elite behavior. The most salient example is the

Qing nobility, over one-third of whom so married. Even among the elite genealogical populations only 10 percent of male marriages were polygynous.[26] By contrast, analysis of over 4,000 marriages among peasants in eighteenth- and nineteenth-century Liaoning found poly-gyny rates of perhaps 1 per 1,000, while polygyny rates among early twentieth-century peasants in Taiwan were only slightly higher (A. Wolf and Huang 1980; Lee and Campbell 1997). Since peasants ac-counted for the vast majority of the population of China, it is unlikely that more than 1 or 2 percent of male marriages were polygynous.[27]

Moreover, recent analysis of polygynous fertility among the Qing nobility suggests that marital behavior in many such marriages was likely to resemble serial monogamy, at least in terms of conjugal rela-tions (Lee and Wang in press). Most polygynous men apparently slept with only one wife at a time, regardless of the total number of wives. The Qing nobility, in other words, practiced polygyny partly to com-pensate for the absence of easy divorce. As a result, adding one wife increased male fertility by only one child. Overall, monogamous no-bles who survived to age 45 and had on average 3 wives had on aver-age 4.6 children. Polygynous nobles who survived to age 45 had on average only 6.8 children. The Western equivalents were 8–10 chil-dren for monogamous men, 15–25 for polygynous men. Monoga-mous fertility, in other words, was only half Western fertility. Poly-gynous fertility was barely one-third Western fertility.[28]

The low level of polygynous fertility is remarkable. Figure 5.4, which tracks male age-specific marital fertility, shows that while poly-gynous fertility was perhaps 20–30 percent higher than monogamous fertility, the contours of age-specific fertility did not begin to differ radically until men were in their mid-thirties, when monogamous fer-tility declined rapidly. Polygynous men in their late forties had the fertility of monogamous men in their mid-thirties; in their late fifties, they were as fertile as monogamous men in their early forties. The mean age at last birth for polygynous men was 45, 10 years older than monogamous men. Clearly, men relied on polygyny largely to extend their reproductive span well into their late middle age rather than to increase their overall fertility. The sybaritic caricature of "traditional" Chinese multiple marriage is also largely a modern, Western fantasy, ironically increasingly accepted in China.[29]

Little-daughter-in-law marriage. Far more common, at least among poor people and at least in some regions, were alternative "minor" marriages such as little-daughter-in-law marriage and levirate, both of which produced brides without the costs associated with major marriage. In little-daughter-in-law marriage *(tongyangxi)*, a woman was adopted as a child, normally before the age of 10, and brought up as a future daughter-in-law.[30] Most parents resorted to such a form of marriage for economic reasons: on the bride's side to avoid having to raise a daughter, and on the groom's side to avoid the high cost of bride price and wedding expenses.[31] Some also found such marriages a convenient way of ensuring that daughters-in-law would be particularly well integrated into their families.[32]

These marriages were particularly popular in some areas in Taiwan, where they accounted for almost half of all marriages (A. Wolf and Huang 1980, 124–125; Chuang and Wolf 1995). They also appear to have been common elsewhere in China, at least during the late impe-

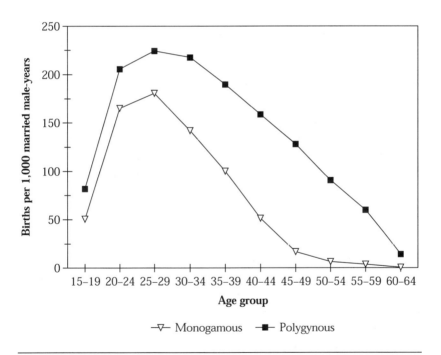

Figure 5.4. Age patterns of fertility among monogamous and polygynous men, Qing imperial lineage, 1700–1840
Source: Wang, Lee, and Campbell (1995).

rial period,[33] although the documented proportions of little-daughter-in-law marriages in the early twentieth century are low, perhaps because of the earlier decline in female infanticide and the greater availability of brides. According to the national land utilization survey conducted around 1930, 5–10 percent of all marriages in the Middle Yangzi and perhaps 0.5–1 percent of all marriages in northern China were little-daughter-in-law marriages (A. Wolf and Huang 1980, 329). While these proportions are low, scattered evidence suggests the greater prevalence of such marriages, even in northern and northeastern China, for specific populations.

Levirate. While there are no quantitative studies or statistics of levirate marriage *(shoujihun),* whereby a man inherits his wife from a deceased older relative, such as his brother or his father, there are documented examples dating as far back as the first millennium B.C. (Gu 1982). Indeed, one of the most famous romances and marriages in Chinese history is that between an eighth-century emperor, Xuanzong of the Tang dynasty, and Yang Guifei, his daughter-in-law. Although this form of marriage was repeatedly prohibited, it persisted, particularly among such non-Han populations as the Manchus and Mongols, but among the Han as well (Ding 1998). Although both levirate and little-daughter-in-law marriages are now illegal in both the Republic and the People's Republic because of their stressful marital relationships and exploitation of women,[34] they continue to be practiced at least occasionally among poor peasants (Yan Xunxiang 1992).

Uxorilocal marriage. In contrast, uxorilocal marriage, whereby a man marries a woman and moves in with her family, has persisted and in some cases increased, especially in urban China. Figure 5.5 shows the proportion of married women by age group who in 1991 continued to live with their family after marriage.[35] From the 1960s to the 1990s uxorilocal living arrangements accounted for 5–8 percent of all marriages in rural areas, and for 7–10 percent of all marriages in urban areas (CASS 1994). While neither husbands nor wives now change their family names, coresident sons-in-law are expected to assume responsibility for supporting and caring for their in-laws.[36]

Overall, the proportions of uxorilocal or proto-uxorilocal marriage arrangements in contemporary China seem in line with the proportions in the past, 10 plus or minus 5 percent of all marriages. Since approximately 20 percent of all marriages would not produce a son, given the demographic rates of a pretransition system (Wrigley 1978), it appears that about half of all sonless families resorted to adopting a son-in-law.[37] The other half probably resorted to adopting a son. Such son-in-law adoption arrangements varied from the complete transfer of allegiance by the son-in-law from his biological to his residential family to shared allegiance, and even contracted temporary allegiance. As we will see in Chapter 7, the forms of son-in-law adoption were as varied as the forms of son adoption. Male hypergamy, in other words, coexisted along with female hypergamy.

Collective and Individual Strategies

The combination of a gender-differentiated marriage market, a tradition of hypergamous marriage for women and even sometimes for men, and a multiplicity of marriage types meant that nuptiality could

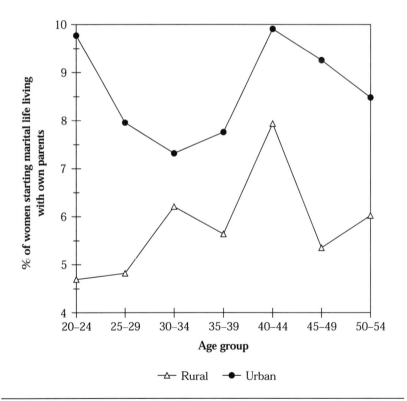

Figure 5.5. Uxorilocal marriages, by wife's age, China, 1991
Source: CASS (1994, table 3.1b).

be as finely differentiated as mortality, especially for males, and at both ends of the social spectrum. Among the Qing nobility and other genealogical populations, the probability of marrying differed clearly by noble status. So did marriage age. Whereas only 6 percent of high-noble sons were still unmarried by age 30–34, the proportion of low-noble bachelors was double, at 12 percent, in the eighteenth and nineteenth centuries (Lee, Wang, and Ruan in press). Similarly, while only 5 percent of gentry sons over age 20 in Anhui were still unmarried, 15 percent of nongentry sons were single (Telford 1994).[38] Low-nobility sons on average began their reproduction two years later than high-nobility sons. Nongentry sons married three years later than gentry sons.

Among commoners, marriage was an even more sensitive measure of privilege, since even fewer males were able to marry (Lee and Campbell 1997). Access to marriage was determined by access to resources, which were distributed unequally both by household position and by occupation. The higher one's occupation or household position, the more likely one was to marry. In rural Liaoning, for example, multiple-family household heads were 75 percent more likely than other household members to be married. Lineage-group leaders were three times more likely to be married than other members of their groups. Occupation was even more important, a reflection of the benefits of having a steady income in a hypergamous society. With both age and position in the household and lineage hierarchies controlled for, the likelihood of marriage for soldiers, village officials, and rural artisans was nine, five, and four times as great, respectively, as for men without such occupations. Whatever their age, men with a profession were more likely than the rest of the population to marry. In fact soldiers and officials were the only men in the population to achieve universal marriage. All officials were married by 36–40 *sui,* as were all soldiers by 46–50 *sui.* Clearly, even in these rural Liaoning villages, marriage was hypergamous. Income was apparently one dimension of male attractiveness. Perhaps so were physical and official powers.

Social stratification in male marriage persists in contemporary China. In the early 1980s, unmarried males were still predominantly the socially and economically disadvantaged, as defined by education and residence. Whereas only 0.5 percent of university-educated men were unmarried at age 40, the proportion among illiterate or semiliterate peasants was 15 percent (SSB 1987, 3326–81). This gap increased slightly in the 1980s along with increases in economic and social inequalities. Despite the tremendous improvements in the probability of marriage for the population as a whole, the percentage of bachelors among the illiterate and semiilliterate rose, from 25 to 29 at age 30, and from 15 to 19 at age 40. One of every five illiterate men in China was still single by age 40 (SSB 1993, 3:217, 232).

In contrast to the West, where marriage has become an increasingly frail institution, marriage in China has remained strong through two political revolutions and untold social and economic revolutions in this century.[39] The rise of romantic love and the decline of the Confucian patriarchal family have replaced parent-child relations with spouse-spouse relations as the most important affective tie. As a result, the search for a spouse has become an obsessive pastime not only for parents and relatives but also for friends, colleagues, and others, played out in a dating culture and a world popular culture that are still new in China though already well developed in Taiwan.

Indeed, although not all Chinese plan their fertility or control the survivorship of their children, all do plan the marriage of their own children and often of other people's as well. From the moment a child is born, parents begin to obsess over their son or daughter's marriage prospects. This obsession, in turn, affects other familial demographic decisions, including how many male and female children to have and to bring up.

The calculus of marriage differs, of course, by class and gender. Girls, for example, earn a bride price for poor families but cost a rich family dowry. The richer the family, the larger the dowry. The pressure of providing a dowry is exacerbated by the hypergamous nature of the female marriage, as Chinese men prefer and most often marry equal- or lower-status brides. As a result, while males at the bottom of the social ladder are left spouseless, women at the top of the social ladder have to wait longer to find a match. This was the case for the imperial nobility, who had so much trouble marrying off their daughters that they created a system of assigned marriage called *zhihun,* which literally assigned such marriages to unmarried young men of good banner families (Ding 1998).

For a boy, the calculus of securing a marriage is even more complex. Given the constant scarcity of brides and the economic resources needed to compete for a spouse, parents have to choose between raising a little daughter-in-law and taking the risk of finding and funding a suitable spouse for their son when he matures. These difficulties, of course, were compounded with each additional surviving son. A poor family that decides not to adopt a little daughter-in-law can avoid the cost of major marriage through levirate or uxorilocal marriage. While neither marriage form appears to have been common among wealthier families, some did choose to give up at least some of their sons in adoption. The less fortunate Chinese males, just like their European counterparts, either remained celibate or resorted to marriage forms other than major marriage.

The joy of many sons must therefore have been muted by the dread prospect of many marriages. It is hardly surprising then that some parents found arranging their children's marriages so burdensome that they preferred to kill or sell their children to avoid such future obligations.[40] The emotional cost of such extreme measures and/or the cost of marriage presumably also made marital restraint, which we will discuss in Chapter 6, less costly and more sensible.

Fertility

Of the preventive checks, the restraint from marriage which is not followed by irregular gratifications may properly be termed moral restraint . . . Promiscuous intercourse, unnatural passions, violations of the marriage bed, and improper arts to conceal the consequences of irregular connections are preventive checks that clearly come under the head of vice.

MALTHUS, *AN ESSAY ON THE PRINCIPLE OF POPULATION* (1803).

Malthusian Legacy

Malthus believed that sexual behavior within marriage was generally uniform in most societies, and that the rare exceptions of fertility control were unintentional consequences of poverty, although he admitted that some secondary sterility came earlier in some societies than in others.[1] While moral restraint was a viable option, marital restraint was not.

Contemporary demographers have by and large accepted this claim that there was little intentional control of fertility within marriage before the fertility transition. Moreover, they have agreed that any variation in ardor from one society to another is largely a function of timing rather than phasing. Couples, in other words, might vary the frequency of their relations per month. As a result, demographers formalized a universal pattern of uncontrolled marital fertility in which only the amplitude of the curve shifts, not the fundamental shape. They therefore identified an age pattern of fertility and named it "natural" fertility,[2] "natural" because the age pattern of fertility conforms closely to the perceived age pattern of human female fecundity. Fertility remains high in youth, when fecundity is high, and tapers off only as aging gradually undercuts the biological capacity to conceive.[3] Numerous studies have confirmed that all pretransition fertility in

Europe was "natural," validating the Malthusian model (Coale and Watkins 1986).

Studies of fertility transition processes in the West have revealed that the fertility transition was a clear shift away from this "natural" fertility regime to an alternative age pattern of controlled fertility, named "family limitation."[4] This age pattern is parity dependent; that is, childbearing stops after an individual or a couple reaches a desired number of children. The age pattern is therefore concave: fertility is high in youth but declines swiftly with age. Such parity-dependent fertility control became possible only after the advent of such reproductive technologies as contraception, sterilization, and abortion.[5]

This model of the fertility transition as a shift "from natural fertility to family limitation" does not, however, fit well with non-Western experience in either historical or contemporary populations. In Japan and China, which we shall examine in detail below, pretransition marital fertility was well below that of pretransition European populations. A variety of descriptive ethnographic and historical studies document the existence of fertility control in these societies,[6] but because these studies are largely nonquantitative, they have been ignored, rejected as anecdotal, or dismissed as unintentional and therefore disqualified as fertility control. Similarly, while a number of contemporary populations are known to use contraceptive methods largely to lengthen birth intervals, these fertility regimes are still considered "natural," since they do not use contraception to stop further births. This is especially the case for a number of African populations.[7] The current model of the fertility transition excludes regulating birth intervals as a means of fertility control.

Chinese Realities

Low Marital Fertility

Contrary to the perception of Malthus and his contemporaries, Chinese fertility overall was probably not much higher than European fertility, while marital fertility was significantly lower. Recent demographic studies have traced fertility measures as far back as the thirteenth century on the basis of retrospective Chinese genealogies.[8] More reliable measures from the archives of the Qing imperial nobility become available beginning in the seventeenth century, and from household registers in the eighteenth century. Table 6.1 summarizes all

Table 6.1 Marital fertility, China, selected periods and populations

Period	Location	Fertility level		Sample size
		TMFR	TFR	
1296–1864	Hunan	6.0	—	2,670
1462–1864	Anhui	6.1	—	1,654
1517–1877	Jiangsu	5.8	—	1,784
1520–1661	Anhui	5.4–8.2	—	11,804
1700–1890	Beijing	5.3	—	3,178
1774–1873	Liaoning	6.3	—	3,000
1929–1931	22 provinces	6.2	5.5	50,000
1950	China	5.8	5.3	300,000
1955	China	6.2	6.0	300,000
1960	China	4.1	4.0	300,000
1965	China	6.3	6.0	300,000
1970	China	6.2	5.8	300,000
1975	China	4.4	3.6	300,000
1980	China	3.2	2.3	300,000
1985	China	—	2.2	500,000
1990	China	—	2.3	70,000
1992	China	—	2.0	—

Sources and notes: Hunan, Anhui 1462–1864, and Jiangsu: Liu Ts'ui-jung (1995b, 99). The TMFR is for ages 15–49. Liu suggests that the actual TMFR was slightly higher because not all the women in the denominator for the youngest age groups would have been married. The discrepancy is unlikely to have been large, since age-specific fertility rates below age 20 were very low.

Anhui 1520–1660: Telford (1992b). Sample size refers to the wives and concubines married to 10,512 males. Telford found a mean of 2.77 recorded male births per married woman, which implies a TMFR of 5.4 assuming a male/female sex ratio at birth of 105. He suggests that the actual TMFR should be higher because of underregistration of male births. Telford (1995) presents an estimated TMFR of 8.2 by excluding some registers with very low recorded fertility and inflating the remaining male births by 50 percent. He provides no explanation of or justification for this procedure.

(continued on next page)

Table 6.1 (continued)

Beijing: Wang, Lee, and Campbell (1995, 395). The TMFR was calculated by adjusting age-specific fertility rates by estimated proportions married in each age group. This is probably an overestimate of the true TMFR because males were included in the denominator in the original calculation only if they had at least one child in their lifetime. Men who married but never had children accordingly contributed no person-years of risk. Moreover, the proportions of males married used in the adjustment were estimated on the basis of whether males had children by specific ages, and accordingly underestimate the actual proportions of males married.

Liaoning: Lee and Campbell (1997, 90). The fertility calculation is based on population registers containing 12,466 individual records and over 3,000 marriages. The number given here, the TMFR, is higher than the TFR (given that not all people are married at all ages). The number reflects a mortality or underregistration adjustment of 33 percent.

22 provinces: Barclay et al. (1976, 614). The TMFR was calculated from age-specific marital fertility rates of women aged 15–49. The survey on which the calculation is based covered some 200,000 Chinese farmers from over 46,000 households in 191 locales. We give the sample size of 50,000 assuming that each household had slightly more than one woman of reproductive age.

China: 1950–1980 TFRs are from Coale and Chen (1987); 1950–1980 TMFRs are calculated for women aged 20–44 from Lavely (1986, 432–433); 1985–1992 TFRs are from Yao Xinwu and Yin (1994). These numbers are based largely on several large-scale fertility surveys.

the available studies from the earliest period when fertility can be estimated relatively reliably. The total marital fertility rate (TMFR) is a synthetic construct based on age-specific fertility rates within marriage, indicating the number of births a married woman could have if she observed the age-specific fertility schedule. The total fertility rate (TFR) is a synthetic measure indicating the lifetime fertility of any woman, including those not married. On average, Chinese women married by age 20 rarely had more than 6 children if they remained married until age 50; their European counterparts had on average 7.5–9 children (Flinn 1981; Wilson 1984; Wrigley et al. 1997).

This low marital fertility is one of the most distinctive features of the Chinese demographic system. Figure 6.1 shows the contrast between age-specific rates for six East Asian and six Western European historical populations. Before 1800 European marital fertility was much higher, especially in the younger age groups, and declined more slowly. Not only is the amplitude of East Asian marital fertility lower than European fertility, but the shape of the curve is fundamentally different.

Low fertility was characteristic of elite marriage, including polygynous marriage. Fertility calculated for monogamous fathers of the Qing imperial nobility ranged between only 4 and 5.5 for 1700–1840. Even polygynous fathers in this elite population had a fertility level of only 6–10 births, comparable only to monogamous men in the West. By contrast, the number of children born to polygynous men in the West was 15–25.[9]

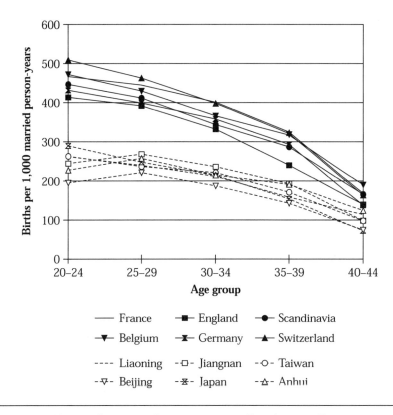

Figure 6.1. "Natural" age-specific marital fertility, East Asia and Europe, ca. 1600–1800
Sources: European populations: Flinn (1981); Japan: Kito (1991); Liaoning: Lee and Campbell (1997); Jiangnan: Liu Ts'ui-jung (1992); Anhui: Telford (1992b); Taiwan: A. Wolf (1985b). The Beijing numbers are monogamous male age-specifc fertility rates but should closely approximate female age-specific fertility. The Anhui and Jiangnan figures are derived from counts of sons multiplied by 1.97. In addition we inflated the Anhui, Jiangnan, and Japanese figures by 20 percent for possible underenumeration.

Surveys conducted in the early twentieth century report similarly low levels of marital fertility. A large survey conducted around 1930 and covering much of China revealed an estimated fertility level of 5.5 per woman. This finding is not only highly consistent with earlier numbers based on married women; it also forced demographers to recognize that fertility in this supposedly natural fertility regime was very low.[10] While others have questioned such low fertility levels, their alternative estimates have not been much different.[11]

Contemporary censuses and survey data provide further confirmation that China's pretransition fertility level was below the level in high-fertility countries. Fertility levels from the mid-twentieth century, when China was still largely noncontracepting, were also quite low despite a possible postwar baby boom. National total fertility, derived from retrospective interviews conducted in 1982, was slightly below 5.0 in the late 1940s and 5.3 in 1950.[12] While fertility increased slightly following land reform and the breakdown of the traditional household collective system of family planning, it rarely exceeded 6.0.[13] This was significantly lower than fertility in other developing countries around the same time.[14]

Marital Restraint

Low Chinese fertility was the outcome of three demographic mechanisms: late starting, early stopping, and long birth intervals. In contrast to pretransition Western couples, Chinese couples did not start childbearing until well after marriage. This feature of Chinese population behavior again can be traced back many centuries. According to the best-documented historical population, the Qing imperial nobility, the gap in 1800 between father's age at first marriage (21) and father's age at first birth (24) was three years.[15] In other less completely recorded historical populations, this gap was even larger.[16] In pretransition Europe the interval between marriage and first birth was only about 15 months.[17] Even in the early 1950s, the mean interval between marriage and first birth in China was 34 months at the national level, and up to 40 months in selected rural populations. Moreover, whereas in historical Europe premarital conceptions and illegitimate births were sometimes common (Flinn 1981), bastardy was largely nonexistent in China.[18]

Despite their late starting, Chinese couples also stopped childbearing far earlier than pretransition couples in the West. Among the imperial nobility, for example, the mean age at last birth was only 33.8 for monogamous wives and 34.1 for polygynous wives (Wang, Lee, and Campbell 1995, 390). The equivalent age among peasant wives was remarkably similar: 33.5 (Lee and Campbell 1997, 93). In contrast, mean age at last birth in historical Europe was usually within one year of age 40 (Coale 1986, 11). Whereas on average a European mother had a reproductive span between first and last birth of 14 years, the average Chinese mother had a reproductive span of only 11 years.

In consequence, at every age the proportion of couples subsequently infertile was much higher in China than in any known historical European population (Leridon 1977, 101–102). Figure 6.2 contrasts the cumulative proportion of monogamous couples in the Qing imperial lineage and in a Chinese peasant population who were subsequently infertile with a European population. The gap between the Chinese and European populations is extremely wide except above age 45. By age 45, over four-fifths of the Chinese couples had stopped childbearing, in contrast to only half of the European couples.

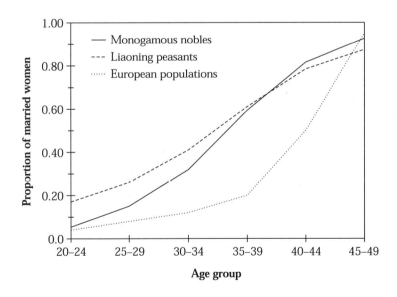

Figure 6.2. Percentage of women subsequently infertile, by age, China and Europe, 1730–1900
Source: Wang, Lee, and Campbell (1995).

The Chinese and European age patterns of stopping are thus fundamentally different. European populations contain few early stoppers and follow an exponential pattern of increase, with a rapidly rising rate after age 35; Chinese populations contain many early stoppers and follow a logistic pattern of increase with a slowly tapering rise. The curves clearly reflect two distinctive fertility patterns and cannot be transformed simply by shifting or compressing.

Moreover, until the 1970s birth intervals were much longer in China than in Europe—on average three years or more.[19] In rural China, for instance, mean birth intervals in 1944–1946 were 39 months between the first and second births and 37 months between the second and third. In 1951–1953 they were 36 and 38 months. In 1963–1965 they were 32 and 34 months.[20] In contrast, interbirth intervals in pretransition European populations were 20–40 percent shorter, mostly in the range of 20–30 months.[21]

As a result of late starting, early stopping, and long spacing, a Chinese couple in the past had at least two to three fewer births than a married couple in the West. Whereas European couples practiced moral restraint but little marital fertility control, Chinese couples practiced no moral restraint but considerable marital restraint.

Health Culture and Reproductive Culture

Chinese marital restraint derives from an even longer cultural tradition of carnal restraint (Hsiung forthcoming). Over two millennia ago Laozi and Mencius argued that, in order to develop mind *(xin)* and spirit *(shen)* and in order to nurture life *(yangshen),* one must control carnal desire *(yü).*[22] This contrast between desire and mind, and this belief in temperate behavior, have been central tenets of all major Chinese philosophies and religions ever since, including Daoism, Confucianism, and Buddhism (Wile 1992).[23]

Sex is one of the foremost such carnal desires. A copious literature on the need to limit sexual activity dates as far back as the first millennium B.C. (Wile 1992; Hsiung forthcoming). In particular, the Chinese believed that sperm contained a life force called *qi,* and that excessive ejaculation led to enervation.[24] Sexual activities therefore needed to be regulated to enhance health and perhaps to prolong life.[25] By the eighteenth century, the long-established consensus in the medical literature appears to have been that male coital frequency should be no greater than three times a month for young adults, less than twice a month for middle-aged adults, and once a month at most for the elderly.[26] To have intercourse more frequently was to risk one's health, perhaps even one's life. The low fertility and long birth intervals of Chinese couples in the past were at least in part the result of their ability and even willingness to regulate coital frequency.

A different conception of the purpose of marriage also underlies couples' ability to limit their coital frequency and consequently their fertility. Coital frequency in China, as in much of Asia, may well be low,[27] in part also because of a tradition of arranged marriage prevalent in many areas until very recently.[28] The primary familial relationship was not that between husband and wife, but that between parents and child.[29] Because filiality was more important than fecundity, East Asian parents accordingly discouraged sexual passion and encouraged moderation.[30] Childbearing in itself was not the only goal of marriage, but rather a strategy of social mobility planning.[31] While European marriages have traditionally required consummation to legalize the union,[32] consummation was unnecessary in China and until recently was frequently delayed.

Chinese mothers also practiced extended breastfeeding, which prolonged postpartum amenorrhea and contributed to the long birth intervals and low fertility (Hsiung 1995a).[33] As we saw in Chapter 4, the Chinese paid increasing attention to breastfeeding for both infant and maternal health. They considered breast milk not only a vital nutritional source, but also a reflection of maternal physiology and psychology. As a result, maternal nutrition, body temperature, health status, even emotional well-being were all matters of serious concern. Though solid food supplements were recommended for infants from an early age, breastfeeding was prolonged and intense. Weaning normally occurred sometime during the second year of life. Moreover, late weaning was considered neither uncommon nor inappropriate.

A wide variety of traditional reproductive technologies may also have facilitated marital restraint. One focus of traditional Chinese pharmacology was to protect women's reproductive health, including the development of methods to induce the abortion of a "bad" fetus. Such techniques included various herbal medicines for contraception, and a wide variety of abortive techniques, including some mentioned by Malthus.[34] These medicines, if effective, could also have been used to end unwanted pregnancies.[35] By the late imperial period, these contraceptive and abortificant medicines were widely sold in some towns and cities (Hsiung forthcoming). According to the well-known Chinese ethnographer Fei Xiaotong, by the early twentieth century abortion was not only widely known and used in some locales, but a woman who did not know how to use abortion to prevent a birth was laughed at by fellow villagers as a "foolish wife" (Fei 1947/1998, 108).[36]

Fertility Transition

The Chinese fertility transition, like the Chinese mortality transition, derived from a long tradition of conscious control, which facilitated the formulation and implementation of a national family planning program dating back to the middle of the twentieth century. While Mao initially dismissed earlier Malthusian concerns,[37] the revelation in 1953 that China's population was almost 600 million convinced him and other Chinese leaders of the need for birth control.[38] The fledgling family planning program, however, became entangled in the ideological debates surrounding the Antirightist Movement from 1957 through 1959, which resulted in a reversal of policy.[39] It was not until the 1960s that the government seriously promoted birth control in urban and densely populated rural areas of China, and it was not until the late 1970s that a forceful government population control policy was formulated and enforced nationwide.[40]

In Shanghai, China's largest metropolis and a pioneer in birth control, fertility started to decline no later than 1955 (Guo Shenyang 1996). Figure 6.3 contrasts the early decline in total fertility rates in Shanghai with the later decline nationwide. Despite the massive interruption and rebound from the Great Leap famine, total fertility fell from above 6 in 1955 to 3 in 1959, rebounded to 4 in 1963, and then fell rapidly to 2.4 in 1964, reaching the replacement level of 2.1 as early as 1967. This decline was accomplished through a combination of early reliance on abortion and a later transition to contraceptive use. The Shanghai municipality established an "official" family planning program in 1964 and reported contraceptive saturation among eligible couples within a few years.

Nationwide, use of modern birth control methods dates back to the early 1950s, when China made abortion available nationally to couples for the purpose of family limitation.[41] Figure 6.4 shows the rise of contraceptive use and abortion for all China from 1960 to 1987. In 1960, long before the formulation of China's current draconian family planning policy, over 10 percent of all urban women already used some form of modern contraceptive. Five percent had experienced at least one induced abortion. By 1970, on the eve of China's first national family planning program, use of contraception and abortion had risen to 35 and 20 percent respectively in the cities. Even in the countryside, over 15 percent of women at age 35 already used modern contraceptive methods. Seven percent had had an abortion. While total fertility was still 5.7 nationwide, it had fallen to 3.8 in cities.

China's fertility transition accelerated greatly after 1970 under the official *wan* (later marriage) *xi* (longer spacing) *shao* (fewer births) family planning program. By the late 1970s, 80 percent of Chinese women had used contraception by age 35. Close to a third of urban women and a fifth of rural women had had at least once induced abortion. China had become one of the highest contraceptive-use societies in the world.[42] The national fertility level declined precipitously, from 5.7 in 1970 to 2.8 in 1979, a record unmatched by any other

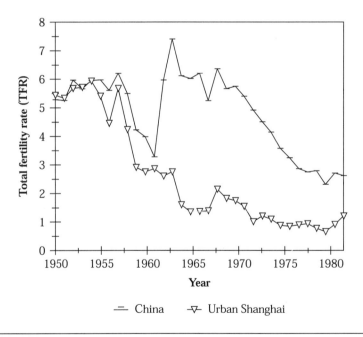

Figure 6.3. Fertility, Shanghai and China, 1950–1982
Source: Coale and Chen (1987).

large population in human history. While this decline was particularly swift among urban Chinese, whose total fertility fell close to replacement level, it was also quite sharp among rural populations in regions with a long tradition of birth control.[43]

Notwithstanding this success in fertility control, in 1979 the Chinese leadership extended their policy goals to reach replacement fertility as rapidly as possible under the slogan "one child per couple," which became the basis for a mass mobilization campaign on the same scale as land reform in the 1950s and economic reform in the 1980s. Because of their strong desire to raise China's living standard to levels comparable with Western industrialized societies, the Chinese leaders elevated family planning to the level of economic planning in state policy. In so doing, they made family planning for the first time in

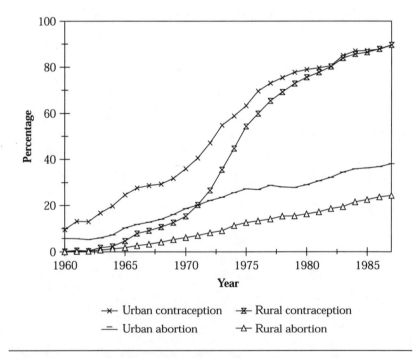

Figure 6.4. Women's use of contraception or first-trimester abortion by age 30–34, China, 1960–1987
Source: Wang (forthcoming).

world history a central component not only of the national agenda but even of national ideology.

As a result, the implementation of the Chinese national family planning program has been more insistent and more compulsory than family planning programs elsewhere. The state not only mandates age at marriage and number of children, but has even promoted mandatory abortion, mandatory insertion and retention of intrauterine devices, and mandatory sterilization to achieve population policies (Banister 1987). This program has led to the well-known excesses of the sterilization campaign of 1983, when cadres used and supplemented mass mobilization to force many people to undergo abortion and sterilization (Hardee-Cleveland and Banister 1988).[44] While recent family planning campaigns have been less overt, cadres continue to be responsible for the implementation of birth control under their jurisdiction; those who fail to fulfill family planning targets face such explicit punishments as monetary fine, demotion, and since 1991 even dismissal. Consequently, even though state family planning rhetoric emphasizes education and voluntarism, local cadres continue to resort to physical coercion to meet the demanding goals set by the state.[45]

Just as these other national economic programs reached different parts of China at different times and with different intensity, the current family planning program has been more effective in some areas and some periods than others.[46] In rural China especially, the needs for familial labor and old age support resulted in negotiations among peasants, cadres, and government officials.[47] As a result, the one-child policy was formally relaxed and modified in 1984 and 1988, with the exception of a few localities. Most of rural China has always followed at least a two-child policy. In contrast, more than 90 percent of all urban couples during the past two decades have had only one child. Such uniform and rapid urban compliance was at least initially a consequence largely of urban dependence on the state for employment, residence, education, and other benefits (Wang 1996). In rural China, where there is no such dependence, there is also no such compliance.

The common assumption that China uniformly follows a one-child policy is simply not true for Chinese rural families, who account for 70 percent of the total population. Figure 6.5 describes the rural period parity progression ratio, that is, the proportion of rural women per 1,000 at each parity (number of births) who continue to have children.

The proportion of women who had a second child, P_{1-2}, was hardly affected by the one-child policy throughout the 1980s. P_{1-2} declined from close to 100 percent in 1979, to 90 percent in 1985, and to 77 percent in 1991. The proportion of women who had a third parity birth, P_{2-3}, declined more substantially, from 81 percent in 1979, to 49 percent in 1985, and to 26 percent in 1991; while the proportion of fourth and higher parity births, P_{3-4+}, declined from 50 percent in 1979 to 18 percent in 1991.

Government intervention largely accounts for the acceleration of the Chinese fertility decline from a TFR of 5.7 to 2.8, and almost entirely for the most recent fall to 2.1. Nevertheless the Chinese fertility transition is fundamentally a consequence of new collective institutions and collective goals, not of new ideas. In contrast to the Western fertility transition, which required a revolutionary extension of individual decision making from marriage to fertility, the Chinese fertility transition required only the extension of collective control from the family to the state. For Chinese, deliberate fertility control has long been within the calculus of conscious choice. China's unusually rapid

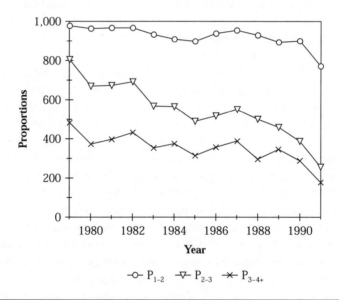

Figure 6.5. Period parity progression, rural China, 1979–1991
Source: Feeney and Yuan (1994).

fertility transition may therefore be attributed to the fact that the Chinese people did not require a change in attitudes, only the establishment of new goals and institutions, along with the diffusion of effective technologies.

Collective and Individual Strategies

Just as Chinese parents planned their child's survival and marriage, they also consciously planned their births. The multiple methods of marital restraint—secondary chastity and traditional methods—after marriage and between births allowed Chinese to vary their fertility according to social and economic circumstances. As a result, not only did the proportion of sons vary by individual, but so did the number of children, even with social status and marriage type controlled for.

This behavior is particularly well documented among the Qing nobility. Low-noble fathers, for example, had on average 2.5 fewer births than high-noble fathers, even with marriage type controlled for.[48] Moreover, while rich polygynous nobles could adjust their fertility according to economic circumstances by marrying fewer spouses, poor monogamous nobles adjusted their fertility by having fewer children. As a result, poor nobles, in addition to increasing female infanticide by a factor of three in the late eighteenth century, also reduced their overall fertility from 5 or more children in the early eighteenth century to just 4 children in the late eighteenth and early nineteenth centuries (Wang, Lee, and Campbell 1995).

Such marital restraint was even more widespread among commoners.[49] In rural Liaoning, for example, registered births even for males rose and fell in inverse proportion to grain prices, with more births in low-price years and fewer births in high-price years. Household structure, an indicator of wealth and an important determinant of a couple's social context, played a key role in fertility decision making. Larger and more complex households reduced their fertility less during poor harvest years and increased their fertility more during good years by comparison with smaller and simpler households.[50] Individual household position and occupation also greatly influenced the number of births. Soldiers, artisans, and officials had substantially more children than did commoners (Lee and Campbell 1997, 180–183). While such patterns are less obvious in genealogical populations, which may well underrecord polygyny, one study of three lineage populations in Zhejiang, from 1550 to 1850, documents that those branches with more degree-holders had many more births than others (Harrell 1985).

Chinese parents at both ends of the social spectrum not only controlled their fertility according to their social and economic circumstances; they also planned their births by the number and sex of their existing children. Both among the Qing nobility and the Liaoning peasantry, fathers who had no sons had shorter birth intervals than those who had sons (Wang, Lee, and Campbell 1995, 397). Moreover, Liaoning peasants who had a son were much more likely to stop further childbearing altogether. This gender-differentiated stopping pattern resulted in a sex ratio at last birth as high as 500 boys to 100 girls (Lee and Campbell 1997, 96). Such stopping behavior has revived under the current family planning program. As a result, the sex ratio of third and fourth births, for example, has risen from 109 in 1976–1980 to 123 in 1985–1989 (Coale and Bannister 1994, 468).

Such a pattern of deliberate marital fertility control also shows clearly in a large national sample of almost 30,000 uneducated rural Chinese women born in 1914–1930, whose reproductive behavior was unaffected by government family planning and uninfluenced by modern contraception. Women with both sons and daughters, compared with those with only daughters or only sons, demonstrated a consistent pattern of control. Not only did a significantly lower proportion of these women proceed to the next birth at every parity; they also had longer birth intervals and an earlier age of completed childbearing (Zhao Zhongwei 1998).

It is perhaps not surprising that such socially differentiated behavior has persisted even during the recent Chinese fertility transition. Individual education, residence, and occupation were important factors in explaining both fertility and contraception use from the 1950s to the early 1970s.[51] Urban and educated individuals used both contraception and abortion much earlier and more frequently and therefore had low fertility from the 1960s on. The difference in using abortion, for instance, was 10 to 1 between college-educated urban women and noneducated rural women in the 1960s and early 1970s, before the nationwide family planning program was enforced (Wang forthcoming).

Because of the Chinese preoccupation with biological perpetuation, scholars often mistakenly assume that the only purpose of marriage in

China is procreation. In fact the immediate concern for all parties is to integrate the spouse into the family for both consumption and production rather than for reproduction.[52] Explicit and excessive intimacy is therefore strongly discouraged, as family order takes precedence over individual indulgence. The number and timing of births moreover depends upon circumstances. Births have to be negotiated with coresident kin according to collective goals and constraints. Couples, in consequence, often have to exercise marital restraint, and resort to infanticide when such restraint fails.

Fertility control in both imperial and contemporary China, in other words, was possible because such decision making has almost never been an individual prerogative. Rather it has been a familial or community decision or a national policy. In that sense, the current family planning program is merely an extension of the familial mode of reproduction to the local community or beyond.

Part III explores the larger implications of Chinese demographic behavior for our understanding both of comparative population processes and of comparative social organization. In so doing, we not only analyze the historical context of the Chinese demographic system; we also contrast the legacy of Western individualism and Chinese collectivism.

PART III

Implications

CHAPTER 7

System

> . . . taking the preventive check in its general acceptance, as implying an infrequency of the marriage union from the fear of family, without reference to its producing vice, it may be considered in this light as the most powerful of the checks which in modern Europe keep down the population to the level of the means of subsistence.

MALTHUS, *AN ESSAY ON THE PRINCIPLE OF POPULATION* (1803)

Malthusian Legacy

For Malthus, moral restraint explained the success of the European demographic system, and England was the most conspicuous example of such behavior and such affluence. Malthus begins his analysis of English society with the assertion that "throughout all ranks the preventive check to population prevails to a considerable degree" (1826/ 1986, 236). He then elaborates on the differing rationales for such behavior among each rank, from the higher classes, down through gentlemen, tradesmen, and farmers, to laborers and servants. According to Malthus, such behavior encouraged savings and discouraged poverty, by restricting population growth. More important, delayed marriage kept the price of labor and savings rates high and assured general prosperity.[1]

Recent studies by E. A. Wrigley and R. S. Schofield have confirmed the Malthusian model of English population processes (Wrigley and Schofield 1985; Schofield 1985; Wrigley et al. 1997). Not only did many women (5–25 percent) never marry, but the proportions fluctuated considerably according to economic conditions. These changes in nuptiality had a great influence on population growth rates in all periods, and a dominant influence in the eighteenth century, both because of a decline in the proportion of unmarried men and women aged

40–44, from one quarter to one-tenth, and because of a decline in the age of marriage from 26 to 23. Until the middle of the eighteenth century, the substantial swings in nuptiality that occurred were produced almost exclusively by wide variations in the proportions of women never marrying. Thereafter there was little change in the proportions, only a change in marriage age.

These studies have also advanced the understanding of the relationship between real wages and marriage rates. While Malthus' supposition that marriages would rise and fall more or less in line with the price of labor is correct, there is a significant lag between the two, "about 15 to 20 years at each of the major turning points" (Wrigley and Schofield 1981, xxi). People, in other words, married according to the state of the economy when they were children rather than according to its state when they were adults. The lag between their wages and their date of marriage may therefore have been linked to the timing of their entry into the job market and their subsequent rate of savings. Once they amassed the necessary resources to establish an independent household, they married regardless of current conditions. But while good times and bad times may not have influenced current marriages, they accelerated or delayed accumulation, and therefore influenced both the timing and probability of future marriages.

Wrigley and Schofield differentiate between two contrasting ideal models of the relationship between population and economy, based on the Malthusian distinction between positive and preventive checks. "High"-pressure demographic regimes are situations in which both fertility and mortality are high, population is large relative to available resources, and growth is curbed principally by the positive check. "Low"-pressure regimes are the reverse. Since low-pressure regimes are more able to accommodate the tension between production and reproduction in the long run, they are also better able to resist price shocks. In contrast, in high-pressure regimes, particularly one variant that Wrigley and Schofield call the "Chinese situation" (1981, xxiv), social conventions made early and universal marriage mandatory. Although the disease environment was less deadly than in other high-pressure regimes, fertility was high, and because rapid growth had to be short-lived, mortality was high too. In the "Chinese" case, in other words, high fertility was caused by high nuptiality, and in turn caused high mortality.

Chinese Reality

The problems with this Chinese ideal model are now obvious. As a result of China's long history as the largest national population and the most densely settled nation,[2] the Chinese evolved a demographic system early on of low marital fertility, moderate mortality, but high rates of female infanticide, and consequently of persistent male celibacy. While the roots of such a system have yet to be traced in detail, we can identify specific characteristics such as infanticide from the first millennium B.C. In contrast to the European system, in which marriage was the only volitional check on population growth, the Chinese demographic system had multiple conscious checks, and was therefore far more complex and calculating than Malthus or his successors thought. As a result, even though Chinese female marriage was universal and early, population never pushed the economy to subsistence levels.

We have already identified the existence of a Chinese demographic system in the past and traced its legacy to the present. We can further differentiate two variant models. "Endogenous restraint" describes the interrelationship of the four salient components: infanticide, which we discussed in Chapter 4; male celibacy and fictive kinship, which we discussed in Chapter 5; and marital restraint, which we discussed in Chapter 6. "Exogenous stress" describes their interrelationship when the system is subject to short-term exogenous pressure from climatic, economic, or epidemic causes.

Endogenous Restraints

Under the endogenous model, Chinese families constantly adjusted their demographic behavior according to their economic and social circumstances and expectations. Figure 7.1 presents a schematic of such endogenous restraint. Chinese relied on marital restraint to keep fertility low to moderate. Not only did married couples wait a substantially longer time to initiate reproduction than their European counterparts; they also ended their reproductive life much earlier. Influenced by a different culture of sexuality, and under the close supervision of the collective family, Chinese couples were able to control the "passion between the sexes." When they wanted to have a child, they could accelerate childbearing. Otherwise they could abstain, and wait. Chinese couples also had access to traditional contraceptive and abortive technologies. Marital fertility was consequently much lower than European fertility.

In addition, Chinese families also killed some of their children. As a result, they could not only reduce family size, but also control family composition by sex. Consequently, while some couples resorted to infanticide when marital restraint failed, others engaged in infanticide to reduce the number of daughters or sometimes sons. While the incidence of infanticide varied considerably over space and time, the combination of infanticide and marital restraint meant that the number of children who survived to adulthood per couple was significantly lower than in other societies with similar model mortality levels.

Female infanticide caused a shortage of marriageable women and consequently an increase in the variant forms of marriage. While a significant number of Chinese men in the past married very late or never, Chinese women generally married quite early. Competition in the marriage market was so intense that the only way some men could marry was uxorilocally or to previous agnate or adopted kin. These variant marriages were in turn characterized by fertility rates that were lower, sometimes considerably lower, than for major marriages and divorce rates that were two to four times higher than for major marriages. Thus the imbalanced marriage market checked population growth not only by increasing the shortage of females but also by lowering marital fertility.

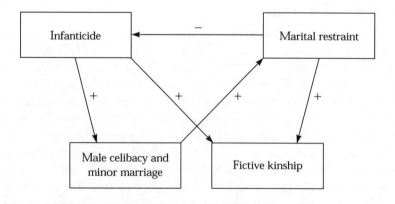

Figure 7.1. Constrained population growth, endogenous restraints

Such low marital fertility rates provided a major check to population growth in the Chinese demographic system. According to William Lavely and R. Bin Wong (1998), a female infanticide rate of 10 percent could reduce the annual population growth rate by approximately 30 percent. Similarly, an extension of their analysis to include fertility would suggest that if Chinese had followed European marital fertility rates, population growth could have been 50 percent higher. Low marital fertility, in other words, had a greater effect on population growth than female infanticide. While sex-selective infanticide was responsible for the differential pattern of nuptiality by sex in the Chinese demographic system, fertility was more directly responsible for China's low to moderate growth rates.[3]

Adoption, the last distinguishing characteristic of the Chinese demographic system, was also a product of both female infanticide and low marital fertility.[4] The effect was sex specific. Chinese couples adopted girls because as a result of female infanticide they could not obtain daughters-in-law. They adopted boys because as a result of low fertility they might not be able to produce an heir. Indeed, the number of couples finding themselves without direct biological descendants exceeded the proportions normally predicted for such low fertility and high infant mortality. Among the imperial nobility, for example, as many as 20 percent of all couples had no male descendants, almost twice the predicted proportions (Wrigley 1978). Some of these sonless couples were biological. Others incorrectly predicted their own subsequent fertility or the subsequent survivorship of their children. Still others were victims of the excessive demands of the Confucian family for denial and sacrifice.

In consequence, the Chinese developed high rates of fictive kinship in addition to variant marriage forms to overcome the limitations of biology, imperfect decision making, and dictatorial abuse. In addition to the approximately 10 percent of sons who were allied by fictive kinship through uxorilocal marraige and the similar or larger proportion of daughters who were allied by fictive kinship through little-daughter-in-law marriage, Chinese families adopted several percent of all births directly. Table 7.1 summarizes the proportion of adoption exclusive of marriage. Although the rates vary by location, period, and population, they indicate that at least 1 of every 10 to 100 Chinese children in the past was given up for adoption, a share almost an order of magnitude larger than any early modern Western population.[5]

Table 7.1 Adoption rates, China, selected periods and populations

Period	Location	%	Number
1730	Beijing	5.9	662
1750	Beijing	6.1	897
1790	Beijing	11.8	1,145
1840	Beijing	6.2	1,087
1906–1910	Taiwan	5.8	666
1911–1915	Taiwan	7.2	758
1916–1920	Taiwan	5.6	750
1921–1925	Taiwan	5.9	819
1926–1930	Taiwan	4.5	968
1931–1935	Taiwan	3.1	1,070
1929–1933	Southern China	0.8	2,679
1929–1933	Southwest Plateau	2.7	2,100
1929–1933	Lower Yangtze	1.3	14,321
1929–1933	Northern Plain	1.2	18,985
1970	China	0.7	50,100
1980	China	1.1	35,104
1986	China	2.2	43,560

Sources and notes: Beijing: Wang and Lee (1998). The rate is the number of adopted sons per 100 sons who survived to age 5. Years refer to year of birth. Taiwan: A. Wolf and Huang (1980, 207); years refer to year of birth. China 1929–1933: A Wolf and Huang (1980, 328), based on a survey of 35,976 families in 101 localities in China by J. Lossing Buck. China 1970, 1980, and 1986 are calculated from China's nationally representative 1988 Two-per-Thousand Fertility Survey conducted by China's State Family Planning Commission. Rate refers to the ratio of reported adoptions to live births, and sample size refers to the number of live births.

While contemporary recording of adoption is incomplete, the scale of adoption appears to be only slightly lower than in the past.

Such adoptions serve many purposes besides charity or parenthood. Chinese parents also adopt children to obtain family labor or support in old age, to marry their children, and to maintain ritual and religious continuity.[6] Consequently, they adopt children at all ages, from infancy well though adulthood, and on rare occasions even into old age.[7]

We can distinguish as many forms of adoption as there were of marriage. Parents can adopt daughters as well as daughters-in-law, sons as well as sons-in-law.[8] So can widows, widowers, never-married men, even eunuchs. The entitlement to children and, most important, to a patrilineal male descendant was so important that it overrode the limitations of human and social biology.

Most adoption was therefore among relatives rather than strangers. This was partly because of the importance of the patrilineal descent line,[9] partly because of the collective familial mentality, and partly because the joint social pressure from both biological and adopting families constrained adopted children to live up to their parental expectations. Intralineage adoption was also a legal requirement.[10] As a result, adopted children, unlike in the West, are often aware of their biological origins. Even today, Chinese continue to differentiate between adoption between relatives *(guoji)* and nonrelatives *(baoyang)*.[11] In any case, the high prevalence of adoption in all its various forms was not only a product of the desire of some parents for fewer children, but also important insurance that no one went childless.

Adoption, in other words, was not only a prominent feature but also an integral part of the Chinese demographic system. Adoption rates therefore depended on the level of both fertility and mortality. Figure 7.2 illustrates the relationship between fertility, infanticide, and adoption in one well-documented population, the Qing imperial nobility from 1700 to 1850. At the beginning of the eighteenth century, when fertility was high and female infanticide was low, the adoption rate was low, less than 2 percent. It rose gradually during the first half of the eighteenth century as fertility declined and infanticide increased, peaked at 12 percent in the late eighteenth century, and returned in the early nineteenth century, along with infanticide, to the levels of the early eighteenth century.

Thus the Chinese demographic system was characterized by a multiplicity of choices that balanced marital passion and parental love with arranged marriage, the need to regulate coitus, the decision to kill or give away children, and the adoption of other children. Chinese families constantly adjusted their demographic behavior according to their familial circumstances to maximize their collective utility. Such demographic adjustment allowed them to prosper even under stress, if at the cost of considerable individual sacrifice.

Exogenous Stress

Chinese parents, moreover, not only had to balance the competing entitlements of family members; they also had to adjust this balance according to external economic conditions. Economic fluctuations affected demographic behavior. Figure 7.3 depicts the Chinese demographic system under one such exogenous economic stress, a rise in grain prices. The result was an increase in both marital restraint and infanticide and a slight postponement of marriage.

In most pre-industrial societies, when grain prices increased, death rates usually rose, and marriage rates and fertility rates decreased (Dupâquier et al. 1981; Bengtsson, Fridlizius, and Ohlsson 1984; Weir 1984a; Bengtsson and Ohlsson 1985; Landers 1986; Galloway 1988, 1994). China was no exception. Grain prices had a large effect on both fertility and mortality in late imperial Chinese populations. Moreover,

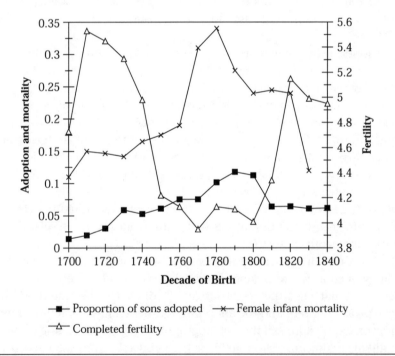

Figure 7.2. Adoption and population behavior, Qing imperial lineage, 1700–1850
Source: Wang and Lee (1998).

they did so instantaneously. Table 7.2 shows that male and female crude birth rates in rural Liaoning were negatively correlated with grain prices and that male crude death rates were positively correlated with grain prices. The lack of overt correlation between female crude death rates and grain prices is largely a result of poor registration of female infanticide. As prices rose, so did female infanticide, resulting in lower recorded female births. Other studies have found that female infant and child mortality correlated strongly with grain prices (Lee, Campbell, and Tan 1992; Lee and Campbell 1997). This combination of infanticide and late registration explains the even stronger negative correlations of birth registration, especially female births, with grain prices.

The multiple opportunities in the Chinese demographic system to control specific births, marriages, and deaths, however, meant that the response to economic conditions could vary greatly from individual to individual. There is already a body of techniques available to analyze such individual-level response.[12] Most studies of Chinese population history to date, however, have focused on populations exclusively in Liaoning Province and on mortality (largely excluding infanticide), which is less responsive than fertility, and maybe even nuptiality, to

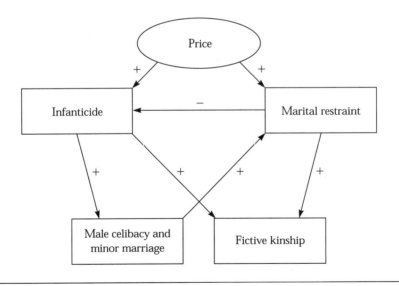

Figure 7.3. Constrained population growth, exogenous stress

Table 7.2 Correlations of grain prices and death and birth rates, rural Liaoning, 1774–1873

| | Household death rate | | Household birth rate | | | | | |
| | | | All | | Complex[a] | | Simple[b] | |
Grain	Female	Male	Female	Male	Female	Male	Female	Male
Rice								
High	—	—	−0.62	—	−0.46*	—	−0.46*	−0.36
Low	—	—	−0.60	−0.37*	−0.48	—	−0.54	−0.46
Millet								
High	—	—	−0.65	−0.37	−0.55	−0.33*	−0.50*	−0.56
Low	—	0.32	−0.49	—	−0.42*	—	—	−0.45
Sorghum								
High	—	—	−0.57	—	−0.46*	−0.33*	−0.39*	−0.39
Low	—	0.26	−0.58	−0.40*	−0.54	—	−0.46*	−0.49
Wheat								
High	—	—	−0.68	—	−0.36*	—	−0.54	−0.34
Low	—	0.43	−0.44	−0.38*	−0.48	—	—	−0.39
Soybean								
High	—	—	−0.45*	—	−0.63	—	—	−0.51
Low	—	0.39	−0.57	−0.40*	−0.36	—	−0.40*	−0.47

Source: Lee and Campbell (1997).

Note: All correlations have a significance of 0.001 unless marked with an asterisk, in which case the significance is 0.01. —indicates correlations with a significance of less than 0.01. Our calculations begin from 1774 for all households and from 1789 for the breakdown by simple and complex households, and end in 1840 for female births and in 1873 for male births. The prices are adjusted annual averages from Fengtian prefecture; the birth and death rates are annual rates from Daoyi and surrounding communities.

a. Households with two or more conjugal units.
b. Households with only one conjugal family unit.

social and economic differentiation and less sensitive to temporal change (Campbell and Lee 1996, forthcoming). Nevertheless, these results have already identified a variety of social relations or combination of relations who were particularly vulnerable to changes in economic conditions.

As a result, we can now appreciate the subtle nuances of discrimination, privilege, affect, and alienation partially hidden by the facade of Confucian hierarchy. As we might expect, for example, male orphans were cared for by other family members, while female orphans were neglected. Liaoning female orphans had much higher death rates than females with at least one parent present, while the death rates of male orphans were similar to those of other male children. More surprisingly, mothers-in-law were beneficial to their daughters-in-law. Married women had lower mortality if their mother-in-law was alive regardless of age. Young (16–35 *sui*) widows had substantially higher death rates than married women of the same age, while older (36–55 *sui*) widows had death rates similar to those of married women of the same age. Old men were more dependent on their wives than their wives were on them: elderly women (56–75 *sui*) were unaffected by whether their husband was still alive, but elderly men had much higher mortality if they had been widowed. Meanwhile, even though male children and grandchildren were supposedly a form of old-age security, neither male nor female mortality among the elderly appears to have been reduced by the presence of living sons or grandsons.

Such analyses reveal the degree to which the household was able to allay the impact of immediate economic conditions (Lee and Campbell 1997; Campbell and Lee forthcoming). Mortality differentials by household and lineage context in Liaoning were generally narrower when prices were high than when they were low, perhaps because when times were good, household members did not share the bounty equally. Privileged members of the household appropriated a disproportionate share of the surplus, leaving less privileged members not much better off than when times were bad. As prices increased, differentials narrowed because the consumption of resources by privileged members of the household fell to the level of less privileged members of the household. Pressure, in other words, reduced the benefits of hierarchy.[13]

Population Growth

Historically, a set of demographic mechanisms, primarily low female survivorship and low marital fertility, enabled China to maintain low population growth at the aggregate level—an annual growth rate of less than 5 per 10,000, far lower than population growth rates elsewhere—until modern times.[14] These adjustments perpetuated a homoeostatic demographic regime in China for almost two millennia. In the first century A.D. there may already have been as many as 75 million Chinese. By 1700, notwithstanding a frontier expansion that more than doubled China's territory, Chinese population had also only doubled.

Beginning in the eighteenth century all this changed. Between 1750 and 1950 China's population almost tripled, from 225 to 580 million, an annual rate of 5 per 1,000. Since 1950 China's population has doubled, from 0.58 to 1.2 billion, an annual rate of almost 2 per 100. Population growth, in other words, increased in each period by an order of magnitude.

The Chinese fertility transition is quite different from the stylized Western transition. Figure 7.4 replicates a matrix drawn by Judah Matras and others and contrasts the Chinese transition with transitions elsewhere. The matrix identifies four types of fertility regime, classified by early or late marriage age and high or low fertility control (Matras 1965; Macfarlane 1986). As Malthus would have predicted, the transition in Western European, particularly English, society followed the path from C to D: marriage age was already relatively late, and the fertility transition essentially involved only a shift from uncontrolled to controlled fertility. By comparison, fertility transition in

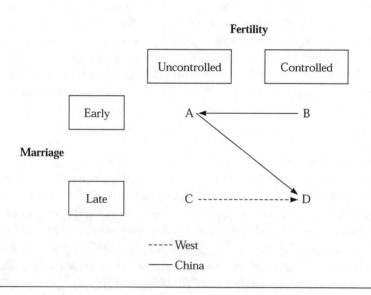

Figure 7.4. Fertility transition, China and the West

most developing countries requires both fertility control and a postponement of marriage age, which means a move from A to D.

China followed a far more complex path. The Chinese fertility transition did not resemble either the Western one or the general pattern
prescribed for developing societies. Rather, it shifted first from B to A,
and only then from A to D. Fertility was originally low. But with the
rise of economic opportunities in the eighteenth century and the deterioration of familial authority in the twentieth century, Chinese fertility control relaxed, shifting the fertility regime from B to A. This
resulted in two stages of population growth: a slow rise in population
over two centuries, from 150 million in 1700 to 500 million in 1900,
and the recent population explosion, which has doubled population in
just fifty years, from 580 million in 1950 to over 1.2 billion. This
explosion, however, in turn generated a collective desire to renew
population control and produced the current family planning program, moving China from A to D.

Phase one: The rise of economic opportunities. The first stage, from
B to A, appears to have been largely a response to economic opportunity. Figure 7.5 illustrates the response of the Chinese demographic
system. Marital restraint and infanticide declined as parents identified
the rise in employment possibilities. With the decline in female infanticide, marriage opportunities opened for unmarried males. There was
less rationale to engage in variant marriages. There was also less need
for fictive kinship of any kind.

In China this shift occurred in a variety of locations and in two
phases. First, increased economic opportunities from frontier expansion attracted people to leave their homes and settle the Chinese pe-
riphery. Simultaneously the increasing division of labor and consequent rise in commerce gave these settlers incentives to cultivate large
surpluses so they could exchange grain and a variety of commercial/in-
dustrial crops for finished products and money. Infanticide subsided,
fertility control relaxed, and population consequently grew. This
phase took place gradually, though not monotonically and universally,
between the eighteenth and early twentieth centuries.[15]

As a result of these processes of agricultural expansion and rural
labor intensification, described in Chapter 3, much of the spectacular
increase in China's population occurred in the countryside, wherever
empty land was available. The initial rise in China's population, unlike
the rise of Western population, was not a product of industrialization

and concomitant urbanization. The urban proportion of China's population grew slowly in comparison with other large populations in similar stages of growth. In 1700 the urban proportion of the population was at most 5 percent—roughly the same as in England. But whereas the urban population in England soared to 85 percent of the national population in 1900 and to over 90 percent today, the urban population in China increased to only 10 percent in 1900 and to 30 percent today (De Vries 1984; G. Skinner 1986). In China, large-scale urbanization is a relatively recent and still incomplete phenomenon.

Instead, most population growth during the last two to three centuries has occurred in China's frontier provinces. Map 7.1 shows the growth rates by province from 1776, the first year with relatively complete population reporting, to 1990, the most recent modern national census available. Most provinces in China proper grew at rates roughly commensurate with the national average, 0.5–1 percent a year. The only major exceptions are the Lower Yangzi provinces, where population growth rates were exceptionally low.[16] By contrast,

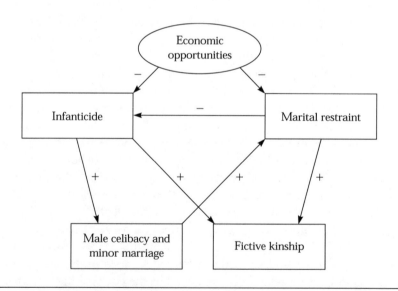

Figure 7.5. Population growth and the Chinese demographic system, eighteenth to early twentieth centuries

most provinces in greater China grew at much faster rates, between 1 and 2 percent. In the Upper Yangzi, southwestern, and especially northeastern provinces, population growth rates were exceptionally high. From the late eighteenth to early twentieth centuries, while the regional proportion of national population shrank in the Lower Yangzi, from 28 percent to 17 percent, the regional proportions tripled from 6 to 15 percent in the southwest, quadrupled from 3 to 12 percent in the Upper Yangzi, and swelled by almost an order of magnitude, from less than 1 percent to 9 percent, in the northeast.[17]

Such high rates of population growth along the frontier were a product of migration as well as of natural increase. We can identify several successive waves of internal migration and frontier settlement

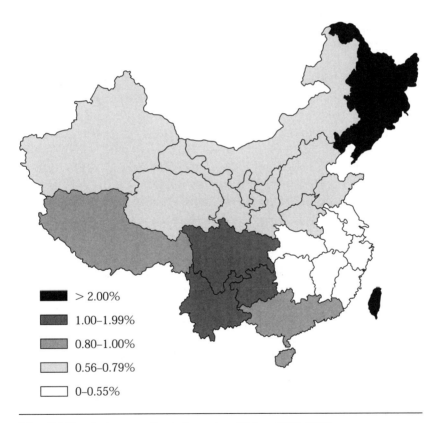

> 2.00%

1.00–1.99%

0.80–1.00%

0.56–0.79%

0–0.55%

Map 7.1. Population growth rate by region, China, 1776–1990
Sources: Liang Fangzhong (1980); Yao and Yin (1994).

during the last three centuries (Lee and Wong 1991; Ge, Cao, and Wu 1993; Ge 1997). Ten million migrants, principally from the Middle Yangzi, settled the Upper Yangzi. Three million migrants from the Middle Yangzi and the Upper Yangzi settled the southwest. Another 12 million migrants from northern China settled the northeast. Millions more moved shorter distances—from Fujian to Taiwan, from Jiangbei to Jiangnan, from Guangdong to Guangxi, from Shaanxi to Gansu, from Gansu to Xinjiang—while others moved abroad to Southeast Asia and even beyond. While the overall number of settlers is impossible to reconstruct completely, the impact of these migrations on China's demographic map was profound. In the mid-eighteenth century, the six most popular provinces for frontier settlement (Sichuan, Yunnan, and Guizhou in the west and southwest; Liaoning, Jilin, and Heilongjiang in the northeast) accounted for only 5 percent of the national population. By the early twentieth century they accounted for 25 percent of all Chinese (Liang Fangzhong 1980).

Population increase, in other words, was tied to a sharp increase in geographic mobility in late imperial China (Lee 1978, 1982b). We have not yet identified the specific mechanisms that produced such migratory waves.[18] We do know that they differed considerably by region. Most settlers came largely from northern China and the Middle Yangzi. Together they accounted for a residential population of some 120 million people in 1776 and 180 million in 1912—that is, between 40 and 45 percent of the registered population—and an emigrant population, including descendants, that by the early twentieth century was almost as large. In these regions, people perceived new economic opportunities on China's internal and external frontiers and responded by increasing their numbers to fill these jobs.

Phase two: The decline of the familial collective. The second phase of China's population growth was the product of the combination of new economic opportunities arising from Communist reforms and a revolution in social relations that the Chinese euphemistically call socialist reconstruction. Frontier settlement continued until 1960. In Heilongjiang, in the northeast, the annual in-migration rate from 1954 to 1960 was above 100 per 1,000—double the national average. By 1960 one of every six residents in Heilongjiang had been born elsewhere. Net in-migration was similarly high in five other popular frontier provinces (Neimenggu in the north; Gansu, Ningxia, and Xinjiang to the northwest; and Qinghai to the west) until 1960 with the establishment of the household registration system (Zhuang 1995). With the exception of Shandong, which continued to export migrants,[19] however, most of these new migrants came from the provinces settled during the first wave of frontier migration. Moreover, overall, their impact on Chinese population growth and distribution was far less than previous migrations. Together these six provinces accounted for 6 percent of the national population in 1950. By 1990 they had grown to only 9 percent.

In contrast with the rise in population during the late imperial period, urban migration during the twentieth century was numerically more important than frontier migration. Between 1949 and 1957, while the total gross value of agricultural products did not even double, total industrial value increased almost sixfold, heavy industrial output increased tenfold.[20] This process of rapid industrialization added 30 million urban jobs between 1949 and 1962, tripling the urban labor force (SSB 1982b, 17). By comparison, rural labor during the same time increased only 29 percent, an order of magnitude less.[21] Urban population consequently grew by 215 percent, from 58 million in 1949 to 124 million in 1959, while the rural population increased by only 13 percent, from 484 to 548 million (Zhuang 1995, 3). Fertility in the 1950s, in other words, like fertility in the 1850s and the 1750s, was largely a response to increased economic opportunity. If these rates had persisted in China through the 1960s, China's population would not have grown as fast in the last half-century and might already be below that of India.

That is not the case because of a population explosion in the countryside that started in 1961, in the aftermath of the Great Leap Forward, and continued unchecked for over a decade until the successive family planning campaigns of the 1970s and 1980s. Figure 7.6 contrasts the total fertility rate in urban and rural China from 1950 to 1987. In the early and mid-1950s, urban and rural rates were roughly similar, with a TFR of 6 or just below. They then fell together during the Great Leap famine from 1959 to 1961 and rebounded to 7 or higher in 1963. But whereas urban fertility subsided rapidly to below 5 in 1964 and below 4 in 1965, rural fertility remained above 6 until 1972, resulting in a net increase in rural population of 150 million, over four-fifths of the national population growth during this time.

Persistently high rural fertility, in other words, was largely responsible for China's population growth during the 1960s.[22] Rural fertility,

moreover, declined far more slowly than urban fertility and stalled in
the late 1970s, leading the state to resort to the more coercive and
extreme measures associated with the one-child campaign. Such high
levels of rural fertility were historically unprecedented. So was the gap
between rural and urban fertility, which accounted for almost 500
million births between 1962 and 1992, 90 percent of China's population increase during those 30 years.

Unlike the rise in population in cities or along the frontier, this
massive increase in rural population seems to have been less a response
to economic opportunity and more a consequence of the deterioration
in familial collectivity and familial control produced by rural collec-

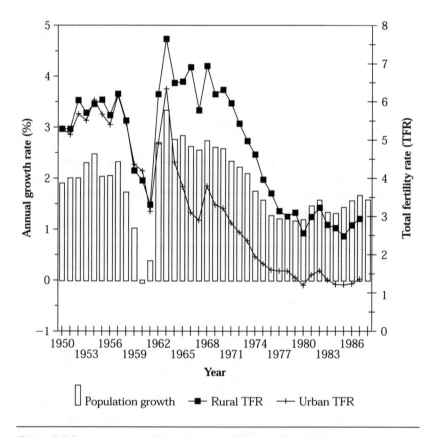

Figure 7.6. Population growth and fertility, China, 1950–1987
Source: Coale and Chen (1987), Yao and Yin (1994).

tivization under People's Communes. Land reform carried out in the late 1940s and early 1950s emancipated numerous farmers from the collective constraints of the traditional Chinese family, producing a widespread upsurge in marriage and household division. As a result, the number of registered households increased from 86.21 million in 1947 to 133.85 million in 1953 (Guo Zhigang 1995, 12).[23] Household size correspondingly shrank from 5 or more in the 1930s and 1940s to 4.3 in 1953 (ibid., 11).

Familial authority deteriorated further. Parents no longer had legal claim over their children's property, or person (Levy 1949; C. K. Yang 1959). A new marriage law explicitly banned arranged marriages and gave individuals the right to choose their own marriage partner (Buxbaum 1978; Whyte 1990, 1993). Compensation for participation in collective production, either in urban work units (in the form of wages or salaries) or in rural communes (in the form of work points), was tied or made directly to individuals, not their families (Parish and Whyte 1978). This revolution in household structure and household control, though unintended, was also one of the most important consequences of the Chinese revolution in 1949.

Land reform was soon followed, moreover, by the planned formation of the collective farming system, culminating in the establishment of the People's Communes in 1958. Under this collective farming system, which embraced over 99 percent of the rural population and persisted until 1978, Chinese peasant families no longer had to plan their demographic behavior as they had before. Collectivization and communization made food, shelter, and employment no longer primarily a familial responsibility. In most villages, food grain was distributed on a per capita basis, which meant that an additional birth entitled the family to increased food supply and increased economic welfare.[24] Not only were families with more children rewarded by more grain distribution from the commune, but those who overdrew were not punished. The collective farming system, in other words, penalized those couples with lower fertility (Nee 1985). By providing free public education and health care, the commune and the state relieved families of a large portion of the cost of raising children. Moreover, by guaranteeing all members a right to employment, the commune system allowed peasants to reproduce without much thought of individual let alone aggregate consequences.[25] While the People's Communes may represent the apogee of rural economic collectivization, especially from 1957 to 1959, they also appear to be responsible for the apogee of individual demographic maximization, producing a population explosion throughout the 1960s that was unprecedented in Chinese history.

The collapse of the traditional collective unit of population control, the family, along with the collapse of the traditional fertility disincentives resulted in the fastest population growth in China's history. Because of this unconstrained high fertility and a simultaneous drastic reduction in mortality, China's population doubled, from 500 million to 1 billion, in only three decades. It took more than a decade of unrestrained rural growth and the addition of over 150 million more people before the new collective, the state, realized fully the consequences of such a breakdown. Today the state has replaced the family as the collective unit of population control and has instituted the most ambitious, coercive, and successful birth control program in human history. Family planning has finally become socialist state planning.

Whereas the Malthusian transition requires individual decision making, the Chinese transition is a product of a renewed collective consciousness. The rapid progress of the Chinese family planning program was facilitated by a long Chinese tradition of collective calculus and control. China has consequently been able to complete the largest demographic transition within the shortest time of any large human populations. Collective demographic processes in the Chinese context have been remarkably effective both in the past and in the present at preventing overpopulation and impoverishment.

But while the shift in Chinese fertility from A in 1965 to D in 1985 resembles the classic demographic transition model, it in fact follows a fundamentally different pattern. The hallmark of the Chinese fertility decline is the renewal of absolutism and coercion in family planning, not ideational or consensual cultural change. And yet this tightening of family planning occurred at the same time as equally aggressive actions at economic reform. In contrast to the common perception that markets lead to individualistic demographic behavior, China shows the anomalous juxtaposition of heightened collectivity and rapid economic growth.

CHAPTER 8

Society

> The improved state of society . . . is to be effected . . . by a direct
> application to the interest and happiness of each individual. It is not
> required of us to act from motives to which we are unaccustomed; to
> pursue a general good, which we may not distinctly comprehend, or the
> effect of which may be weakened by distance and diffusion. The
> happiness of the whole is to be the result of the happiness of individuals,
> and to begin first with them. No cooperation is required. Every step tells.
> He who performs his duty faithfully will reap the full fruits of it, whatever
> may be the number of others to fail.
>
> MALTHUS, *AN ESSAY ON THE PRINCIPLE OF POPULATION* (1803)

Malthusian Legacy

For Malthus, a demographic system based on individual calculation
and self-interest could guarantee the collective good. By deferring marriage to accumulate the capital both to improve their station and to
support their family, people could check population growth at the
same time that they improved living standards. Correct decisions, in
other words, require self-interest, not cooperation. The alternative,
decision making motivated by a collective good and at the expense of
individual self-interest, Malthus thought unrealistic.

Malthus' emphasis on the role of individualistic, self-interested calculation was hardly new. Neither was his commitment to improving
human welfare. The late eighteenth and early nineteenth centuries saw
a shift from a concern with state interests to the welfare of the individual. The early classical economists accordingly sought to promote individual welfare and the mitigation of poverty and misery.[1]

Malthus identified several collective societies, both in the non-Western world and in the nonmodern West, that were able to check population growth, but he believed that they were effective at only a small

scale (1826/1986, 140), and he found their utilitarian and eugenic solutions—infanticide, planned births, restricted marriage, large-scale adoption—highly distasteful. Moreover, he thought that while collective property arrangements would encourage production, they would also accelerate "distress and degradation" (1826/1986, 502–503). China, for Malthus, exemplified such a collectivity. On the one hand, the Chinese state maximized production of whatever could be grown.[2] On the other hand, "the extraordinary encouragements that have been given to marriage, have caused the immense produce of the country to be divided in to very small shares and have consequently rendered China more populous in proportion to its means of subsistence than perhaps any other country of the world" (ibid., 369). Malthus believed that such subsistence societies were the product of weak individual property rights and strong collective polities.

Chinese Realities

The Chinese system, however, despite its size and its collective nature, was able to regulate population growth, through first family and later state control, and thus largely avoided impoverishment. Moreover, when population expanded in response to collective needs for increased labor, such growth was a reflection of affluence rather than impoverishment. Chinese demographic success, in other words, was based on collective control rather than individual restraint. Such control operates in China at several levels of social organization. In this chapter we discuss the two extreme and probably most effective levels: the family and the state.[3]

Family

Chinese demographic behavior past and present is largely a product of the family system. In contrast to Western Europe, where social organization has evolved from a long ideological tradition of individualism, Chinese collective organizations are rooted in a political economic tradition centered on the family. A hierarchical and patriarchal social institution, the Chinese family specifies clear lines of duty, responsibility, and entitlement for each member according to principles of age, birth order, gender, and generation. As roles change over the life course, individual entitlements and obligations change according to their position in the hierarchy. Family socialization therefore requires a multiplicity of individual roles according to a complex set of principles.

The ideal household consisted of married sons living with their parents. While inheritance in theory was partible, many households, both on the island province of Taiwan and in the frontier province of Liaoning, remained together even after the death of the household head (Finegan 1988). Empirical longitudinal studies of Chinese household formation on both provinces before the early twentieth century have revealed that the majority of the population lived in complex multiple-family households (A. Wolf 1985a; Lee and Campbell 1997). While this pattern may not have been as strong elsewhere, even where households were relatively simple, familial relationships and obligations remained complex.

While individual roles might change according to household structure, the family did not change as a collective institution. The Chinese family was a unit, regardless of residence. Family decisions were based on family and household interests, not the interests of a particular individual. Family members supported one another materially and emotionally. They also required individual sacrifice and loyalty for the family collectivity. As a result, the extended family and the household, not the individual or the individual couple, was the basic decision-making body.

Such collective decisions were especially common in demographic behavior. Demographic events, such as birth, marriage, migration, and death, all had direct and critical implications for family life and the family economy. They determined the size, composition, and ultimately the well-being of the family and were therefore too important to be left in the hands of individuals.[4] Marriages, births, even death were decided by individual negotiation and collective decision making. Individual gratification was subordinate to the collective interest.

To ensure enforcement of such decisions, all households, regardless of the configuration of relationships, were under the control of the household head. The head had absolute authority over all members of the household, including his wife, his children, his junior relatives (brothers, sisters, cousins, and nephews), and their families. He controlled the family economy both as a unit of production and as a unit of consumption. He served as the family priest and as the family judge. The fundamental organizing principle repeatedly cited in numerous classic books of family instructions simply states, "All junior and inferior relatives must consult the head of the family about every event, large or small. Before they do anything, they should ask his permission even when he is not their parent. The family can be in order only when the orders come from one person."[5]

The organizing principles of Chinese society came from Confucian tradition and were summarized by the Five Human Relationships *(wu-lun):* ruler-minister, father-son, elder brother–younger brother, husband-wife, and friend-friend.[6] The three general principles are well known: generation, that is, parents over children; age, that is, senior relatives over junior relatives; and gender, that is, men over women, especially husbands over wives. Parents, for example, had the legal right to punish physically and even to kill their children when they were disobedient.[7] Only parents who killed their children without any cause were punished, but by at most 100 blows of a bamboo rod or, under the revised "reformist" code of 1910, by a fine of 15 ounces of silver. On the other hand, the minimum punishment for unfilial behavior was also 100 blows. Disobedience or impoliteness could be punished by banishment. Cursing or physically resisting a parental beating could be punished by death. Parents, at least in theory, had absolute power over their children.

Successive Chinese dynasties from the Qin (221—206 B.C.) through the Qing (A.D. 1644—1911) relied on the family to enforce social order. They therefore followed familial principles in designing political institutions. Imperial law codes, for example, were designed to reinforce familial prerogatives over individual personal and property rights. According to the surviving remnants of Qin law, the first imperial legal code, parents had control over their children's property.[8] They also had authority over their children's bodies.[9] Unfilial behavior was a capital offense.[10] Moreover, such authority extended beyond parents at least to grandparents.[11] Children of all ages, in other words, had no "human rights"; they had only filial obligations.

By the time of the Qing dynasty and the last imperial legal code, parental authority over the person and property of "children" had grown to encompass a wide range of kin relations delineated by sex, seniority, and degree of kinship.[12] Qing law required even distant family relationships to be identified in all legal proceedings with incredible precision.[13] Qing criminal case records accordingly reported routinely any family relationship within the "fifth degree" *(wufu),* that is, common great-great-great-grandparents, and occasionally even beyond such spacious boundaries.[14] The definition of many crimes depended as much on the familial relationship between the criminal and the victim as on the specific act itself.[15] An act of violence committed by an inferior against a superior might be a capital offense. The same act committed by a superior against an inferior might be a misdemeanor or not even a crime. The closer the relationship, the greater, or the lesser, the offense.[16]

But although the family head was an autocrat, his actions were also bound by a highly developed moral code of obligations and responsibilities. He was responsible for the well-being of the family. His role was to be a leader and distributor, not a self-maximizer. This is succinctly expressed in the Confucian instruction that "the head of a State or a Family, should not be concerned that his people are poor, but only that what they have is unequally divided" (XVI, 138).[17]

Among the most basic entitlements the autocratic leader needed to provide family members, especially if they were female, were the universal demographic entitlements to marriage and family. The Chinese deeply believed that marriage and children were universal entitlements. We have already seen how these entitlements overcame the limits of human biology and also overrode property rights. Indeed, one of the reasons China did not develop a system of unfree labor similar to slavery in the West derived from the obligation to give up female serfs and servants in marriage to new masters—their husbands (Elvin 1973).

Moreover, as a family leader the household head was obliged to subordinate even his personal behavior to family interests. Tables 8.1 and 8.2, which summarize the share of married men and the number of sons in rural Liaoning by age group, show that household position clearly influenced both the timing and probability of marriage and fertility. Among senior relatives, household heads married earlier and had more children than anyone else in their generation. Similarly, among junior relatives their sons generally married earlier and had more children than anyone else in their generation. But while the household head could take the lead to marry and have children earlier, he could not deny this privilege to others. As a result, while there is a distinct gap in the younger age groups between the head and his immediate family and other coresident kin, this gap virtually disappears by middle age. Furthermore, as we saw in Figure 4.7, while other family members might be allowed to have a virtually normal sex ratio among

Table 8.1 Men ever married, by age and family relationship, Liaoning, 1792–1873

Relationship	16–20 *sui*		26–30 *sui*		36–40 *sui*		46–50 *sui*	
	%	No.	%	No.	%	No.	%	No.
Multiple-family households								
Head	52	54	86	196	93	394	97	613
Brother	27	183	76	427	89	595	92	507
Cousin	37	257	73	286	86	210	93	94
Uncle	—	—	88	52	90	81	93	132
Son	34	957	81	995	87	612	90	186
Brother's son	26	634	75	395	79	151	87	23
Cousin's son	38	115	72	54	81	16	—	—
Total	31	2,874	78	2,772	88	2,287	94	1,680
Non-multiple-family households	10	1,282	50	1,063	70	1,232	76	1,112
Total all households	25	4,156	71	3,835	82	3,519	87	2,792

Source: Lee and Campbell (1997).
Note: Calculations for specific relationships include only households in which the head is alive.

their children, household heads were required to have more sons and therefore presumably to kill more daughters. Infanticide was therefore a corollary of higher fertility.

State

In contrast to many past states that relied primarily on tax extraction and territorial conquest for revenue, the Chinese state depended more on labor extraction than on material appropriation.[18] Chinese state power was therefore based especially on its ability to mobilize and organize population.[19] This fiscal philosophy contributed not only to state building but also to the longevity of the Chinese political system.

In order to organize the population for efficient mobilization, the Chinese state as early as the fifth century B.C. developed and perfected a national household registration system. As a result, all Chinese people not only possessed family and personal names from a very early period; they were also highly socialized to state organization and regulation of population processes. Indeed, each dynasty formulated explicit laws and policies to intervene in various aspects of the demographic process. Some dynasties stipulated the desired age of marriage.[20] Others specified rewards for childbearing,[21] prescribed the

Table 8.2 Boys already born, by age of father and family relationship, Liaoning, 1792–1873

Relationship	16–20 *sui*		26–30 *sui*		36–40 *sui*		46–50 *sui*	
	%	No.	%	No.	%	No.	%	No.
Multiple-family households								
Head	0.20	35	0.82	182	1.49	385	1.94	601
Brother	0.25	51	0.60	325	1.30	520	1.69	461
Cousin	0.09	96	0.48	211	1.00	172	1.60	85
Uncle	0.11	9	0.64	45	1.36	85	1.83	127
Son	0.21	332	0.73	797	1.31	521	1.72	160
Brother's son	0.17	179	0.64	285	1.12	121	1.50	18
Cousin's son	0.17	46	0.42	38	0.73	15	—	—
Total	0.18	936	0.66	2,158	1.29	2,013	1.80	1,562
Non-multiple-family-households	0.15	62	0.60	330	1.00	607	1.23	593
Total all households	0.18	998	0.65	2,488	1.22	2,620	1.64	2,155

Source: Lee and Campbell (1997).
Note: Calculations for specific relationships include only households in which the head is alive.

occasions for marital restraint,[22] prohibited the practice of infanticide,[23] and established control over migration.[24]

Most important, because the organization of the Chinese state focused on persons more than materials, the Chinese legal and social system defined a hierarchy of personal entitlements and obligations both more powerful and more sophisticated than individual or property rights. According to this conception, there were no human rights, only human entitlements and obligations. Indeed, most individuals had no absolute property rights.[25] Just as Chinese parents had property rights over their children, so the Chinese state had property rights over individuals. In theory, the Chinese state, like the Chinese family, was highly autocratic. There were no institutional checks on imperial power, just the realities of distance, history, personality, and technology, whose limitations are well documented in numerous case studies.[26]

At the same time, much like the Chinese family, the Chinese state based its legitimacy and existence on the premise that it also served a collective interest. Derived from the Confucian doctrine, one of the most fundamental responsibilities of a good government was to guarantee the most basic human entitlements: food, clothes, and shelter.[27] Failure to do so not only violated a basic moral conduct code imposed on the government, but also could lead to social unrest and eventually the downfall of the regime. Consequently, past Chinese states organized large public works projects such as irrigation and road construction and also provided regular relief within the system of an extensive state granary (Will 1990, Will and Wong with Lee 1991).

In this respect, state policy in the past half-century simply continues and extends this tradition. Initially, however, the modern state was concerned primarily with liberating individuals, particularly women, from the oppression and authority of "feudal" society. Some of the earliest laws therefore not only legislated minimum marriage age, but also regulated marriage types. They explicitly banned arranged marriage and minor marriage, and encouraged uxorilocal postmarital living, in the interest of raising women's status.[28] They required female participation in the work force and promoted equal pay for equal work.[29] While these laws substantially weakened household authority, the family itself was not targeted by the state. Indeed, the modern Chinese state is the only one in the world to specify in the constitution children's responsibility to support their parents.[30]

Otherwise the state did not intervene in demographic planning and population control until after the population explosion of the 1960s. It tightened control over migration and instituted a family planning program that mandated not only late marriage and long birth intervals but even small family size. The success of these efforts is a testimony to the authority and legitimacy of the Chinese state. It is also a product of its authoritarian structure and coercive capabilities. While the contemporary Chinese state is ostensibly bound by a constitution and the rule of law, the government has rewritten the constitution at least half a dozen times during the first fifty years of its existence.[31] Inspired by a revolutionary goal to create a fundamentally new form of society and economy, the state has extended its activity into virtually every form of social organization and individual behavior. However, unlike the imperial Chinese state, whose social mobilization policies were based on patriarchy, the contemporary national mandate is to create not only a prosperous economy but also an egalitarian and cohesive society. The state has accordingly mobilized the general public to articulate national goals and collective interests and relied on mass participation to implement them.

The extension of coercive power from the formal organization of the state to "the masses" required the paradoxical juxtaposition of an unparalleled devolution of power from the center to the general public with the increased concentration of authority under the Communist Party.[32] On the one hand, the state centralized family planning as part of national social and economic planning. On the other hand, the state made the general public responsible for implementing these goals. Individuals are responsible not only for their own demographic behavior but also for monitoring the behavior of those around them. Restraint is no longer simply an individual demographic decision, but a national political goal.

What has enabled the modern state to exercise a degree of population control unparalleled in the past is its unprecedented degree of direct control over the economy (Riskin 1986). A collective national economy has not only created a system of organizations through which the state exercises its control, but has also produced a heightened sense of collectivity and responsibility. Seizing on this new sense of collectivity, the state has been able to mobilize the masses through political campaigns to silence opposing views and to internalize state goals and policies. Consequently, the masses have turned into mutual enforcers of the newly articulated collective goals.

The immediate level at which such coercion was articulated was no longer at the level of the Chinese family, but at the level of the "unit," or *danwei,* in urban areas and in villages in the countryside.[33] By organizing the population into these state-controlled units, the state has effectively combined economic, social, and political control in one institution. These organizations are units not only of production but also of consumption and distribution. They are not just economic entities, but also social and political institutions. Individuals are dependent on their work unit not just for income, housing, food subsidies, and health care, but for permission to get married and have children. Consequently, individuals who violate the family planning policy run the risk not only of being denied promotion or losing their job or farm, but also of losing such benefits as public housing, public education, and guaranteed health care.

In some ways, of course, the "unit" resembles the traditional Chinese family. Unit heads, like past household heads, organize production, redistribute welfare, and exercise moral control. Unit members share the same entitlements and obligations and are expected to sacrifice, if necessary, for the collective good. Contemporary Chinese therefore have developed both strong dependency on and expectation from these units.[34] However, while these entitlements are still allocated according to the same set of principles—age, gender, and generation— they have expanded to include such criteria as political attitude and moral performance.[35] More important, while the family was a largely universalistic organization defined by kinship, the unit has evolved into an increasingly particularistic institution based on personal relations called *guanxi*.[36]

To avoid such favoritism, the state has extended and intensified its oversight of politicians. Since 1991 state officials at all levels have been responsible not only for their own compliance with the policy, but also for the compliance of those under their jurisdiction. Failure to meet family planning quotas means demotion, even dismissal. As a result of this system, popularly known as *yipiao foujue*, or "one strike, you're out," local officials utilize all the means available to them to enforce the family planning program as much for their own interests as for the collective's.[37] Whereas officials in cities are able to enforce such a policy relatively easily, given the economic and political leverage of the *danwei*, in isolated rural locales, where there is no such leverage, officials have resorted to physical force and violence (Aird 1990).

Moreover, whereas the traditional Chinese state relied on the gentry to disseminate and enforce Confucian mores in rural society, the contemporary state, in addition to relying on the intermediate work units and cadres, depends upon an interwoven web of work and residential social controls to circulate public opinions and to exert social pressures.[38] The articulation of collective interests and national goals, however, extends well beyond work units and deeply permeates contemporary society. As a result, any individual who violates public policy is placed under constant public scrutiny and public humiliation in almost any venue where he or she has human contacts. Such pressures from public opinion, called *yülun*, play an increasingly important role in a collective society. This shift from Confucian consensus *(wulun)* to contemporary assent *(yülun)* parallels the transformation of Chinese society from familial to public culture.

The Chinese demographic system has always operated on collective, not individual, principles. In late imperial China, the collective goals were at the family level and were implemented through the daily negotiation and cooperation of coresident family members. In contemporary China, the collective has been elevated to the national level. While implementation has relied to a large degree on the cooperation and coercion of intermediate organizations such as the "unit" or the village, it also depends heavily on the omnipresent pressure of public opinion.

The family planning program is undoubtedly one of the most successful and most effective of the Chinese government's recent policies. One analysis has estimated that well over half of the decline in fertility between 1970 and 1987 was a direct consequence of the family planning program (Feeney and Wang 1993, 94). Within China, the need for some kind of program to limit population growth is widely accepted, and unhappiness with the policy is focused largely on the fact that the goal is one, not two, children per family. What discussion there has been of the program in government and academic circles has focused not on whether the policy is necessary, but on how it should be implemented.[39] Thus there has been debate over the precise target for the number of children per couple in rural areas, how strictly to enforce limits, and what combinations of penalties and incentives should be offered to obtain compliance, resulting in numerous adjustments (Greenhalgh 1986, 1993; Zeng 1989, 1996). The need for some kind of family planning policy is so widely accepted that during the spring of 1989, when millions of Chinese took to the streets of Beijing and elsewhere to voice their dissatisfaction with the government over a wide variety of political and social issues, virtually none of the criticism was aimed at the family planning policy.

While the Chinese state has attempted to disseminate a wide variety of contemporary policies and Communist values through similar campaigns, none has been remotely as successful as the family planning program. Other campaigns for political or economic goals are perceived to benefit some more than others.[40] The family planning campaign is regarded as benefiting everyone equally. Other campaigns require more sacrifice from specific portions of the population.[41] The family planning program requires sacrifice from everyone.[42] While other campaigns have been characterized by particularism, the family planning program is designed to be universal. There are virtually no exceptions.[43] And unlike other campaigns there is little corruption.[44] Everyone, regardless of political influence and economic affluence, is required to limit fertility. Indeed, leaders in particular have to serve as individual models of correct behavior.

Moreover, just as the imperial state reinforced the Confucian values of *wulun* through a combination of legal sanction and moral suasion, so the contemporary state has reinforced the family planning program with extreme public enforcement and extensive public education. In addition to the formal family planning apparatus and apparatchiks discussed in Chapter 6, family planning is part of premarital counseling. It is also a principal component of sex education beginning in primary school.[45] Indeed family planning has almost replaced revolutionary rhetoric in contemporary media. Advertisements, billboards, blackboards, books, cartoons, cassettes, CDs, comics, movies, news, paintings, plays, poems, posters, radio, songs, television, videos, VCDs, even web sites, numerous speeches, and, of course, endless group meetings are devoted to the exhortation to have only one child. As a result, family planning not only resides at the core of civic and political culture in contemporary China; it has become an important strand of popular culture as well as popular opinion.

For the Chinese public, the broadly accepted and deeply believed goals of the family planning program legitimate the use of state and public coercion. While many Chinese sympathize with the victims of state coercion when such pressure leads to excess, unlike Western observers they also believe that such sacrifices are necessary and that such excesses are probably unavoidable.[46] In that sense, their ambivalence toward forced abortion and sterilization probably resembles that of family members in the past when a young couple had to kill or abandon an infant. All collective societies exact numerous individual sacrifices in the name of the greater good. In Chinese culture, however, such sacrifices are not only deemed necessary; they are also routinely glorified.[47] While this is less true of family planning now, that is only because such control has become a universal and routinized achievement.

Couples who violate their local family planning norms are almost universally reviled. While people who have more children are not formal criminals in the eyes of the state, they are maligned as irresponsible free-riders in the eyes of the public. Not only are they more selfish and more "feudal," but by taking advantage of everyone else's sacrifice, they have violated a cardinal principle of Chinese society—egalitarianism within the same collective.[48] The tradition of familial entitlement, fortified by a Communist ideology and empowered through mass mobilization, has only reinforced a tradition of egalitarianism.

This strong sense of equity has produced an atmosphere of public intimidation that is probably more effective and more influential in enforcing family planning policy than the most punitive coercive measures of the contemporary state.

The family planning program may therefore be a model of a new level of collective activity for Chinese society. The combination of coercion and consensus motivated by a collective strategy to attain a common good under the family planning program and the elevation of this program from the family to the nation has been one of the great successes of the contemporary state. The viability of the current government probably depends on its ability to conceive similar strategies and to design similar programs in other policy areas. To the extent that it is successful, the government will achieve its goal of maintaining the legitimacy of the current collective autocracy while allowing increasingly individualistic behavior.

Whereas Western society has evolved from a self-conscious tradition of individual rights that are now perceived as universal human rights, Chinese society has evolved from an equally long tradition of individual entitlements that are now perceived as universal human obligations. Whereas Western governments have evolved from particularistic to universal democracy based on individual participation, Chinese government has evolved from the particularistic collectivism of the family to more universal collectivism of socialist society based on participation and mobilization. Whereas Western societies adhere to the assumption of Malthus and Smith that the collective good can be achieved only through individual calculation based on self-interest, Chinese societies follow an even longer belief that the collective good requires a combination of egalitarian allocation and authoritarian implementation. Whereas individualistic society requires the rule of law to protect human rights, collective society requires the rule of autocracy to enforce collective goals. Whereas individualistic society tolerates some social injustice and economic inequality as a necessary cost of individual freedom, collective society requires individual sacrifice and dedication as a cost of collective welfare.

The study of Chinese demography therefore is not just a window on comparative population dynamics but also on comparative social structure and social behavior. Two tenets seem to inform utilitarian social science theory, which has become so popular in the West: first, that people universally desire economic affluence, which in turn requires a market economy, private property, and the rule of law; second, that such complex economies and societies require broad-based individual participation to endure, and that such public political participation is fundamentally antithetical to authoritarianism. For these thinkers, in other words, the rise of democracy and individualism are inevitable along with the universal triumph of Western political and social ideologies (Fukayama 1992). To the extent that this is not true, they also believe that the existence of any alternative system portends an ultimate clash between world civilizations (Huntington 1995). In their world view, compatibility, compromise, and coexistence are not possible.

The mythology of China as a binary "other" is commonplace to many attempts at social theory. Malthus, in that regard, was simply more careful, more thoughtful, more powerful, and more successful than others.[49] For two centuries the Malthusian paradigm has shaped our understanding of social and economic behavior, with far-reaching consequences. Moreover, while Malthus' specific understanding of Chinese population dynamics was mistaken—hardly surprising given our limited understanding of China two centuries ago—his intuition that Chinese behave differently from Europeans was correct. What distinguishes China from Europe, however, is not the nature of demographic checks, but rather the social context of demographic behavior. The distinctive features of Chinese demographic behavior—high female infant and child mortality, universal female marriage, low female marital fertility, and high female and male adoption—are the products of collective interests and collective institutions. By contrast, the distinctive features of Western, especially English, population behavior identified by Malthus—the low prevalence and late age of marriage—are the product of individual interests and strategies. To the extent that there exists a binary contrast between China and the West, it is not so much in these population behaviors per se, but in the different social and political orientations of each society.

Our elaboration of Chinese reality and our comparison of Western individualism and Chinese collectivism therefore have important implications for our understanding not only of comparative population dynamics but also of comparative civilizations. With one-fifth of current humanity and at least one-fourth of historical humanity, the Chinese experience provides an important corrective to cultural particularism masquerading as scientific universalism.

CHAPTER 9

Demography, Ideology, and Politics

Any attempt to reduce human experience to a simple binary opposition requires caution and qualification. While individualism and collectivism may explain many of the demographic differences between China and the West, they are also universal dimensions of human behavior.[1] Even in the contemporary West, where individualism seems rampant, few if any individuals are able to live free from social and political regulations and constraints. Conversely, even in China, where collectivism appears triumphant, individuals have always been able to exercise personal initiative. Nevertheless, the comparison of demographic behavior and demographic systems in the preceding chapters illustrates the social consequences of the cultural, ideological, and political orientations in the East and West and measures these consequences quantitatively.

Demography

Demography provides a new perspective on comparative social organization and social behavior. Until recently a paucity of data has impeded such research on China, and what few records of their social behavior or individual thoughts have survived come from the elite.[2] Less flawed are the contemporary demographic data recently collected in the Republic and People's Republic of China and the historical demographic data discovered in large quantities in their historical archives.[3] Consisting largely of events whose definitions are simple and constant—birth, marriage, and death—these records provide a more objective window on peasant as well as elite behavior in the past. Moreover, what biases and errors persist are often systematic, therefore identifiable, and sometimes even correctable. Demography thus gives us a new lens through which to examine human experience, while demographic techniques and data processing in particular provide the tools to adjust this Malthusian lens to a degree unanticipated two centuries ago.

In Europe, such researches have documented increasingly individualistic behavior: the prevalence of late marriage and nuclear families in northwestern Europe, especially England, and of early marriage and joint families in southern and eastern Europe (Laslett and Wall 1972; Wall and Laslett 1983). John Hajnal (1965, 1982) linked the Western European marital system to a premarital life-course sequence of service and savings based on individual decision making, while Peter Laslett (1983) has ascribed the major difference in family systems to the ability or inability of the domestic group to control familial labor. According to Jack Goody (1983), this prevalence of individualistic marriage was a product of early Catholic church policy against concubinage and collective control. As a result, as early as the eighth century, marriage, which had previously been regarded largely as the unification of two families, was already widely regarded as the unification of two individual souls. Even where arranged marriage remained common and patriarchy predominant, consent and conjugality were required (Ozment 1983; Burguière 1987).

Others have documented the origins and expansion of fertility decline in Europe. While the broad underlying processes of historical causation are still unclear, many scholars have attributed the fertility transition to the rise of individual family planning within marriage and the expansion of individual privacy and individual agency at the turn of the twentieth century (Gillis, Tilly, and Levine 1992). The process began in eighteenth-century France but did not spread to the more developed regions of Europe—northern Italy, England, Belgium, Germany, and Scandinavia—until the late nineteenth century, and to the rest of southern and eastern Europe until the early twentieth century.[4] In each area, however, the process was roughly similar, with an initial fertility decline spearheaded by specific social groups—Jews, nobles, urban bourgeois—followed by the population at large (Perrenoud 1979; Bardet 1983; Livi-Bacci 1986; Bardet and Dupâquier 1997). Wherever fertility fell by an initial 10 percent, it continued to fall monotonically without reversal.

In China, by contrast, marriage, fertility, and even mortality have always been subject to human agency, exercised not by individuals but by such collective social organizations as the family and the state. Chinese households in the past married their children through a variety of unions to serve familial and other interests. They required that married couples limit their fertility either through sexual restraint or contraception, a policy continued at the state level today. Such collective strategies forced Chinese parents to kill or abort some children and nurture others according to collective economic and social constraints. They also encouraged Chinese parents to adopt children as either a consequence or a circumvention of such constraints. Collective control is so strong that couples today not only cannot decide if or when to marry or how many children to have; until very recently they also could not decide their place of residence, occupation, or political preferences.

Ideology

Some Western social theorists building on such research have suggested that the roots of English and, by extension, Western individualism can be traced to these demographic and familial origins. Alan Macfarlane (1978, 1986, 1987) in particular has elaborated the Malthusian model to argue that the English demographic system and the English individualistic orientation are inextricably linked.[5] Emmanuel Todd (1982) has gone so far as to suggest that globally the difference in comparative political systems can be traced to comparative familial systems. According to this conception, while nuclear family societies are more conducive to democracy, joint family systems are more inclined to autocracy and communism. As a result, Western democracy and Eastern autocracy are virtually predetermined by their respective demographic and familial cultures.

Although the attraction of such far-reaching claims is clear, the authenticity of both the similarity between demography and ideology and the contrast between East and West requires further examination. While individualism has triumphed and predominated in the West, a rich intellectual and philosophical tradition of collective behavior can be traced from the works of Plato and Aristotle to those of Thomas Hobbes and Karl Marx.[6] Even democracy, according to Machiavelli, was originally designed to articulate the collective desires of the citizenry, much as feudalism enforced the individualistic wishes of the nobility.[7] Western political philosophy, in other words, featured many collective elements that predated or dominated modern political concepts of individual freedom and civil liberty, which were largely the product of Enlightenment, especially English, theorists (Berlin 1958; Q. Skinner 1997).[8]

Similarly, while collectivism has been at the core of Chinese classical political philosophy, individualism was also fundamental to Confucian ideology (De Bary 1970; Munro 1985). Traditionally, the Chinese valued individual ability and achievement as strongly as familial and political hierarchy. Confucius himself insisted that the ideal society was one in which an intellectual and moral elite should rule, but in which access to such education should be open to all. Successive Chinese states acting on such Confucian principles opened political office to the able and accomplished and, beginning in the seventh century, established a system of highly competitive formal examinations to select candidates for higher office. According to Ho Ping-ti's well-known analysis of 40,000 officials who served during the late imperial period, half achieved office through competitive examinations, a rate of elite social mobility higher than that in Tudor and Stuart England (Dibble and Ho 1961).[9] In China, in other words, collective social institutions hardly precluded advocacy of individualistic principles and appreciation of individual achievement.

Moreover, Chinese family behavior was so malleable that early imperial governments were able to modify important collective relationships such as those between siblings and even between parents and children. A well-known example was when the Qin, the first imperial dynasty, assessed a multiple-household tax on households with more than one coresidential conjugal unit and prohibited fathers, sons, and brothers from living together (*Shi Ji* 68.5a). Within two years, customs had changed to the point that "when a son reached adulthood [and married], he set up his own household with a share of the property if his family was rich and married uxorilocally if his family was poor. If he lent his father a rake or hoe, he behaved as if he acted magnanimously. While if his mother borrowed a dustpan or broom, he would reprove her. Daughters-in-law would bare their breasts and feed their children in front of their fathers-in-law. Mothers-in-law and daughters-in-law did not speak to each other, but argued constantly instead" (*Han Shu* 48.2244).[10]

Politics

Population behavior is hardly predetermined by either political ideology or social tradition. Rather it is a path-dependent phenomenon shaped by tradition and modulated by politics, and in exceptional circumstances can even fundamentally change. Such revolutions in demographic behavior are infrequent. They are also a testament to the adaptability of human social behavior when confronted by political inflexibility or social and economic change. The Catholic church's stipulation of monogamous marriage and the contemporary Chinese family planning program are good examples of such demographic revolutions.

So is the rise of individualistic demographic behavior in the West in the twentieth, especially the late twentieth, century. Divorce rates, for example, summarized in Figure 9.1, have risen dramatically in most, but not all, Western societies.[11] In the United Kingdom the divorce rate quadrupled between 1960 and 1980, from 3 to 13 divorces per 1,000 married females; while in the United States the divorce rate rose an order of magnitude, from less than 2 per 1,000 married females in 1950 to over 20 in 1980. Lower rates of divorce elsewhere, such as in France and Sweden, were a consequence of an increase in nonmarital unions, as shown in the increase in nonmarital fertility summarized in Figure 9.2. In France the proportion of unions that began out of wedlock increased from 10 percent in 1970 to 90 percent in 1995.[12] The proportion of nonmarital unions among females aged 20–44 increased from 2 percent in 1975 to over 20 percent in 1995 (Touleman 1996). While the proportions are less clear elsewhere, nonmarital fertility in Sweden in 1990 accounted for almost half of all births, while the share in France, the United Kingdom, and the United States was about one-quarter of all births.[13]

This revolution in individualistic demographic behavior is the outcome of both political and social change. On the one hand, a succession of Western governments facilitated divorce and legitimated nonmarital unions and nonmarital fertility, beginning in the late 1960s, as an affirmation of individual over collective rights (Glendon 1989).[14]

On the other hand, such social and economic transformations as the rise of industrial and postindustrial employment, increased geographic and social mobility, and declining religious influence also enhanced awareness of individual, especially female, rights. While these state laws alone did not create changes in demographic behaviors, by making divorce, nonmarital cohabitation, and even nonmarital procreation easier, they validated the view of marriage as a temporary contractual relationship between individuals, rather than a lifelong collective commitment to family.

At the same time, by legislating to protect individual rights, Western governments have ironically also encroached on the traditional spheres of patriarchal behavior. Within the family, by making individual physical well-being a state responsibility, governments have

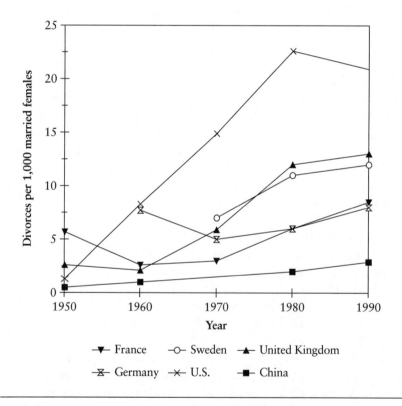

Figure 9.1. Divorce rates, selected countries, 1950–1990
Sources: China: Feng Fanghui (1996); other countries: Goode (1993, 27, 139).

stripped away traditional parental power to punish their children. They oppose the husband's rights to control his spouse physically and stipulate that all conjugal relations be consensual. The state now not only legislates on parental responsibilities to support biological children, even in the case of divorce, but routinely pursues and coerces "deadbeat dads" to fulfill these obligations. Even the individual "right to die" is a subject of heated public debate, forcing individuals who dread the prospect of life without sentience to complete legal formalities in advance. As a result, collective control, despite such recent rampant individual emancipation, has a greater jurisdiction over certain facets of individual behavior than ever before.

The opposite is true in China. Despite the expansion of the collective sphere into individual demographic behavior, a series of legal ac-

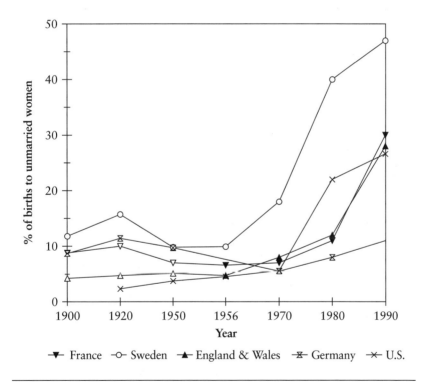

Figure 9.2. Nonmarital fertility, selected countries, 1900–1990
Sources: 1900–1956: Goode (1963, 38); 1970–1990: U.S. Bureau of the Census (1997, 834).

tions has also liberated individual demographic behavior. This legislation occurred in two steps. Beginning in 1950, the Chinese state legally banned arranged marriages and polygyny and gave individuals the right to choose their own marriage partners (Meijer 1978). Beginning in 1980, the state facilitated divorce by broadening the grounds for dissolution as well as streamlining what had previously been a tedious process (Wu Deqing 1995).[15]

Individualistic demographic behavior in China, as in the West, has therefore increased, if not as radically. Figure 9.3 summarizes the trend from 1955 to 1992 in divorce in selected provinces. Though still very low, divorce has risen from 2 per 1,000 married females in 1982 to close to 3 in 1992,[16] a level comparable to that in England and France in the 1960s. In such urbanized Chinese provinces as Liaoning,

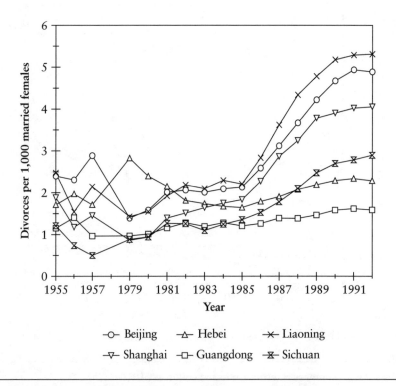

Figure 9.3. Divorce rates, selected Chinese provinces, 1955–1992
Sources: Divorce numbers: Feng Fanghui (1996, 418–451). Number of married females, estimated from female population in 1953, 1982, and 1990: Fan (1995).

as well as Shanghai and Beijing, divorce rates in the early 1990s reached as high as 6 per 1,000 married females, a level comparable to that in France, Germany, and England in 1970. Premarital sexual behavior has also increased. According to one estimate, the proportion of premarital conception has risen from 11 per 1,000 first births in 1970 to 34 in 1980 and to 51 in 1987 (Wang and Yang 1996). By the late 1980s, in other words, 5 of every 100 first births in China was conceived before marriage, a veritable revolution in individual premarital behavior.[17]

The binary contrast between a collectivist East and an individualist West and the linkage between demography and ideology can therefore be overdrawn—even in the late twentieth century. Nevertheless, the comparison of human experience over time and place remains important to all social scientific enterprises. It was only through his explicit comparison of population behavior in the non-Western and nonmodern Western world and in the modern Western world that Malthus was able to identify the distinctive differences between Western and non-Western population behavior and to produce his influential demographic model of positive and preventive checks. It was only through similar comparisons, largely between East and West, that subsequent scholars were able to link Malthusian population processes to social organization and economic behavior. Without such comparisons, they and Malthus would have written only population history, not social theory.

The explanatory power of the Malthusian or neo-Malthusian models lies partially in the simplicity of the binary model. In contrast, the current fashion in history, and even in some social sciences, is to use comparison to generate complexity. This is true even in the quantitative social sciences, where sophisticated multivariate techniques of analysis are used to measure the multiple dimensions of human motivation and experience. We are now confounded by a multiplicity of coefficients and explanations at the individual and aggregate levels organized by class, ethnicity, gender, geography, and history. The challenge of such approaches is that in the absence of any larger organizing principles or narratives, it is increasingly hard to fit each story into a global or even historical context. Ironically, while the world has grown increasingly smaller, our understanding of our shared experience has grown increasingly complex, so complex as to defy simple synthesis.

This book uses the history of population behavior of one quarter of humanity both to examine the century old Malthusian opposition of China and Europe and positive and preventive checks, and to propose an alternative opposition between Western individualism and Chinese collectivism.[18] Unlike Malthus, however, we do not mean to link these features exclusively to any specific society or time according to a predetermined teleology. Rather, we suggest that they define a universal spectrum with which we can contrast and explain social organization and behavior in the East and the West. By so doing, we hope to produce a partial understanding of human demographic experience during the last three centuries, and at the same time to avoid the ethnocentric and teleologic traps so common to earlier social science.

Appendix · Notes
References · Index

Chinese Population Sources, 1700–2000

Historical Demography

For almost half a century, two advances in population and family history have been central to the rapid expansion of population studies, population history, and quantitative social-scientific history.[1] First, in the late 1950s, demographers developed a body of analytic techniques known as family reconstitution to calculate demographic rates from records of weddings, baptisms, and burials (Gautier and Henry 1958). Then, in the late 1960s, a group of historians and anthropologists proposed and propagated a series of analytical classifications of household structure to measure changes in household complexity (Laslett and Wall 1972). These two sets of techniques were among the first quantitative methods of social scientific analysis that were easily accessible to nearly all historians. Together they inspired many historical studies of fertility and mortality, marriage and migration, household structure and household formation, individual and domestic cycle in Europe. The results have produced a new set of objective measures of Western life in the past. At the same time, they have provided generalizable standards with which to compare the historical experiences of societies in different parts of the world.

Such studies have greatly expanded our appreciation of history from below. On the one hand, population history has defined the patterns of demographic behavior among the common people and has also redefined our understanding of many social customs and economic conditions. On the other hand, family history not only has shown what types of households and household formation were common in the past, but also has shed new light on the organization of production, the transmission of property, and the rise of familial affect. European historians, in particular, have linked such changes to the transition from feudalism to capitalism. They have shown that this process was tied inextricably both to changes in demographic rates from high to low fertility and to changes in household function from a unit of production to a unit of socialization. In consequence, much of our theoretical understanding of the modern transformation of the Western world is rooted in population and family history.

Chinese scholars have, of course, long been aware of the centrality of family and household in Chinese society. In China, the concepts of family and household date back to prehistory (Ho 1975). The importance of the family was reaffirmed by Confucius and further elaborated by Mencius in the fifth and fourth centuries B.C. respectively. Indeed Mencius elevated the centrality of the family by making three of the five fundamental human relationships familial: those of father and son, elder brother and younger brother, and husband and wife.[2] Ever since, Chinese have modeled their behavior according to a social hierarchy of parents over children, senior relatives over junior relatives, and men over women. Historians of China have accordingly invested great efforts in defining both the formal kin structure and the corresponding system of behavioral norms in traditional society (Freedman 1966). But because of lack of appropriate data, there has been little study of formal family and household structure, even in the late imperial period.

Chinese scholars have also long recognized the importance of population history to the Chinese past, if only because there have always been so many Chinese. Indeed the dramatic rise in population from 160 million in 1700 to almost 500 million by 1900 is probably the most frequently noted achievement of the late imperial period. Nevertheless, despite such research we still know very little about the demographic characteristics of late imperial China. Until very recently, it was fair to say that the Chinese of the late imperial period were among the least known of any major historical populations.

The change has been sudden. New data and new methods have begun to illuminate China's historical demography. Major advances in China, as in Europe, have been inspired by the discovery and analysis of nominative records. Three types of sources have been especially important: retrospective genealogies, contemporary household registers, and continuous vital records. On the basis of these sources historical demographers have already reconstructed the population history of some 500,000 people primarily from six geographic areas summarized in Table A.1, that is, roughly 2 per 10,000 of China's population during that time. Research on such sources has already advanced our knowledge about population behavior in China.

Most of these data come from genealogies that have the broadest spatial coverage but are also the most imperfect (Telford 1986).[3] Genealogies have the least correlative information on their historical circumstances. Worst of all, since the data are retrospective and highly incomplete, long-lived married men with many surviving sons are far more likely to be remembered and recorded than their unmarried or childless counterparts. Unknown patterns of survivorship can bias any demographic analysis of these data (Pope 1989).

The second most commonly available source of historical demographic data, household registers, offers far more complete demographic information than do retrospective genealogies, as well as more detailed information on occupation and a variety of other indices. Moreover, they are the only source to provide detailed information on family context. To date, research on household registers has been confined almost solely to Taiwan from 1895 to 1945 and Liaoning from 1750 to 1909.[4] Whereas the Taiwan registers are a unique product of the Japanese colonial occupation, registers similar to those in Liaoning exist for Beijing and for Jilin, Heilongjiang, Inner Mongolia, and Hebei Provinces (Thatcher 1998). Other sorts of household registers have also been identified, particularly from the *baojia* registration system common throughout much of China proper.[5] These registers were usually of peasant populations and in that sense are probably more "typical" than genealogical sources. At the same time, they also require a far more laborious process of data entry and linkage.

The vital registration archives of the Qing imperial lineage, the third source of population data, are the most completely recorded population in Chinese history and offer the most socioeconomic information.[6] They are also undoubtedly atypical, since the Qing imperial lineage was an elite population that depended solely on the state for financial support, was highly regulated, and was required to live largely in two cities: Beijing or Shenyang. Nevertheless, the Qing impe-

Table A.1 Reconstituted Chinese historical populations

Period	Location	Population size	Data type
1000–1749	Undetermined	4,265	Retrospective genealogy
1200–1900	Jiangnan	261,420	Retrospective genealogy
1250–1900	Xiaoshan	6,592	Retrospective genealogy
1300–1900	Suzhou	6,000	Retrospective genealogy
1520–1661	Anhui	40,000	Retrospective genealogy
1600–1920	Beijing	100,000	Vital registration
1600–1900	Manchuria	5,000	Contemporary genealogy
1760–1910	Liaoning	50,000	Household register
1905–1935	Taiwan	50,000	Household register
Total		523,277	

Sources and notes: Undetermined: the *Wangshi Tongpu* genealogy, reconstructed in Zhao Zhongwei (1997); according to Zhao, the Wang had no specific place of residence.

Jiangnan: 147,956 men and 113,464 women recorded in 49 retrospective genealogies from 12 provinces, including Anhui (3), Fujian (1), Guangdong (5), Hebei (4), Henan (2), Hubei (2), Hunan (3), Jiangsu (9), Jiangxi (3), Shandong (3), Taiwan (1), and Zhejiang (13), reconstituted by Liu Ts'ui-jung (1992).

Xiaoshan: the He, Lin, Shi, and Wu lineage genealogies, reconstructed in Harrell (1985) and Harrell and Pullum (1995). The He genealogy, compiled in 1893, covers 3,078 cases, but only 3,300 of the population have recorded vital events.

Suzhou: the *Shanghai Caoshi zongpu* and *Dengjiang Fanshi zongpu* genealogies, reconstructed by Hou Yangfang and Peng Xizhe and reported in Hou (1997).

Anhui: 41 retrospective Tongcheng County genealogies, transcribed by Telford (1990b).

Beijing: 43,950 sons and 34,765 daughters born into the imperial lineage and some 30,000 spouses recorded in the vital registration records from the Archives of the Office of the Imperial Lineage. See Lee, Campbell, and Wang (1993) and Lee and Guo (1994) for a detailed description of the data and the institutions that produced them.

Manchuria: the Niuhulushi genealogy reconstructed by Lai Huimin (1991).

Liaoning: household registers for 10 populations preserved in the Liaoning Provincial Archives and available through the Utah Genealogical Society. See Lee and Campbell (1997, 223–237) for a description of these data for one population, Daoyi. Since each individual on average has seven or eight observations, the number of records is far larger, around 500,000. In Daoyi we entered 114,272 individual records. The numbers for the other populations are 29,578 records for Chengnei, 25,378 for Dami, 100,000 for Feicheng Yimian cheng, 37,188 for Gaizhou, 22,558 for Gaizhou Mianding Guo Santun, 70,000 for Niuzhuang Liuerbao Lama Yuan Yuding (70,000 records of 10,000 individuals), etc.

Taiwan: Japanese household registers reconstructed in Chuang and Wolf (1995). See A. Wolf and Huang (1980) for a description of these data for one population, Haishan.

rial lineage is also one of the largest and longest longitudinal populations.

None of these populations is "typically" Chinese. Each is a prisoner of its specific circumstances—age, class, climate, culture, ethnicity, geography, history, institutions, occupation, sex, residence type, or time period. Nationally representative Chinese populations become available only after the advent of the censuses and sample surveys in the second half of the twentieth century (discussed later). Many population historians have documented significant variation in marital and fertility behavior by land ownership, occupation, or social status (Harrell 1985; A. Wolf 1985b; Telford 1990a, 1990b, 1994, 1995; Lee, Wang, and Campbell 1994; Lee and Campbell 1997). Simple aggregation can therefore be quite misleading and misrepresentative. Individual level event history analytic techniques, however, allow demographers to control for most such circumstances and are exemplified in a variety of recent publications (Wang, Lee, and Campbell 1995; Campbell and Lee 1996, forthcoming).

Moreover, generalizations based on such historical data are still possible when these "atypical" populations share behaviors that are not associated with any specific population characteristic. Thus, when all Chinese populations regardless of location, period, and social and economic background demonstrate low marital fertility and universal female marriage, it is reasonable to conclude that such behavior was typical of the Chinese demographic system. Similarly, when different populations exhibit common behaviors that are tied to a specific characteristic, it is also reasonable to conclude that other populations with this characteristic may exhibit similar behavior. For example, since state populations, which were not allowed to migrate, generally had high rates of female infanticide and particularly low rates of marital fertility, it would be reasonable to conclude that the populations that were less free and less mobile also exercised more collective control over their population behavior.

Contemporary Demography

In contrast to most historical population data, which are localized, virtually all contemporary population materials are national or nationally representative by definition or by design. During the past half-century, China has produced a wealth of social and demographic data.

The progress in accumulating large-scale, often nationally representative, demographic data has been especially rapid during the past fifteen years, aided by two methodological and technical advances. The first such advance is the use of probability sampling designs in conducting high-quality surveys. These scientifically designed sample surveys not only allow more in-depth questions, such as retrospective birth histories; they also can be carried out more frequently and at lower cost. The second advance, the use of computers to store and to analyze data, has allowed much more sophisticated record linking and modeling at the individual level and better examination of both past and present patterns of demographic behavior. Contemporary Chinese demographic data can be broadly classified according to three major sources: population registration, censuses, and large-scale national representative sample surveys.

Until recently, population registration was the main source of contemporary Chinese demographic data. With the exception of the 1953 and 1964 censuses, until the 1980s household registration data were the only source of national as well as regional population counts and vital rates.[7] Beginning in 1949, state efforts to integrate population registration with national economic planning and to use the registration system as a tool of social control were based on a centuries-old tradition of household registration.[8] Since the late 1950s the household registration system has evolved into a nationwide institution encompassing virtually every individual.[9] This system has allowed the Chinese government to tabulate annually updated demographic profiles, including not only national and regional population totals, but also systematic vital information on such events as birth, death, and migration.[10]

Population registration is therefore known in China as household registration, because every individual is registered either through a resident household *(jumin hu)* or an institutional household *(jiti hu)*, such as a factory dormitory or a military unit. Every individual registered is also assigned a household registration status *(hukou)*, indicating not only geographic location but also agricultural or nonagricultural affiliation.[11] This household registration status in turn formed the basis of a person's economic entitlements, as well as such social privileges as food and cloth rationing, land allocation, public education, and heath care (Cheng and Selden 1994).

The second major source of contemporary Chinese demographic

data is the census. Censuses have been used not only to enumerate the country's population but also to cross-examine and to update the population registers tabulated from household registration. Over the past five decades China has conducted four censuses, in 1953, 1964, 1982, and 1990. Over the years the coverage of population has improved; the more recent censuses also include far more information than the household registers.[12] The utility of census data has also greatly increased beginning with the 1982 census, as individual-level data have become available in machine-readable format.[13]

The third data source, scientifically designed probability sample surveys, is particularly useful for social demography. Table A.2 lists the surveys cited in this volume. Such sources have become available only during the past two decades. Recognizing the limitations of household registration and census data, various Chinese government and academic institutions launched a series of major surveys utilizing newly introduced probability sampling techniques. Unlike registration and census data, which are expensive to collect and can cover only a limited number of questions, these surveys are more resource efficient, and therefore suitable for asking more detailed questions. In contrast to the most recent Chinese census, which included 21 questions, for example, some recent national surveys contain well over 100 questions.

These sample surveys not only provide current demographic data sources; in several cases they also allow construction of a nationally representative demographic history of the recent past. This is especially the case for two large-scale national fertility surveys: the 1982 Fertility Sample Survey, known also as the One-per-Thousand Survey, of over 300,000 ever-married women aged 15–67; and the 1988 survey of fertility and birth control, also known as the Two-per-Thousand Survey, of nearly half a million women aged 15–57. These two surveys have provided detailed pregnancy, birth, and contraceptive history data for Chinese women as far back as the late 1940s, enabling researchers to trace the process and origins of China's rapid fertility decline (R. Freedman et al. 1988; Wang 1988; Lavely and Freedman 1990; Zhao Zhongwei 1998).[14]

Using these data, demographers have been able to reconstruct marriage and fertility histories for China at both the national and subnational levels for the four decades since the 1940s.[15] Results from these reconstructions have generally corroborated findings from earlier,

Table A.2 Contemporary Chinese demographic surveys

Year	Location	Sample size	Example of content
1982	China	~ 1 million, 300,000 ever-married women	pregnancy and birth histories for women aged 15–67
1985	Hebei, Shaanxi, and Shanghai	13,300 ever-married women	marital, pregnancy, birth, and contraceptive use history
1987	China	~ 2 million, 500,000 ever-married women	pregnancy, birth, and contraceptive use history
1987	Beijing, Liaoning, Shandong, Guangdong, Gansu, and Guizhou Provinces	~ 36,000 ever-married women	marital, pregnancy, birth, and contraceptive use history
1987	China	1 percent of national population, ~110 million	current population, marriage, birth, and death
1992	China	380,000	birth and contraceptive use history
1995	China	1 percent of national population, ~120 million	current population, marriage, birth, death, migration

more localized data sources, such as fertility level (Coale and Chen 1987) and fertility behavior (Coale, Li, and Han 1988; Wang and Tuma 1993; Wang and Yang 1996; Zhao Zhongwei 1998).[16]

Moreover, the simultaneous availability of three data sources—allows scholars to cross-examine data quality from any single source. For example, by using death rates derived from survival ratios between the 1982, 1964, and 1953 censuses and fertility rates from the independently conducted 1982 fertility survey, Ansley Coale (1984) was able to construct a national population for China for 1982 implied by these birth and death rates. He then compared this population at each age to population enumerated by the 1982 census. Coale found the agreement between the two independent sources of data "extraordinary" (ibid., 21).[17]

By comparison with historical data sources, however, these contemporary demographic data also have important limitations. Not only are they by definition less longitudinal; they are also less detailed than the best historical data. Contemporary surveys, for example, are generally incapable of generating retrospective information on such socioeconomic variables as occupational attainment, household composition and structure, and kinship relationships. Contemporary survey data therefore have more limited usefulness in exploring and understanding past interactions between demographic behavior and social context at the individual level.

Nevertheless, these survey materials hold promise for future research. Together with time series of historical data already available for selected locales in China, it is now possible to combine historical data with available contemporary survey data for the same populations and to construct detailed, uninterrupted, data series for some locales. Such research will further refine our understanding and appreciation of Chinese demographic behavior.

Notes

1. Introduction

Epigraph: Malthus (1826/1986, 61).

1. These numbers are derived from data from the United Nations Population Division, Department of Economic and Social Information and Policy Analysis. See too Durand (1974), Coale (1975), McEvedy and Jones (1978) and Biraben (1979).
2. Overbeek (1974) summarizes the history of population theory during the last three centuries and vividly describes the theoretical debate's focus on overpopulation.
3. See National Research Council (1986) and Easterlin (1996) for the most recent National Academy report on the relationship between population and economic constraints, and Royal Society and National Academy of Sciences (1991) for the most recent National Academy report on the relationship between population and environmental constraints. Keyfitz (1992 and esp. 1996) offers an elegant analysis of both concerns.
4. Malthus published the first edition of *An Essay on the Principle of Population* anonymously in 1798 and a substantially revised second edition in 1803. This was followed by revisions in 1806, 1807, 1817, and 1826 (James 1979). We quote the 1798, 1803, and 1826 editions, incorporated in Winch (1992) and the definitive edition by Wrigley and Souden (1986), now unfortunately out of print.
5. China is largely missing from the first, 1798, edition, but has a chapter more or less to itself from 1803 on.
6. Macfarlane (1997, 363–367) provides the most recent reformulation of this contrast, this time between China and Japan.
7. See Lavely, Lee, and Wang (1990) for a detailed discussion of the state of

Chinese demography. The major changes since 1990 have been the rapid rise in population mobility and a corresponding increase in migration studies such as Solinger (1999).

8. The most important work is by the Cambridge Group for the History of Population and Social Structure, summarized in two volumes: Wrigley and Schofield (1981) and Wrigley et al. (1997). They conclude (549): "Had he but known it, Malthus might well have dubbed a preventive-check society, in which marriage acted as the demographic regulator, as 'English' to balance his designation of a positive-check society, where the regulator was mortality, as 'Chinese.'"

9. Goody (1996) describes the rise of this binary opposition between East and West and identifies a variety of similar misunderstandings.

10. The 1982 and 1990 censuses and the 1982, 1988, and 1995 fertility and population surveys are particularly noteworthy. See the Appendix.

11. The major advances in Chinese historical demography, as in the West, have been inspired by the discovery and analysis of nominative records, in particular genealogical and household registration records. Many of these sources are now available through the Genealogical Society of Utah. See Finegan and Telford (1988) and Thatcher (1995, 1998) for detailed descriptions of the GSU holdings and information on accessibility.

12. See the Appendix for a general introduction to and appraisal of the sources for Chinese population history.

13. China will soon lose its standing as the most populous on earth. According to current projections, India will replace China before the mid-twenty-first century. Whereas China's population is projected to plateau by 2030 at 1.6 billion, India's at current rates will continue to grow indefinitely.

14. For much of human history world population has been remarkably sparse. While we currently trace our origins as far back as 1 million years, we believe that as recently as 5000 B.C. there were no more than 5 million people, concentrated largely in Asia and Africa. These numbers grew slowly. A demographic regime of high mortality and low fertility restricted global population growth to below 2 per 10,000 a year. Although the rate of population growth increased with the rise and spread of settled agriculture during the fifth millennium B.C. and of literate civilization during the first millennium B.C., it required a millennium for population to double. In A.D. 1, world population was still only 150 to 200 million. As late as 1700, 300 years after the Renaissance and 200 years after the Age of Discovery, world population was no more than 600–700 million (Durand 1974; Coale 1975; McEvedy and Jones 1978; Biraben 1979).

15. Here and elsewhere we follow the stylistic lead of the neo-Malthusians and use "East" to refer to China and "West" to refer to Western Europe, especially England (Schofield 1989, 284–285).

16. By "system" we mean the defining characteristics of "Chinese" demographic behavior during the past 300 years in contrast to the "European demographic system, 1500–1820," identified by Flinn (1981).

17. See Chapter 4 for a detailed discussion of sex differential mortality. The Chinese preference for male descendants dates back at least four millennia. According to Ho (1975, 323), "Oracle texts reveal that Shang kings frequently asked about the sex of infants yet to be born . . . The word 'good' was used to denote a boy and . . . 'not good' to denote a girl."

18. As far as we know to date, the only Chinese populations that clearly did not practice infanticide are from the twentieth century, in particular from Taiwan. See B. Lee (1981) and Li Bozhong (forthcoming) for a summary of the qualitative evidence. However, since many populations did not record female children, quantitative evidence is confined to the specific populations discussed in this book: approximately 125,000 people.

19. Langer (1974a, 1974b) provides the classic survey on this subject. While vestiges of such behavior, which was common in the classic Mediterranean world, persisted for some time, Kertzer (1993) documents the gradual disappearance of sex-selective behavior by the seventeenth century even in such patriarchal societies as Italy.

20. See Chapter 5 for an analysis of universal marriage in China and a detailed comparison with the Western marriage system.

21. These estimates are based on the shares of married females aged 45–49 for France, Italy, Spain, and the United Kingdom in 1982 and 1990 (United Nations 1984, 1992).

22. See Chapter 6 for a detailed discussion of the Chinese low marital fertility regime and the rationale and mechanisms that perpetuated such behavior.

23. Wilson (1984, 228) summarizes the TMFR for a dozen seventeenth- and eighteenth-century European populations aged 20–49, which ranged from 6.6 to 10.8 with a mean of 8.5 and a mode of over 8. Flinn (1981, 31) aggregates 86 historical European populations aged 20–44 by nationality. While his aggregation is dubious because of different sample size and population definition, he concludes that TMFR ca. 1750 was 7.6 in England, 8.1 in Germany, 8.3 in Scandinavia, 8.9 in Belgium, and 9 in France. In 1997 Wrigley, Davies, Oeppen, and Schofield completed a large-scale reconstitution of couples from 26 English parishes ca. 1600 to 1824 and concluded that the TMFR aged 20–49 was 7.4 (355, 450).

24. While unmarried females in the West could also have a substantial number of births, further increasing Western fertility, in China they generally did not. The illegitimacy rate in almost all the available historical and contemporary Chinese populations is virtually zero. The only notable exception is the island province of Taiwan under Japanese occupation, which in the early twentieth century had a bastardy rate of less than 5 percent. The share of illegitimate births in Austria, Sweden, Denmark, Germany, Hungary, and Portugal was higher during this period, and considerably higher in the eighteenth and nineteenth centuries (Barrett 1980; Flinn 1981).

25. According to Coale and Treadway (1986, 42–44), it took 60 years for the marital fertility rate for Europe as a whole to drop from 7.5 in 1900 to 4.3 in 1960.

26. See Chapter 7 for brief discussion of this phenomenon. For more details see A. Wolf and Huang (1980) for a detailed description of adoption in rural Taiwan during the early twentieth century, and Wang and Lee (1998) for a description of adoption among the Qing nobility in the eighteenth and nineteenth centuries.
27. See Chapter 8 for a discussion of these collective traditions and their demographic consequences.
28. See Coale and Watkins (1986) for the summary book of a large multivolume demographic study of the European fertility decline, and Gillis, Tilly, and Levine (1992) for a recent symposium volume of similar historical studies.
29. See Chapter 9 for a more textured discussion of the rise of Western individual and Chinese collective demographic behavior. The historical process was complex and in the West had much to do with female emancipation and the rise of a private familial sphere, described in Perot (1990). Gillis, Tilly, and Levine (1992) discuss how these processes intertacted to produce the European fertility decline.
30. World population in 2025 thus will probably be 8.5, not 9.5, billion (United Nations 1993). The number of averted births China has contributed to world population control is, of course, higher, between 1 and 1.5 billion.
31. Malthus recognized that the preventive check could take many forms. Most, however, were either unintended, impossible, or, to Malthus, immoral and uncommon. See our discussion of preventive checks in Chapters 2 and 6.
32. Lee and Campbell (1997) describe the demographic patterns associated with the consequent tension between hereditary familial privilege and individual-level ability and initiative in several rural populations in northeast China during the eighteenth and nineteenth centuries.
33. See Wrigley (1986) on Malthus' contributions to such diverse fields as biology, economics, geography, history, and social anthropology.

2. Malthusian Myths

Epigraph: Malthus (1798/1986, 315; 1803/1992, 23 and 1826/1986, 16).

1. While this idea was by no means original to Malthus, his elegant formulation of the principle and his iteration and reiteration of its importance in five subsequent editions, as well as in other essays, created a paradigm whose intellectual legacy has been remarkably persistent (Overbeek 1974).
2. Malthus (1803/1992, 40; 1826/1986, 312). Although Malthus believed that the passion between the sexes was high and constant and that sexual restraint within marriage was impossible, he recognized other types of preventive checks, including such unintended forms as sterility as a result of contact with prostitutes, and subfecundity as a result of malnutrition. Finally, while he recognized that there were means of averting conception, he believed that they were immoral, and uncommon because they involved either what he regarded as unnatural sexual acts or the use of contraceptive devices.

3. While Malthus is indefatigable in these chapters both in his presentation of ethnographic and historical detail and in his citation of sources, he refrains from classifying specific behaviors as positive or preventive.

4. In contrast to his treatment of the non-Western world, Malthus ordered his discussion of the Western world geographically, beginning clockwise with Norway and then proceeding to Sweden, Russia, Middle Europe, Switzerland, France, England, and concluding with Scotland and Ireland.

5. Although Malthus does not say so explicitly, he appears to have organized these chapters according to his understanding of the most primitive to the most sophisticated human civilizations, beginning with Tierra del Fuego and concluding with the Greek and Roman world. In between the chapters deal with the American Indians, the islands of the South Sea, the ancient inhabitants of the North of Europe, modern pastoral nations, Africa, Siberia, the Turkish Dominions and Persia, Indostan and Tibet, and China and Japan. Malthus' explicit conclusion was: "it appears that in modern Europe the positive checks to population prevail less, and preventive checks more, than in past times, and in the more uncivilized parts of the world" (1803/1992, 43; 1826/1986, 315).

6. For example, the Tierra del Fuegans, whom Malthus called "the lowest stage of human society," "are driven to such resources for subsistence, where the supply of animal and vegetable food is so extremely scanty, and the labour necessary to procure it is so severe, it is evident, that population must be very thinly scattered in proportion to the territory" (1826/1986, 24).

7. For example, in Siberia, "where the market for corn is extremely narrow, and the price very low, the cultivators are always poor; and though they may be able amply to provide for their family in a single article of food, yet they cannot realize a capital to divide among their children, and enable them to undertake the cultivation of fresh land" (ibid., 106). And in Turkey, "its tyranny, its feebleness, its bad laws and worse administration of them, together with the consequent insecurity of property, threw such obstacles in the way of agriculture that the means of subsistence are necessarily decreasing yearly . . . The general land tax paid to the sultan is in itself moderate; but by abuses inherent in the Turkish government the pachas and their agents have found out the means of rendering it ruinous . . . To these constant oppressions are added a thousand accidental extortions . . . The consequence of these depredations . . . is that the food of the peasants is almost everywhere reduced to a little flat cake of barley or doura, onions, lentils, and water" (ibid., 110–111).

8. In India, for example, "marriage is very greatly encouraged, and a male heir is considered as an object of the first importance . . . The tendency to early marriages was still always predominant, and in general prompt every person to enter in to this state who could look forward to the slightest chance of being able to maintain a family. The natural consequence of this was, that the lower classes of people were reduced to extreme poverty, and were compelled to adopt the most frugal and scanty mode of subsistence. This frugality was

still further increased, and extended in some degree to the higher classes of society, by its being considered as an eminent virtue. The population would thus be pressed hard against the limits of the means of subsistence, and the food of the country would be meted out to the major part of the people in the smallest shares that could support life. In such a state of things every failure in the crops from unfavorable seasons would be felt most severely; and India, as might be expected, has in all ages been subject to the most dreadful famines" (ibid., 118–120).

9. Thus Malthus emphasized the paradox that "the richest and most flourishing empire of the word is notwithstanding, in one sense the poorest and the most miserable of all" (ibid., 130).

10. "Extraordinary encouragements . . . given to marriage . . . have caused the immense produce of the country to be divided into very small shares and have consequently rendered China more populous, in proportion to its means of subsistence than perhaps any other country in the world" (ibid., 128). See also ibid., 126, 130.

11. "The effect of these encouragements to marriage among the rich is to subdivide property, which has in itself a strong tendency to promote population . . . Property in land has been divided into very moderate parcels, by the successive distribution of the possessions of every father equally among his sons . . . These causes constantly tend to level wealth, and few succeed to such an accumulation of it as to render them independent of any effects of their own for its increase. It is a common remark among the Chinese, that fortunes seldom continue considerable in the same family beyond the third generation" (ibid., 129–130).

12. "The price of labor is generally found to bear as small a proportion everywhere to the rate demanded for provisions as the common people can suffer . . . They are reduced to the use of vegetable food, with a very rare and scanty relish of any animal substance" (ibid., 130).

13. "Notwithstanding the great sobriety and industry of the inhabitants of China, the prodigious number of them occasions a great deal of misery. There are some so poor that being unable to supply their children with common necessaries, they expose them in the street" (ibid.). Malthus concluded: "Respecting the number of infants which are actually exposed, it is difficult to form the slightest guess; but if we believe the Chinese writers themselves, the practice must be very common" (ibid., 134). Malthus apparently thought that infanticide functioned both as a positive check and as an incentive for marriage. "This permission given to parents thus to expose their offspring tends undoubtedly to facilitate marriage, and encourage population. Contemplating this extreme resource beforehand, less fear is entertained of entering into the married state" (ibid., 129).

14. "The positive checks to population from disease, though considerable, do not appear to be so great as might be expected" (ibid., 133). In contrast, "Famines here are but too frequent, millions of people perish with hunger . . . All

writers agree in mentioning the frequency of the dearths in China" (ibid., 131, 132). Malthus also quoted a Jesuit writing to a member of the Royal Academy of Sciences: "Another thing that you can scarcely believe is that dearths should be so frequent in China . . . If famine did not, from time to time, thin the immense number of inhabitants which China contains it would be impossible for her to live in peace" (ibid., 135–136).

15. The only preventive check Malthus recognized in China was the practice of celibacy by Buddhist monks (ibid., 132). As a result, he thought that the preventive check did predominate in at least one contemporary Chinese province—Tibet (ibid., 122–123). Of course, for Malthus Tibet was clearly part of South Asia, not East Asia.

16. Goody (1996) discusses this much larger myth of the superiority of the West over the East in detail and Malthus' contributions in particular (190–191). However, while he devotes one-sixth of his text to a discussion of neo-Malthusian theory's perpetuation of this myth, he does not seem to accord much importance to Malthus' own contributions to such ethnocentric social theory.

17. Ansley Coale (1973) has most recently reformulated this Malthusian premise. According to Coale, there were three preconditions for the fertility decline: it must be within the calculus of conscious choice, it must be advantageous, and the technology must be available (65).

18. Efforts to establish alternative approaches to these individual decision-making models include McNicoll (1984, 1992), Greenhalgh (1995), and Mason (1997).

19. Nevertheless, despite decades of empirical research along such individual lines, some demographers remain unsatisfied with the utility of such research for developing countries (McNicoll 1992; Greenhalgh 1995, 1996; Mason 1997).

20. In an important article on Bangladesh, however, Mead Cain (1982) has also shown that in some rural populations, the rise of the nuclear family and the consequent loss of familial labor from other kin can also serve as an incentive for population growth. See also Schultz (1983).

21. Hajnal's model has been highly influential. Schofield (1989) provides an elegant and succinct reformulation. See the 1987 symposium issue of the *Journal of Family History* for an assessment of Hajnal's model and Goody (1996) for a recent critique.

22. The term "Malthusian revolution" belongs to Macfarlane (1986), who devotes one-quarter of his book to discussion of the Malthusian marriage system.

23. See Demeny (1986) for a dissenting view.

24. "[By 1800] after the Chinese population had reached 400 million, the over-all opportunities for gainful employment in the nation began to be drastically reduced amidst continual population increase and technological stagnation. At the point where the margin above bare subsistence became so much

smaller than the traditional or customary living standard, the effect of irrational land tenure on the marginal segments of the population presumably became disproportionately greater" (Ho 1959, 226).

25. The only significant exception is the Maoist scholarship that dominated China ca. 1950–1975, which stressed class struggle and virtually ignored population growth. During the last twenty-five years, however, even Chinese historians have increasingly emphasized the importance of demographic constraints. See Li Bozhong (1996c, 1998) for detailed discussion of recent Chinese emphases on "population pressure" and their similarities with Western scholarship.

26. See Ho (1959), G. Skinner (1964, 1965a, 1965b, 1977, 1985), Perkins (1969), Elvin (1973), Myers (1980), P. Huang (1985, 1990), Chao (1986), and Liu Ts'ui-jung (1986).

27. Chao (1986) and P. Huang (1990) are the most articulate examples of such thinking.

28. Elvin (1973) was the first to single out the economic implications of the low cost of labor. The most rigorous attempts to document labor costs, however, are Chao (1986) and (1990).

29. Population change has also been identified by some as a determining factor in shaping Chinese social and political processes, at least in the past (P. Huang 1990). Dynastic cycles coincided with the rise and fall of population (G. Skinner 1977).

30. The well-known economic historian and social critic Richard Tawney, for example, observed after a year in China: "Chinese habit and doctrine put a premium on the growth of population, which appears to Western eyes unnatural and artificial. Sentiment, hallowed by immemorial tradition, makes it a duty to leave sons, and the communism of the patriarchal family dissociates the production of children from responsibility for their maintenance. Hence prudential restraints act with less force than elsewhere and population, instead of being checked by the gradual tightening of economic pressure on individuals, plunges blindly forward, till whole communities go over the precipice" (1932, 104). See Chao (1986), quoted in Chapter 5, note 9, for a more recent formulation of this understanding.

31. For example, P. Huang suggests "that China's demographic change was driven by alterations in the mortality rate, not in the fertility rate as in early modern Europe" (1990, 329).

32. While Ho (1959, 270–278) may be the classic example of such views, they have recently been reinvigorated by Harrell's reevaluation of Chinese mortality rates (1995, 7–9, 14). Harrell's findings, however, are based solely on highly restricted retrospective reconstructions of specific eighteenth- and nineteenth-century populations by Chinese genealogists during the very late nineteenth century and the twentieth century.

33. In a very brief essay, Hong Liangji (1746–1809) made an observation highly similar to Malthus' formulation of the positive check, without, however, any

mention of the preventive check and without Malthus' exhaustive documentation or extensive argumentation (Ho 1959). More recently, Ma Yinchu (1882–1982), the former president of Peking University, made a strong plea for population control in 1958. Mao, however, criticized Ma as Malthusian and dismissed him from his post. He was rehabilitated only in the late 1970s.

The refutation of Hong Liangji by Bao Shichen (1775–1855) is typical: "The land of China is sufficient to support the people of the country. More people mean more labor; and labor is the basis of wealth, not the cause of poverty" *(Anwu sizhong,* 26.2b).

34. See Chen Pi-chao and Kols (1982) and Lavely and Freedman (1990) on the early development of the Chinese government's family planning program.

35. Given this income target, Chinese "think tanks" produced a variety of optimization studies based on the economic growth rates of the 1970s. 1.2 billion was the compromise consensus. Some extreme estimates claimed that China's optimum population was 600–700 million (Song, Tuan, and Yu 1985).

36. Having arrived at a 1.2 billion target population for the year 2000, the think tanks calculated that each couple could have no more than two children. They formulated the one-child-per-couple policy on the assumption that this was a target and not an immediate goal (ibid.).

37. See Chapter 8, esp. notes 20 and 21, for examples of this policy tradition.

38. Banister (1987) and Aird (1990) document this resistance in some detail.

39. See too the well-known popular works by the Ehrlichs (1968/1971, 1990).

40. Critics of Brown point to the fact that during the last two decades China's grain output has increased at twice the rate of population growth. Moreover, Brown's calculations seem to use unrepresentative or even incorrect data. See Smil (1995) and Alexandratos (1996) for more balanced discussions.

41. The mythology that China is a leader in intellectual piracy and illegal immigration is an example. While intellectual property laws are very new to China and much remains to be done (Alford 1995), China is hardly the leader in such transgressions—especially when we remember that the Chinese are one-fifth of current world population. According to the Motion Picture Association of America, the per capita rate of Chinese illegal video production of United States movies in 1995 was $0.10, less than one-tenth the rate in Italy or the United Kingdom, and one-sixth the rate in Russia. According to the International Federation of the Phonographic Industry, the per capita rate of Chinese illegal CD and cassette production in 1995 was $0.12, one-hundredth the rate in Mexico or Brazil, one-tenth the rate in Russia, and approximately the same rate as in the United States. Meanwhile, according to the Business Software Alliance, the per capita rate of Chinese illegal software production in 1995 was $0.59, less than one-twentieth the rate in the United States, Japan, or South Korea (International Herald Tribune, July 4, 1997, 6). Put differently, while Mexico pirates ten times as many CDs and Japan pirates twice the software as China in total, they receive far less press. This disparity is even more apparent in accounts of illegal immigration into the United

168 · Notes to Pages 27–29

States. According to estimates by the United States Department of Immigration and Naturalization Services, in 1996 China was not even in the top twenty countries of origin for illegal immigration into the United States and accounted for less illegal immigration than other Asian countries such as the Philippines, Pakistan, India, and South Korea (INS 1997).

3. Subsistence

Epigraph: Malthus (1798/1992, 57–58).

1. "Notwithstanding the great sobriety and industry of the inhabitants of China, the prodigious number of them occasions a great deal of misery. There are some so poor that being unable to supply their children with common necessaries they expose them in the street, especially when the mothers fall sick or want milk to nourish them; so that these little innocents are in some sense condemned to death as soon as they begin to live" (Du Halde 1738, 1: 277).

2. Thus according to Adam Smith (1776/1979, 174–175), "The poverty of the lower ranks of people in China far surpasses that of the most beggarly nations in Europe . . . The subsistence which they find . . . is so scanty that they are eager to fish up the nastiest garbage thrown overboard from any European ship. Any carrion, the carcase of a dead dog or cat, for example, half putrid and stinking, is as welcome to them as the most wholesome food to the people of other countries."

3. According to official Chinese statistics, by the middle of the eighteenth century, population density was already over 500 people per cultivated square kilometer (Liang Fangzhong 1980, 400, 546). While these numbers are undoubtedly exaggerated because of underregistration of cultivated acreage (Ho 1995), the contrast with eighteenth-century Europe, where one cultivated square kilometer supported seventy people, is quite extreme (Braudel 1979, 56–64).

4. The classic passages by Smith and Malthus cited above reflect this common observation.

5. While the mean stature of Chinese has yet to be determined for the eighteenth century, it was no more than 163 centimeters in the late nineteenth century (A. Chen and Lee 1996). By contrast, European stature in the late nineteenth century was approximately 170 centimeters (Floud, Wachter, and Gregory 1990).

6. Both Malthus and Ricardo defined overpopulation as the point at which average output fell below the minimum subsistence level, so that mortality levels rose or marriage was deferred and population growth was halted (Grigg 1980).

7. Ho wrote in 1959 that "there is reason to believe that the optimum condition (the point at which 'a population produces maximum economic welfare') at

the technological level of the time, was reached between 1750 and 1775" (270). Mark Elvin (1973), however, was the first to elaborate it as a formal model for Chinese economic history. Coincidentally, similar views were also extremely popular in China during the late 1970s, when the draconian population control policy was first formulated (Song 1981).

8. Among Chinese historians, Philip Huang (1985, 1990) is probably the most important exponent of this definition of overpopulation. See Chao (1986) for a formal specification of the model in a Chinese context.

9. Whereas many scholars agree more or less with the "national" pattern first proposed by Ho Ping-ti, there is enormous disagreement over the location as well as the timing of overpopulation. For instance, many scholars identify China proper, especially the eastern provinces of Jiangsu, Zhejiang, Fujian, Shandong, and Hebei, as the loci of overpopulation, and the late imperial period (seventeenth to early twentieth centuries) as the main period of overpopulation. Others argue that overpopulation occurred much earlier and in a number of different regions (Cong 1984). Most historians agree that overpopulation was especially characteristic of the Lower Yangzi, the region with the highest population density in China and the region on which we will focus in this chapter. Li Bozhong (1996c, 1998) summarizes these different views.

Until recently our knowledge of China's population and economy was based on studies of institutional histories such as Ho (1959), G. Skinner (1986), and Jiang Tao (1993) on Chinese population history, and Wang Yeh-chien (1973), Chuan (1974, 1976), and Liang Fangzhong (1980, 1984) on Chinese economic history, and on estimated broad contours of China's population and economic growth such as Ho (1959); Liu Ta-chung and Yeh (1965); Aird (1968); Eckstein, Galenson, and Liu (1968); Perkins (1969); and Schran (1978).

10. See Lavely, Lee, and Wang (1990) for an overview of the state of Chinese historical and contemporary demography. Unfortunately, we know of no equivalent article on studies of the Chinese economy.

11. Agricultural production increased not only during a period of population growth, but also during a period of contraction of sown land. For example, Walker (1988) describes how between 1978 and 1986 national grain production increased by 24 percent, while the total sown area shrank by 8 percent, mostly as a result of industrial and housing construction use. Li Bozhong (1998) describes a similar process for the Jiangnan region from 1700 to 1850.

12. While Perkins (1969) argues that per capita productivity was relatively stable during the last three centuries, Chao et al. (1995) document a slight dip in productivity per acre during the late eighteenth and early nineteenth centuries, followed by a recovery in the late nineteenth and early twentieth. See Li Bozhong (1998), however, for a critique of both of these findings.

13. A *shi* was a unit of volume in late imperial China and has been estimated to be slightly less than 200 pounds of milled rice (Chuan and Kraus 1975, 98).

14. Li Bozhong's well-documented findings call into question one of the major

conclusions in Perkins (1969). Relying on a variety of indirect evidence, Perkins suggested that agricultural expansion from the fourteenth through nineteenth centuries was as much a result of rising land productivity as of increased cultivation. Specifically, he suggested that grain yields more than doubled nationwide, with most of the increase taking place before the eighteenth century (pp. 14–23). Li's findings, backed by the findings in Chao et al. (1995), suggest that this is unlikely to have been the case and that cultivated acreage must have increased far more than Perkins thought.

15. Calculated from Walker (1988, 608). In 1978, for example, Zhejiang Province had a per capita grain output of 391 kilograms, 19 percent higher than the national average of 329. In Jiangsu Province, it was 25 percent above the national average. Moreover, from 1978 through 1986 per capita grain production for Jiangsu increased by an additional 29 percent, to 533 kilograms, 44 percent above the increased national average. In Heilongjiang and Jilin Provinces in the northeast, grain output per capita was 472 and 426 kilograms respectively in 1978, 43 and 29 percent above the national average. By 1986 per capita grain output had risen to a new high of 533 and 604 kilograms, 44 and 63 percent above the national average.

16. These numbers are in 1955 *yuan*, worth approximately 40 cents in U.S. dollars. We thank Tom Rawski for this information.

17. The average rate of growth in per capita agricultural output was 4.8 percent for 1978–1986 and 0.4 for 1957–1978 (Field 1988).

18. In 1978 per capita grain output in Shaanxi was 87 percent of the national average, in Gansu 80 percent, in Guizhou 73 percent, and in Yunnan 85 percent (Walker 1988, 608). According to Lee (forthcoming), this process of deterioration did not begin in southwest China until the second quarter of the nineteenth century.

19. The fact that such measures are currently unavailable for the eighteenth and nineteenth centuries does not mean that there was no improvement in nutrition during this period.

20. Except in brief periods of severe famine, such as the one in 1959–1961, there is no clear evidence that China, given its widely recorded impoverishment in the first half of this century, ever experienced a consumption level below that of subsistence. The Food and Agriculture Organization of the United Nations considers 1,600 kcalories to be the level of minimum subsistence. A large-scale survey conducted in 1929–1933 gives an estimate of 2,365 daily available kcalories (Buck 1966, 11).

21. A. Chen and Lee (1996). The extrapolation for the population at large follows Wachter (1981) and Wachter and Trussell (1982). These are mean calculations, and the variance is relatively large—over three centimeters. Numerous similar records, however, are available in the Chinese archives, and we are in the process of collecting and analyzing these data.

22. In 1915 the Research Committee of the Chinese Medical Missionary Association (CMMA) issued a call for "physical measurements on as large a number

of individuals and from as widely scattered a group of Chinese as possible" (Stevenson, 1926, 95). The CMMA realized that the physical growth standards available at that time had been derived from studies of European and American children and were almost useless as standards for Chinese children. The CMMA's call for an anthropometric survey of the Chinese was the first step in establishing reference standards of physical growth for healthy Chinese. Altogether, doctors and medical workers associated with the CMMA responded to the call by collecting physical measurements on more than 11,000 Chinese in urban areas during the period 1915–1925. The mean heights of 18-year-old males and females were 163.1 and 151.1 cm, respectively. Not until after 1949 were massive publications of anthropometric data on rural populations exploited.

23. According to A. Chen and Lee (1996), between 1900 and 1950 the mean height of urban males and females increased 0.5 and 1 cm per decade respectively on the mainland and 0.8 cm per decade regardless of sex on Taiwan.

24. According to A. Chen and Lee (1996), between 1950 and 1990 the mean height of males and females increased 1 and 1.3 cm per decade respectively on the mainland and 1.4 and 1.2 cm respectively per decade on Taiwan.

25. A 1979 survey of Anhui Province found that from 1958 to 1979 height had increased 4.2 cm a decade in rural areas and 2.3 cm per decade in urban areas (Research Group 1982, 508, cited in Piazza 1986, 156–157). More recently, a similar survey of Sichuan Province found that from 1985 to 1995 the height of rural males and females had increased 4.3 and 3.5 cm respectively, compared to only 1.21 and 1.31 cm in urban areas (UPI press release, November 5, 1996).

26. These handbooks include an anonymous work from about 1630 titled *Shenshi nong shu* (Mr. Shen's agricultural treatise) and a supplementary 1658 work by Zhang Luxiang titled *Bunongshu* (Supplements to [Mr. Shen's] agricultural treatise), both annotated by Chen Hengli and Wang Da and published as *Bunongshu jiaoshi* (Beijing nongye chubanshe, 1983), as well as Jiang Gao's 1834 work titled *Pu Mao nongzi* (Report on agriculture in the Huangpu River and Maohu Lake region) (Shanghai tushuguan, 1963) and Tao Xi's *Zuhe* (The truth about rents), written sometime between 1864 and 1884 and published anonymously in 1927.

Rural wages in the Lower Yangzi often consisted of food, cash, and kind. While the portion in kind does not appear to have changed greatly during the seventeenth, eighteenth, and nineteenth centuries, the portions in food and cash increased (Luo 1989; Fang 1996). Indeed, according to a recent analysis by Pan (1997), adult male farm laborers consumed on average more than 4,000 kcalories a day.

27. The number of meat days was slightly lower in the slack season, but the trend was the same: 7–8 days a month in the sixteenth century and 10 days a month in the seventeenth.

28. In the seventeenth century "meat" consisted of 63 grams (one-eighth of a

catty) of preserved meat or 100 grams (one-fifth of a catty) of animal intestines or fish a day. In the nineteenth century the portion was 250 grams (one-half a catty) of pork, that is, two and a half to four times as much food.

29. Year laborers ate 125 grams (one-quarter of a catty) of pork on meat days and of fish on nonmeat days.

30. According to Fang Xing, before the seventeenth century, for example, the daily serving of wine was one-third cup. In the seventeenth century the daily serving of wine during the busy season was one cup for hard labor and half a cup for ordinary labor. By the late seventeenth century laborers received 1.2 taels of silver to purchase wine and firewood. By the late nineteenth century wine money alone had increased to 1.25 taels a year (1996, 98).

31. Again according to Fang Xing, expenditure on nongrain food—oil, meat, fish, salt, vegetables, alcohol—expanded from one-fifth to almost one-third of an ordinary peasant family's food budget (measured in constant prices) between the seventeenth and nineteenth centuries. Altogether such items cost a "typical" nineteenth-century family of five persons 7 taels of silver a year (1996, 93, 97).

32. According to Pomerantz (forthcoming), Chinese ca. 1750 consumed 6–8 pounds of cotton cloth per capita compared with 5 pounds in Germany and 8 pounds in France. See Buck (1937, 456) and De Vries (1975) for a comparison of per capita home furnishings.

33. Previously, the rural standard of living was assumed to have been poor, in particular in the Lower Yangzi, where the person-to-land ratio, land ownership, and land rent were especially high. For some scholars this was the result of a process of increasingly feudal exploitation of rural labor (Chen Zhenhan 1955; Fu Zhufu and Gu 1956; Fu Yiling 1991, 92, 95; Xu 1991, 40–44, 105–106; Wang Tingyuan 1993). For other scholars this was a product of Malthusian or neo-Malthusian overpopulation (Chuan 1958; Hong 1989, 91; P. Huang 1990). According to Huang's particularly lucid account, the development of rural industry and commercialization in the Lower Yangzi were merely byproducts of excess labor at the microfamilial level and only aggravated and accelerated impoverishment at the macrosocial level.

34. Thus Harrell claims (1995, 6) that "[the late imperial] demographic regime is driven primarily by mortality factors rather than fertility factors." Philip Huang places similar emphasis, though without any direct evidence, on the function of mortality in the Chinese socioeconomic regime: "China's demographic regime was driven by alterations in the mortality rate, not in the fertility rate as in Early Modern Europe" (1990, 324).

35. Retrospective genealogies suffer from particularly severe biases in the recording of mortality. The longer the period from the date of compilation and the younger the person's age at death, the less likely a person is to be recorded or to be recorded in any detail. This is particularly true for those who die without progeny. Pope (1989), using retrospectively compiled genealogical sources for North America, demonstrates the consequent weaknesses of

analyses of mortality history based on such sources, particularly for infant and child mortality and especially for the last century or so before the date of compilation.

36. In France, according to Blayo (1975), life expectancy in 1770–1779 was 28.2 for males and 29.6 for females at birth, 38.6 for males and 38.5 for females at age one, and 46.0 for males and 45.6 for females at age five. Life expectancy in 1780–1789 was 27.5 for males and 28.1 for females at birth, 37.6 for males and 37.1 for females at age one, and 45.5 for males and 44.3 for females at age five. By contrast, in England, according to Wrigley and Schofield (1981), life expectancy at birth was higher for both sexes—36.3 in 1750–1775, 37 in 1775–1800, and 41.5 in 1800–1825. In Sweden life expectancy at birth was roughly similar to that in England: 33.7 for males and 36.6 for females in 1751–1790, 39.5 for males and 43.6 for females in 1816–1840, and in the low forties for men and the mid-forties for women from 1840 to the 1890s (Statiskiska Centralbyrån 1969, 61).

37. This conclusion stands in contrast to one important claim to the contrary. Harrell and Pullum's 1995 analysis of male death rates recorded in three late nineteenth-century retrospective genealogies from Xiaoshan County, compiled in 1888 (Shi), 1897 (Lin), and 1904 (Wu) respectively, appear to show higher mortality in the late eighteenth century than in the late seventeenth and in the late nineteenth than in the early nineteenth century (7–10, 146–149). The problems with their results concern selection—they restrict this analysis to males with both a recorded birth and death date, although many of these males are likely to have lived more recently—and representativeness. Xiaoshan was a major battle area during the Taiping rebellion with consequent higher mortality. Harrell and Pullum themselves acknowledge these problems: "The apparent decline over time in the expectation of life in each genealogy is so great that it must be regarded as spurious. It is likely that in the seventeenth century, the chance that an individual would be included in the genealogy was positively related to that individual's longevity" (1995, 148).

38. This is true for males and for females from age one onward.

39. The paucity of famines was first identified by Ho (1959). Will and Wong with Lee (1991) suggest that this was at least partly the result of the state welfare system's annual distribution of almost 5 percent of the national food supply to manipulate food markets for the benefit of the needy. See Liu Ts'ui-jung (1992) for many examples of limited impact. Malthus in fact made the same general observation: "The traces of the most destructive famines in China are by all accounts soon obliterated" (1798/1992, 49; 1826/1986, 323). Watkins and Menken (1985, 1988) have shown through simulation studies that famines, even severe ones, are not the causes holding back population growth unless they occur extremely frequently (more than once every 50 or fewer years). They conclude that "the causes of the normal high levels of mortality, rather than their unusual sharp peaks, should be sought as the explanation

for slow growth or population stagnation" (1988, 170). See Menken and Campbell (1992) for a recent refinement of their simulation model.

40. For analysis of the causes and the consequences of the 1958–1961 famine, see Ashton et al. (1984), Bernstein (1984), Peng (1987), and D. L. Yang (1996).

41. The worst famine in the nineteenth century occurred from 1876 to 1879. Severe drought (little rain for three years) spread in northern China, including Shaanxi, Shanxi, Zhili (current Hebei), Henan, and part of Shandong Provinces. Deaths resulting from hunger, disease, or associated violence were estimated at 9–13 million. According to Walter Mallory, who served as the secretary of the China International Famine Relief Commission in the 1920s, "the tremendous death rate must be ascribed to lack of communications. . . . it took months for the news of the distress in the interior to reach the capital and ports. People were actually dying in great numbers over a wide area before any concerted action was taken to bring aid from the outside" (1926, 29). In 1920–21 analogous climatic conditions obtained throughout the same territory, but because of a newly established 6,000-mile railway system and better relief organization, known deaths were less than half a million.

42. According to Jiang Zhenhua, Li, and Sun (1993), materials from the 1990 census suggest that life expectancy in 1990 nationwide was 68.4 for males and 71.7 for females.

43. See also Lee, Campbell, and Tan (1992); Lee, Campbell, and Wang (1993); Lee and Guo (1994); Lee, Wang, and Campbell (1994); Wang, Lee, and Campbell (1995); Campbell and Lee (1996); Wang and Yang (1996); and Lee and Campbell (1997).

44. These proportions are derived from Lee (1982a, 1982b) and include his estimates of the unregistered population. They therefore differ from the registered population figures in Map 7.1.

45. While the original idea came from Boserup (1965/1996), it was Perkins who first applied this formulation to China (1969, 23).

46. Li Bozhong (1996c) confirms similar conclusions in Faure (1989) and directly contradicts P. Huang's claim (1990, 1) that "peasant farming for subsistence-level returns persisted in China's advanced Yangzi deltas area through six centuries of vigorous commercialization and urban development between 1350 and 1950, and three decades of collectivization and agricultural modernization between 1950 and 1980. Only in the 1980s did transformative development begin to come to the delta countryside, to result in substantial margin above subsistence in peasant incomes."

47. Li Bozhong (1998) focuses in particular on the use of fertilizer and specific combinations of crops and seeds. Shiba (1991) focuses on irrigation. See Bai, Du, and Min (1995) and Liang Jiamian (1989) for an overview of agrarian technology during the late imperial period.

48. This policy was based on the Marxist ideological belief that women's position in society is determined by their relation to the means of production and that female liberation therefore requires female participation in the labor force.

49. Rawski (1979) gives two estimates for 1975, a high one of 284 days and a low one of 215. The 250 we give is roughly the average of the two. See also Rawski (1979, 118). Peter Schran's (1969) estimate of the average peasant's work days per year for the early 1950s is even lower, only 119.

50. According to Rawski (1979), the index of multiple cropping rose from 1.31 in 1952 to 1.50 in 1977 or 1978.

51. Li Bozhong (1998, chap. 8) summarizes studies by other scholars estimating that in the late nineteenth and early twentieth centuries, village women in the Lower Yangzi worked on average 200 days a year in cotton handicrafts. See Yang Lien-sheng (1955) for a classic article on work and rest in imperial China.

52. In some parts of China, output per workday, though not per year, may indeed have decreased. P. Huang (1990) has seized on this possibility to suggest that economic processes in the Lower Yangzi were therefore on a downward involutionary spiral. His argument, however, ignores one important fact: while output per workday may not have increased, the number of workdays did increase substantially (Rawski 1979, 115). As a result, annual output and annual income also increased.

53. Western travelers made similar observations. Sir John Barrow, for example, wrote about the widespread use of silk clothing in the Lower Yangzi at the turn of the nineteenth century in *Travels in China* (London: Caldwell and Davies, 1806), 572.

54. See Bao Shichen, ca. 1840, *Anwu sizhong* 26.3b–5a, for a vivid description of the increase in luxury consumption in the Lower Yangzi. According to Spence (1975, 154), opium addiction nationally was as high as 10 percent in the late nineteenth century.

55. This pattern held true not only in terms of calories but also in terms of taste. Despite the dissemination of American food plants, for example, maize and sweet potato remained unpopular in Jiangnan, where they were regarded as coarse grain. Despite the high price of rice, which had to be imported from such faraway provinces as Hunan and Sichuan, even poor peasants in Jiangnan continued to eat fine grain and not coarse grain.

4. Mortality

Epigraph: Malthus (1803/1992, 16).

1. Malthus placed particular importance on infanticide and disease as the two most important intermediate checks. He discussed infanticide in more than a dozen passages (1826/1986, 25–26, 31, 50, 54, 56, 120–122, 130–131, 134–135, 140–141, 146–147, 151–152).

   Malthus recognized that while infanticide was strictly speaking a positive check on population growth, the custom could, paradoxically, encourage population increase: "It is a very just observation of Hume, that the permission of infanticide generally contributes to increase the population of a country. By removing the fears of too numerous a family, it encourages marriage" (ibid., 51).

2. In his description of Tahiti, Malthus noted: "From the small proportion of women remarked by the missionaries, we may infer that a greater number of female infants had been destroyed . . . This scarcity of women would . . . strike most effectively at the root of population" (ibid., 54).

3. Among the Eariioie of Tahiti, for example, while infanticide was "permitted to all," it was particularly "prevalent among the upper class" (ibid., 50).

4. Thus in Tahiti, "the distresses experienced from one or two unfavorable seasons, operating on a crowded population, which was before living with the greatest economy, and pressing hard against the limits of its food, would, in such a state of society, occasion the more general prevalence of infanticide and promiscuous intercourse; and these depopulating causes would in the same manner continue to act with increased force for some time after the occasion which had aggravated them was at an end. A change of habits to a certain degree gradually produced by a change of circumstances, would soon restore the population" (ibid., 54–55).

5. While Malthus listed war as "the most prominent and striking" of the positive checks (ibid., 153), in more sophisticated societies, "we well know that wars do not depopulate much while industry continues in vigour" (ibid., 149). He singled out China as a society particularly prone to famine (ibid., 131, 135).

6. Whereas in India epidemics resulted from "indigence and bad nourishment" (ibid., 121), in societies of "savages" such as those of American Indians the prevalent causes were "extreme ignorance, the dirt of their persons and the closeness and filth of their cabins" (ibid., 34).

7. On smallpox see ibid., 26–27, 34, 86–87, 95, 102, 115. On plague see ibid., 113–114. In addition, there were unnamed diseases endemic to specific populations. For example, in Turkey there were "epidemic and endemic maladies . . . which make as dreadful ravages as the plague itself" (ibid., 114). See also the many specific examples from the Persian Gulf (ibid., 94–95).

8. In his discussion of India, for example, he differentiated diseases that made "great ravages" among young children (ibid., 121).

9. The initial topic inspiring study of historical demography (e.g., Goubert 1960) was "subsistence or rural crises," first developed in Meuvret (1946).

10. Paradoxically because Malthus went to considerable trouble to prove that the positive check was more important in non-Western societies. He believed that famine was infrequent in western populations. Several articles, (Walter and Schofield 1989; Schofield and Reher 1991; and Johansson 1994) describe this important school of Western social history and population history in detail.

11. Sen (1992) is of course the best known, but see too Greenough (1982), L. Li (1982), McAlpin (1983), Will (1990), and Will and Wong with Lee (1991).

12. Major contributions to our understanding of the structure of cause of death,

albeit during a more recent period, are the studies of French mortality by Vallin and his colleagues (Vallin and Meslé 1988; Vallin 1991) and a more general comparative analysis in Preston (1976).

13. See Preston and van de Walle (1978) and Preston and Haines (1991) for two specific studies, one at the city level and the other at the national level.

14. This is much the same conclusion as Saito (1996, 543). Schofield and Reher (1991), Johansson (1994), and Preston (1996b) are three recent surveys of the state of mortality studies—each with distinctly different approaches.

15. See, however, Szreter (1988) and Woods, Watterson, and Woodward (1988/1989) for more textured explanations of the mortality decline in Britain.

16. The most important technique is probably event history analysis. Allison (1984) and Yamaguchi (1991) are the standard textbooks.

17. Bengtsson (1993) and Campbell and Lee (1996) are early examples. See Bengtsson and Saito (forthcoming) for a preliminary comparison of individual-level mortality in Belgium, China, Italy, Japan, and Sweden.

18. Flinn (1981) is a major exception, as are Wrigley and Schofield (1981); the authors in Bengtsson, Fridlizius, and Ohlsson (1984); and Wrigley et al. (1997).

19. The historical record of epidemics in China is sparse. This is partly a function of the nature of sources. It may also reflect their genuine scarcity. See Dunstan (1975) and Benedict (1995) for studies of specific epidemics.

20. This traditional concept of health maintenance was prevalent in turn-of-the-century China, where it was known generically as *weisheng* or, for the older population, *yangsheng,* literally, the nurturing of life. According to Rogaski (1996), *weisheng* techniques increased resistance to harmful environmental influences and thus formed the basis for the Chinese response to epidemic disease such as cholera.

21. Most of these practices date back at least to the first millennium A.D. (Needham 1962). There was of course some regional variation. Bathing was much more common in southern China than in the north. Even today, many populations in Heilongjiang do not boil water before drinking.

22. The earliest reference to female infanticide is a well-known repetitive passage in the *Han Feizi* (319): "Moreover, parents' attitude to children is such that when they bear a son they congratulate each other, but when they bear a daughter, they kill her. Both come from the parents' love, but they congratulate each other only when it is a boy and kill if it is a girl because they are considering their later convenience and calculating their long-term interests." See Chen Guangsheng (1989) and Liu Jingzhen (1994a, 1994b, 1995a, 1995b) for detailed studies of infanticide in China during the first millennium B.C. and the first millennium A.D. B. Lee (1981) and Waltner (1995), though less detailed, discuss infanticide in more recent times.

23. In a brief survey of the Qing period, Feng Erkang (1986) lists historical records of infanticide in 27 counties and 7 provinces. Infanticide seems to have

been particularly common in the Lower Yangzi: there are records from seven localities in Anhui, six localities in Zhejiang, and four localities in Jiangsu. Feng has also identified five localities in Jiangxi, one in Hunan, three in Fujian, and one in Guangxi (320–321). Feng quotes a memorial to the emperor, written by Wang Bangxi in 1878, that reports that partly because of the high cost of dowry, killing infants by drowning was prevalent in every province, especially Jiangxi.

24. While the demographic record for Taiwan is only quite recent, beginning with the Japanese occupation in 1895, there is no sign of female infanticide (Barclay 1954).

25. Thus the common saying that "a married daughter is like water spilled on the ground," a resource that one cannot retrieve.

26. The contours of perinatal and neonatal mortality are identical. Perinatal rates, however, are distorted, since the vast majority (2,111 of 2,690) of records of daughters who died during the first month of life do not specify the precise day.

27. See, for example, D'Souza and Chen (1980); L. Chen, Huq, and D'Souza (1981); Bhatia (1983); Das Gupta (1987); and Basu (1989). Most of these studies claim roles for differentials in the allocation of both food and health care. Basu, however, argues that the role of differences in food allocation in explaining childhood mortality sex differences has been overstated, and that other gender-based differences in the treatment of children, in particular parents' greater willingness to seek modern medical care for boys, are more important. Das Gupta points out that discrimination was more severe for girls with older siblings.

28. "The woman's position is usually inferior in the Manchu family and she is subjugated . . . The inferior position of the woman is especially accentuated in the order of taking and serving meals. The woman before eating is obliged to feed every day and in the first place the men, even if they be ordinary paid workmen or slaves. However . . . If the family is not very numerous, all the family members eat together" (Shirokogoroff 1926, 126–127).

29. China, of course, is not the only developing country to have undergone a rapid mortality decline in this century. Death rates have fallen everywhere in the developing world, partly because of economic growth, but mainly as a result of the widespread introduction of new medical and public health technologies beginning in the 1950s and 1960s (Preston 1980). Mortality decline in China was aided, as in many other countries, by the allocation of resources to the health sector (Jamison et al. 1984). What is remarkable about China's mortality decline is that the country is several orders of magnitude larger in terms of land area and population than any of the other societies most frequently noted for the size and speed of their mortality declines: Sri Lanka, Costa Rica, Cuba, and India's Kerala state (Caldwell 1986). China is also distinctive in having been isolated from the international community during much of the time that mortality was falling.

30. This is particularly true for Chinese females. In 1990 life expectancy at birth for females was 71.9 in China and 78.8 in the United States (U.S. Bureau of the Census 1997, 88).
31. Whereas male life expectancy at age five ca. 1800 was 40 for Beijing residents, it was 44 for Liaoning peasants. By contrast, ca. 1920 male life expectancy at age five was 54 for Beijing residents and 40 for northern Chinese peasants; female life expectancy at age five was 47 for Beijing residents and 37 for northern Chinese peasants (Campbell forthcoming).
32. Rogaski (1996) makes a similar point in her analysis of public health in Tianjin in 1860–1960.
33. Bernice Lee (1981) was perhaps the first to document the gradual decline in female infanticide during the Republican period; her information, however, was almost entirely anecdotal. She attributed the decline to a change in female labor: "There was a demand for children's and women's labour in the new factories and more girls were being used in the domestic industry, and the fact that some families were beginning to see girls as an economic asset undoubtedly increased their chances of survival" (176).
34. While no one has studied this important change in moral values, the rising appreciation of human life and the consequent opposition to infanticide can be seen in the local establishment of orphanages and relief institutions for children in nineteenth century China studied by Angela Ki Che Leung (1995, 1997). These institutions, which had not existed previously, proliferated in particular in the late nineteenth and early twentieth centuries as missionary efforts reinforced domestic charity.
35. No one has yet unpacked this spectacular achievement in any more detail by cause of death, location, or year.
36. The disparity in reduction between young adult males (10 percent) and females (40 percent) is a reflection of the unusually high mortality of young females identified in Lee and Campbell (1997, 71–75).
37. By expected male mortality we assume that males die in greater numbers than females—which is true for the vast majority of contemporary populations. According to model life table level 20, which is the level of overall mortality in China today, the male-to-female mortality ratio for ages one to four should be 1.13 (Model North) or 1.15 (Model West). The observed ratio for Japan is 1.11. In China the ratio is only 0.99 for first births and 0.95 for later births, suggesting a 10–20 percent excess in female mortality (Choe, Hao, and Wang 1995, 59).
38. According to Zeng et al. (1993) and Gu and Roy (1995), the main method used to achieve such gender-skewed rates is sex-selective abortion. In South Korea, similar practices have produced sex ratios of 114 for overall births in 1992: 106 for first births, 113 for second births, 196 for third births, and 229 for fourth births (Park and Cho 1995).
39. Extrapolating from the national 2-per-1,000 survey, which reports adoptions as a separate category, Johansson, Zhao, and Nygren (1991) estimated that

the number of adoptions has risen sharply in China from about 200,000 in the 1970s to about 400,000 by 1985 and to over 500,000 after 1987. See too Wang and Lee (1998) and Johnson, Huang, and Wang (1998).

40. One conspicuous example of such behavior was reported by Zhu De, one of the two founders of the current Communist state, who told Agnes Smedley, an American journalist, that his mother had given birth to thirteen children. "Only six boys and two girls lived. The last five children were drowned at birth because we were too poor to feed so many mouths" (Smedley 1958, 12). In such cases, of course, it is virtually impossible to distinguish mortality control from marital restraint. The only exception is the imperial nobility.

41. This follows the suggestion of Basu (1989) that differential health care may play a far more important role than nutrition in explaining differential mortality rates in contemporary societies.

42. Lavely, Mason, and Li (1996) is one of the few exceptions.

43. This paragraph summarizes results from Lee, Wang, and Campbell (1994), where we do several multivariate logistic regression calculations to distinguish between the effects of parental noble status and marriage type on child mortality in the imperial lineage.

44. Similar birth-order-specific patterns of gender discrimination have been reported in many contemporary Asian societies, raising the possibility that such behavior is common to most societies with strong preferences for sons. Das Gupta (1987) suggested that in India gender discrimination against girls is more pronounced for later births than for earlier births. Muhuri and Preston (1991) found that in Bangladesh a newborn girl's chances of surviving were reduced if she had older siblings. In the East and Southeast Asian societies in which sex ratios at birth have been rising as the result of sex-selective abortion, including Korea, Taiwan, Hong Kong, and Singapore, gender imbalances have been most pronounced at later births (Zeng et al. 1993).

45. See Lee, Wang, and Campbell (1994) for an analysis of female infanticide by noble status and the essays on government dowry subventions in Lee and Guo (1994).

46. Before the late eighteenth century, the cost of noble daughter dowries was borne at least partially by the state (Lee and Guo 1994). While many people, including Malthus, have identified this link between dowry and death in a wide variety of populations, no one has produced a rigorous quantitative test of this proposition. See Dickeman (1975) and (1979) for an elaboration of the general hypothesis.

47. An imperial edict of 623 in the *Collection of Important Documents of the Tang (618–907)* stated: "When people are born, they are just young animals, *(huang)*. At four *sui* they become minors, *xiao*. At sixteen *sui* they become youths, *zhong*. At twenty-one *sui* they become adults, *ding*. At sixty *sui* they become old, *lao*" (*Tang huiyao* 85.1555). According to a famous passage from the *Rites of Zhou,* a compendium of statements on early political institutions and policies probably completed in the second century B.C., "People should be registered after they have grown their teeth." In a well-known

commentary on this passage Qiu Jun, a fifteenth-century statesman, explained: "The human body is not fully developed until teeth are grown. Boys grow their first set of teeth in the eighth month and their second set in their eighth year. Girls grow their first set of teeth in their seventh month and their second set in their seventh year. They should then all be recorded in the population register" (*Daxue yanyi bu* 13.14). We thank Liu Ts'ui-jung for bringing the passage from the *Tang huiyao* to our attention.

48. The Chinese count age in *sui,* which refers to the number of calendar years during which a person has lived. People are accordingly one *sui* at birth and two *sui* at the next New Year. *Sui* are therefore on average 1.5 years higher than Western years of age.

49. Such attitudes were commonplace elsewhere in China and in East Asia in general. LaFleur (1992) provides the most complete discussion on Japan. But see too Lee and Saito (forthcoming) on infanticide in Qing China and Tokugawa Japan and on abortion in contemporary Asia.

50. Even the earliest Chinese law codes declared infanticide to be illegal except in the case of birth deformities. See the surviving remnants of Qin law, the first imperial law code (Hulsewe 1985). See too the discussion of subsequent law codes in B. Lee (1981).

51. Such advances in medical technology have led to widespread interest in eugenics, particularly in the island republic of Singapore, where government programs explicitly encourage the marriage and procreation of educated elite. Although there are no such public policies in China, and although the Chinese government has proclaimed an explicit ban on human cloning, the cultural tradition of fertility control encourages such discussions.

52. This estimate of morbidity levels is based on the reported morbidity of adult males in eighteenth-century rural Liaoning. Of 2,478 individual observations at risk, 676 reported a major disability, primarily some form of respiratory disease (Lee and Campbell 1997, 77). The proportion of disabilities among urban residents may well have been even larger.

53. Rozman made a similar speculation (1982, 19): "It is difficult to draw definite conclusions about the causes of [population] growth . . . but the materials are suggestive about at least two factors affecting population growth, infanticide and migration." Classical economists, however, thought that infanticide could have had an opposite effect and boosted population growth by encouraging marriage. Thus according to Adam Smith (1776/1979, 175), "Marriage is encouraged in China, not by the profitableness of children, but by the liberty of destroying them."

5. Marriage

Epigraph: Malthus (1826/1986, 369).

1. "The period of delayed gratification would be passed in saving the earnings which were above the wants of a single man, and in acquiring the habits of

sobriety, industry, and economy, which would enable him to enter into the matrimonial contract without fear of its consequences. The operation of the preventive check in this way . . . would give a real value to the rise of wages and to the sums saved by the labourers before marriage" (Malthus 1803/1992, 218; 1826/1986, 475).

2. This was particularly true in Central Asia. "Among the Tartars . . . as parents keep all their daughters till they can sell them, their maids are sometimes very stale before they are married . . . The inability to buy wives must frequently operate on the poorer classes as a check to marriage particularly as their price would be kept up by the practice of polygamy among the rich" (1826/1986, 88).

3. Thus the Middle East and Persia, "It is observed in general that the Christian families consist of a greater number of children than the Mahometan families in which polygamy prevails. This is an extraordinary fact; because though polygamy, from the unequal distribution of women which it occasions, be naturally unfavourable to the population of a whole country; yet the individuals who are able to support a plurality of wives, ought certainly, in the rational course of things, to have a greater number of children than those who are confined to one" (ibid., 113). Malthus mentioned promiscuous intercourse as an obstacle to population growth in the South Sea Islands (ibid., 51, 54).

4. "It is the duty of each individual not to marry till he has a prospect of supporting his children; but it is at the same time to be wished that he should retain undiminished his desire of marriage, in order that he may exert himself to realize this prospect" (1803/1992, 215; 1826/1986, 472).

5. "There is no period of human life in which nature more strongly prompts to an union of the sexes than from seventeen or eighteen to twenty" (1803/1992, 221; 1826/1986, 477). However, "there is in general so strong a tendency to love in early youth, that it is extremely difficult, at this period, to distinguish a genuine from a transient passion" (1803/1992, 221; 1826/1986, 478). Therefore, "if the custom of not marrying early prevailed generally . . . passion, instead of being extinguished, as it now too frequently is by early sensuality, would only be repressed for a time, that it might afterwards burn with a brighter, purer, and steadier flame" (1803/1992, 219; 1826/1986, 476).

6. This explains in part the study, pioneered by Laslett (1977), of bastardy, which was quite common in some periods among European populations. Bastardy has been far less important in the study of Chinese population behavior, since it was less common—except in the island province of Taiwan under Japanese occupation (Barrett 1980).

7. Hajnal's 1953 development of singulate mean age of marriage is such an example. See Flinn (1981, 27–31) for a summary survey on premodern Europe and P. Smith (1974) on contemporary Asia.

8. See, for example, Cherlin (1994) and Goldscheider and Waite (1991) on contemporary American populations, and Dupâquier et al. (1981) on a variety of historical populations.

9. Chao (1986) is a prominent and explicit example of this Malthusian logic. Commenting on the barriers to marriage in the West, he writes (8): "The traditional Chinese family system functioned quite differently. One was the drive for family perpetuation . . . the second was the strength of family feeling, the inescapable obligation of a family to support those members who had no income or jobs. The family as institution often became a multiworker business entity, provider of employment and basis for intrafamily income distribution. Consequently, instead of functioning as an automatic regulator, the Chinese family system tolerated overpopulation."

10. Among the elite, for example, dowry often differentiated wifely status. Concubines not only provided no dowry; they were often purchased in an overtly commercial transaction, different from the transaction involving bride price.

11. The terms major and minor marriage were developed by Arthur Wolf. See A. Wolf and Huang (1980) for his discussion of major and minor marriage in China, especially the island province of Taiwan.

12. While there were no explicit state policies regarding marriage age, the prohibition on arranged marriage undoubtedly contributed greatly to this early rise in marriage age.

13. In the United States, the median age for female first marriage in the late 1980s was 23.7 (U.S. Bureau of the Census 1997, 105).

14. This pattern, as observed by Whyte (1990, 184), "suggests that Chinese marriage customs had begun to change in the direction of patterns familiar in more modern societies, but then became 'stuck' and did not continue to converge toward such patterns."

15. The survey of married men and women aged 20–69, conducted by sociologists from the University of Michigan and Peking University, asked: "Can a woman live a full and happy life without getting married?"

16. Marriage is apparently far less popular in Japan. In 1994 only 18 and 26 percent of ever-married Japanese men and women respectively agreed to a similar statement, "Women should marry to live a full and happy life," in the National Survey of Work and Family Life. Fifty percent of males and 49 percent of females were uncertain, while 32 percent of males and 15 percent of females disagreed (Noriko Tsuya, private communication).

17. Telford (1992a) was the first to observe the similarity in the probability of Chinese and Western European male marriage.

18. This improvement in males' marriage prospects did not occur uniformly across China in the early twentieth century. In one location of north China, Dingxian, by 1930, 20 percent of all males were still single (Gamble 1954).

19. While the figures vary tremendously according to the specific circumstances of individual populations, these proportions seem to be typical of the populations discussed in Dupâquier et al. (1981, 50, 169, 260, 275–277, 294–295, 300, 329, 359).

20. In a study of 49 lineage populations, 11.5 percent of ever-married males remarried. By contrast, 32 of the 49 genealogies did not record any female

remarriage. Among the 17 that did, remarriages accounted for only 0.5–8.6 percent of all female marriages (Liu Ts'ui-jung 1992, 1:48).

21. The percentage of women who remarried varied by their age at widowhood. Of widows aged 24 or under when their husbands died, 58.5 percent remarried. Of those aged 30–34 when their husbands died, only 30.3 percent remarried (A. Wolf 1981, 141).

22. In the United States, for instance, 46 percent of all marriages in the mid-1980s were remarriages (U.S. Bureau of the Census 1997, 106).

23. Another more recent example of the divergent pattern of marriage between females and males is from Dingxian (Ting Hsien), Hebei Province. A survey of 776 couples, carried out in 1926–1933, found that while all females were married by age 23, only 66.3 percent of men that age were married. Even at age 39 only 90 percent of males were married. Yet an extraordinarily high proportion of those men who married did so very young—almost one in six when they were 14 years old and almost half, 47.5 percent, before they turned 17. Consequently, in 70 percent of couples the wife was older than her husband (Gamble 1954, 41).

24. "There are three ways of being a bad son. The most serious is to have no heir" (Mencius 1970, 6.1, 127).

25. Arthur Wolf was the first to identify these variant marriage forms and to analyze them in detail (Wolf and Huang 1980).

26. Proportions vary of course by lineage. Among 8,295 husbands in the lineages of Tongcheng, Anhui Province, 7.5 percent had more than one wife recorded (Telford 1992a, 27), whereas the proportions for five other genealogies reported by Liu Ts'ui-jung range from 8 percent for the Xus from Wuchang, Hubei, to 26 percent for the Mais of Xiangshan, Guangdong (1995b, 105).

27. The previous claim had been 10 percent (Naquin and Rawski 1987, 108). This number, which appears to have originated with work by Liu Ts'ui-jung (1983), does not control for the elite male status of much of her genealogical population and does not distinguish polygyny from widower remarriage.

28. See Wilson (1984) for monogamous fertility. According to Bean and Mineau (1986) and Bean, Mineau, and Anderton (1990), Mormon polygynous marriages included on average 3.9 wives before 1820, 2.9 wives in 1820–1839, and 2.4 wives in 1840–1859, with 6.3, 7.3, and 7.6 children born to each wife respectively. This implies that each Mormon husband who survived to age 45 had on average 24.6 children before 1820, 21.2 children in 1820–1839, and 18.2 children in 1840–1859.

29. One well-known example of such historical distortion is the story by Su Tong filmed as *Raise the Red Lantern*.

30. Arthur Wolf's study of 848 little-daughter-in-law marriages from the area of Haishan in Taiwan (Wolf and Huang 1980) found an age range from 2 to 8. Reviewing the capital cases for two years, 1736 and 1745, Guo Songyi (forthcoming) found 55 cases of little daughter-in-laws, 80 percent of whom were adopted before age 10. In contrast, Feng Erkang (1986) cites a mere 12 specific examples culled from local gazetteers throughout China, but with a

mean age of 11, that is, over 12 *sui* (309–310). To the extent that such older little-daughter-in-law marriages were common (5 of Feng's 12 examples are 14 or older), they may have merely been an excuse to avoid the expenses of major marriage.

31. According to an early nineteenth-century gazetteer from Jixi County, Anhui Province, "The poor are forced to give up their daughters for adoption. These adopted girls become brides when they grow up" (quoted in Feng Erkang 1986, 310). According to a mid-nineteenth-century gazetteer in Ganzhou County, Jiangxi Province, people married this way "so that farm families would not have to prepare bride price, and poor families could avoid the misery of having to kill their daughters" (quoted in Guo Songyi forthcoming).

32. A. Wolf and Huang (1980) document that familial relations are often more harmonious if less ardent in such marriages.

33. A. Wolf and Huang (1980) provide a wide variety of anecdotal evidence of the prevalence of little-daughter-in-law and uxorilocal marriages during the nineteenth century (1–15, 326–339).

34. Both forms of marriage are considered as exploitation because brides have little or no rights of choice, an entitlement guaranteed by the Chinese constitution. See A. Wolf and Huang (1980) for a detailed ethnography of little daughters-in-law in Taiwan.

35. We thank Guo Zhigang for providing these materials.

36. Family surnames have become unusually complicated in recent years as a result of a revolution in the concept of paternity and lineage. It is now even possible for children to take their mother's family name without any formal adoption process.

37. In Japan the proportion of uxorilocal marriages in the past was far greater— almost 30 percent in some Tokugawa populations (Kurosu and Ochiai 1995).

38. These proportions are from a variety of genealogies from Tongcheng County in central Anhui and date from 1300 to 1850. They are therefore not directly comparable to the Qing nobility, who were far more completely recorded.

39. Even with the recent rise in the incidence of divorce, China still is among the countries with the lowest divorce rate. In 1989, for instance, the crude divorce rate (number of divorces per 1,000 population) was 0.68, compared with 4.7 in the United States, 2.86 in England, 1.9 in France, 1.2 in Japan, and 0.96 in Singapore (Wu Deqing 1995).

40. Waltner (1995) discusses the link between infanticide and dowry during the Ming and early Qing dynasties and presents a variety of anecdotal evidence.

6. Fertility

Epigraph: Malthus (1803/1992, 23–24).

1. According to Malthus, "the passion between the sexes has appeared in every age to be so nearly the same that it may always be considered, in algebraic

language, as a given quantity" (1803/1992, 40; 1826/1986, 312). His most prominent exception was the low marital fertility of the American Indian. "It was generally remarked, that the American women were far from being prolific. This unfruitfulness has been attributed by some to a want of ardour in the men toward their women, a feature of character which has been considered as peculiar to the American savage. It is not, however, peculiar to this race, but probably exists in a great degree among all barbarian nations, whose food is poor and insufficient, and who live in a constant state of apprehension of being pressed by famine or by an enemy" (1826/1986, 29). Thus in explaining China's large population he wrote: "To account for this population, it will not be necessary to recur to the supposition of Montesquieu, that the climate of China is in any peculiar manner favorable to the production of children, and that the women are more prolific than in any other part of the world" (ibid., 126).

2. Though he was not the first to make such an observation, Louis Henry (1961) is generally considered the earliest to have documented and identified an age pattern of fertility for populations known to lack any forms of deliberate fertility control. The populations he studied, such as the contemporary Hutterites in Canada, have not only very high fertility (over 10 births per married woman) but also a vigorous marital relationship without contraception or induced abortion and a short breastfeeding period (Henry 1961; Bongaarts and Potter 1983).

3. This ability to conceive is also known as fecundability, which is sometimes used interchangeably with the term "fecundity." Human fertility, however, is affected most directly by several factors that demographers have labeled as the "proximate determinants" of fertility. The most important factors include proportions married (among women), use and efficacy of contraception, use of induced abortion, length of breastfeeding, frequency of sexual intercourse, spontaneous intrauterine mortality, and natural sterility. It is believed that under a natural fertility regime, the fertility-inhibiting effects of these proximate determinants (especially the first three) are minimal. The concept of proximate determinants was first proposed by K. Davis and Blake (1956) as intermediate variables and elaborated in Bongaarts (1978) and Bongaarts and Potter (1983).

4. The most elaborate and influential modeling is that of Coale and Trussell (1974, 1975, 1978). By using fertility age patterns from a wide range of populations, they proposed two indices to describe whether a population is under a natural-fertility regime or a family-limitation regime. Specifically, M indicates the ratio of the overall level of fertility to the highest recorded natural (Hutterite) fertility in the age group 20–24, and m indicates the degree of parity-specific fertility control. While these indices have been widely applied in the studies of fertility transitions worldwide, their validity has also been challenged (Wilson 1985). See Xie (1990) for a vigorous defense.

5. A large body of literature exists on the European fertility transition, showing

the shift from a natural fertility to a family limitation regime. See, for example, Coale and Trussell (1974), Knodel (1983, 1988), and Coale and Watkins (1986). More recently, van de Walle (1992) and Santow (1995) have argued that traditional technologies such as coitus interuptus were responsible for the early decline in fertility. Cultural ideational change, in other words, was more important than technological innovation.

6. Fei (1939) is a good example of such ethnographic accounts. Ho (1959, 58) is a good example of such historical accounts. See B. Lee (1981) for a summary of these and other studies.

7. See Caldwell and Caldwell (1977, 1981), Page and Lesthaeghe (1981), Lesthaeghe (1989), and esp. Bledsoe et al. (1994) for studies on long birth intervals and interpretations of this pattern in African populations. Bledsoe et al., in particular, question the utility of the European-based model of family limitation in understanding fertility dynamics in contemporary Africa.

8. These estimates were pioneered by Liu Ts'ui-jung (1978, 1981, 1985, 1992, 1995a, 1995b), who over the past two decades has analyzed over 50 genealogies, covering more than 260,000 individuals in 12 provinces of China. These data, however, are highly incomplete. Although the records themselves date back as far as the thirteenth century, vital information dates back only to the fifteenth and sixteenth centuries. Moreover, since much of the information appears to have been assembled retrospectively in the late nineteenth and early twentieth centuries, many people may well be missing. Generally the principle is that the earlier the date, the greater the probability of underrecording. In addition, these genealogies generally represent more elite populations, but since the proportions of elite vary considerably by lineage, this bias is uneven. See Telford (1990b).

9. Chinese polygynous fertility is from Wang, Lee, and Campbell (1995, 387). Western fertility is from Bean and Mineau (1986). According to Bean and Mineau, Mormon polygynous marriages included on average 3.9 wives before 1820, 2.9 wives in 1820–1839, and 2.4 wives in 1840–1859, with 6.3, 7.3, and 7.6 children born to each wife respectively. These numbers imply that Mormon husbands who survived to age 45 had on average 24.6 children before 1820, 21.2 children in 1820–1839, and 18.2 children in 1840–1859.

10. Barclay et al. (1976) observed that the Chinese pretransition fertility level was "35 percent below the average of other populations identified as experiencing natural fertility, and about 20 percent lower than any other reliably reported." They remarked that a population with such a low level of fertility and "an age pattern that indicates no reduction that depends on parity constitutes a demographic puzzle" (615). They also noticed that "marital fertility as low as that in China (only 51 percent of the highest recorded schedule) would be expected by demographers only in populations in which some combination of contraception and abortion is practiced" (625).

11. The estimated low fertility of Chinese farmers by Princeton demographers was challenged by other scholars working on Chinese data, notably Arthur

Wolf (1984). In defense of the reassessment, Ansley Coale (1984) pointed out that the fertility estimates given by Wolf himself, while moderately higher, were fundamentally no different. Harrell (1995), however, concurs with Wolf (15). One of Wolf's and Harrell's criticisms is that mortality was not taken into consideration. This is not true. First of all, the fertility figures in the reassessment were based on a question about births in the previous year, not a retrospective survey over a lifetime. Second, the reported numbers were adjusted upward both by sex ratio and by an indirect estimation method known as the P/F ratio. Furthermore, the resulting fertility was used with a very high infant-mortality assumption to derive a crude birth rate under a "stable population" regime. The estimated birth rate not only was consistent across several estimates but also matched very well with the crude birth rates calculated directly from the population using an adjusted fertility rate (Coale 1984). Indeed, as Barclay et al. wrote (1976, 624), "Even allowing for as much as 20 percent concealed mortality at age zero would imply a marital fertility schedule that was only 64 percent of the highest recorded fertility, and would not resolve the question of why fertility, 'natural' in age pattern, should be so low in level."

12. Coale and Chen (1987). The 1982 survey could provide complete age-specific fertility schedules only from 1964. Total fertility rates before this year were estimated by assuming the same age pattern of reproduction.

13. The only notable exception was the unusually high fertility in 1963, 7.4, which was a recovery from the devastating Great Leap famine, which had driven fertility down to only 3.3 in 1961.

14. In 1950, for example, the fertility level in what is now Bangladesh was 6.66; in India, 5.97; in Egypt, 6.56; in Indonesia, 5.49; in Iran, 7.13; in Peru, 6.85; and in Thailand, 6.62 (United Nations 1993).

15. Lee, Wang, and Ruan (in press) summarize the age at first marriage for over 900 males. The mean age was 20.3 for those married before 1840 and 21.2 for those married after 1839. Mean age at first birth was approximately 23 in the late eighteenth century and 24 in the early nineteenth century.

16. In rural Liaoning, for example, the mean interval from marriage to first birth was almost four years (Lee and Campbell 1997, 92, 94).

17. According to the summary calculations by Flinn (1981), before 1750 the mean first-birth interval was 14 months in England and 16 months in France (33).

18. The illegitimate birth rate in 1780–1820 was 6 per 100 live births in England, 7 in Scandinavia and Spain, and 12 in Germany, and the percentage of premarital conceptions was as high as 35 in England, 14 in France, and 24 in Germany (ibid., 82). In China premarital illegitimate births were extremely rare, if only because there were very few unmarried females over age 20. The only exception was Taiwan in the early 1900s, when it was under Japanese rule and when common-law marriages were encouraged, at least for widows (Barrett 1980). On the mainland, even during the 1970s and 1980s premari-

tal conception is estimated to have been very low, no more than 5 percent (Wang and Yang 1996).

19. Mean birth interval for non-last birth for monogamous fathers of the Qing imperial lineage was slightly less than 3 years before the mid-1800s and 3.5 to almost 4 years thereafter (Wang, Lee, and Campbell 1995, 389). Liu Ts'ui-jung's (1992, 1:113) study of lineage populations shows a mean interval for *male* births of 5.5 years for first to second son, 5 years for the second to third son, and 4 years from the third to the fourth son. Assuming an equal number of female births between the male births, the mean birth interval suggested by these numbers for *all* births would be 2–2.5 years. Mean birth intervals among the Liaoning peasantry seem to have been even longer (Lee and Campbell 1997, 93–94).

20. Calculated from Coale, Li, and Han (1988, 15, table 1). This calculation included only birth intervals between children who survived infancy. Since the interval to conception is shorter following an infant death, the overall mean birth interval could be slightly shorter.

21. The mean non-last-birth interval for France was 30 months, for Germany 33 months, and for Switzerland 27 months. The mean interval between first and second birth was 28 months for England, 23 for France, and 21 for Germany (Flinn 1981, 33).

22. Laozi, for example, advocated "thinking sparsely and desiring less" (19.21–22). Mencius proclaimed that "nothing works better in cultivating the mind than to desire less" (1970, 201–202).

23. We thank William Lavely for bringing this book to our attention.

24. Joseph Needham, one of the first Western scholars to discuss these ideas, found that these beliefs were still quite common in China in the mid-twentieth century (1962, 146–152). See also Furth (1994).

25. Hsiung (forthcoming) provides a lucid discussion of reproductive culture in late imperial China.

26. This schedule originates from Dong Zhongshu (179–104 B.C.), who advised in his famous Confucian commentary, *Chunqiu fanlu* (Luxuriant dew on the spring and autumn annals): "Gentlemen [*junzi*] should discipline their bodies and not dare to defy Heaven. As a result, young men have coitus only once every ten days. Middle-aged men have coitus only half as frequently as young men. Young elderly men have coitus only half as frequently as middle-aged men . . . Very elderly men have coitus only once every ten months." Many Chinese took this advice to heart. Gu Yanwu (1613–1682), perhaps the best-known scholar from the Qing period, for example, cited this passage in an intimate letter to a close friend who was contemplating remarriage (*Gu Ting-Lin wenji*, 6.148). We thank Gao Ruohai for bringing Dong's text to our attention and Yuk Yung for giving us a copy of the quotation from Gu.

27. Fertility surveys reveal that even today, when couples have the protection of contraception, Asian couples continue to follow a pattern of coital frequency considerably lower than elsewhere. In Thailand, for example, the mean coital

frequency of all currently married women during the four weeks preceding the 1987 Demographic and Health Survey was 3.2. Newlyweds had a monthly coital frequency of 6, which dropped to 4.2 after one year of marriage and to 3.7 after four years of marriage (Chayovan and Knodel 1991). The comparable number in the United States in 1975 was 8.9 for all currently married women and 10.4 for women in their first five years of marriage (Trussell and Westoff 1980).

28. Rindfuss and Morgan (1983) and Wang and Yang (1996) discuss the effect of arranged marriages on long first-birth intervals in China and elsewhere in Asia. They recognize the effects of low coital frequency on Asian marital fertility and assume that such low frequency reflects lack of marital passion among newlyweds as a result of arranged marriages. Arthur Wolf's (1980) pioneering work on Taiwan has shown that different forms of marriage differed in levels of fertility. Total marital fertility of women in major marriages was 10 percent higher than that in uxorilocal marriages and 30 percent higher than that in minor marriages.

29. Sexual intimacy between spouses was not only difficult to initiate, because of arranged marriage; it was also hard to develop within the corporate family. The Chinese sociologist Fei Hsiao-tung characterized the interspousal relationship in the early part of this century in rural China as follows: "Before the birth of the child, her husband, at least overtly, is indifferent to her. He will not mention her in conversation. Even in the house, in anyone's presence, if he shows any intimate feeling for his wife it will be considered improper and consequently will become a topic for gossiping. Husband and wife do not sit near each other and very seldom talk to each other in that situation. Rather they talk through a third party and they have no special terms for addressing one another. But when a child is born, the husband can refer to his wife as the mother of his child" (1939, 47).

30. Kwon (1993) describes similar behavior in contemporary South Korea. According to Kwon, Korean mothers justify such behavior in terms of concern for their son's health.

31. The idea that fertility was a means of upward social mobility among Chinese populations has already been articulated in the literature. See, for instance, Greenhalgh (1988).

32. See, for example, Macfarlane's 1986 discussion of marriage in England.

33. Prolonged breastfeeding, however, could not have accounted entirely for such long intervals and low fertility. Wang, Lee, and Campbell (1995) compared mothers' subsequent birth intervals in the Qing lineage according to whether or not a child died in the first month of life, and found no difference. Had prolonged breastfeeding been the main factor in explaining long birth intervals in the lineage, the death of a child in the first month of life should have dramatically reduced the subsequent birth interval, because the mother would no longer be breastfeeding and would quickly resume menstruating. More generally, while there are examples of populations with prolonged breastfeed-

ing for which the associated period of amennhorea lasts until breastfeeding ceases (Bongaarts and Potter 1983, 26), a retrospective fertility survey carried out in Taiwan in the 1960s found that women there who had breastfed for more than 24 months resumed menstruating after an average of only 14 months (Jain et al. 1970; Jain, Hermalin, and Sun 1979). The implication is that while breastfeeding in Taiwan was prolonged, in later months it was not intense enough to have a contraceptive effect. To the extent that breastfeeding patterns and associated durations of amennhorea in Taiwan were similar to those in the lineage and other Chinese populations, they cannot account for the birth intervals of three or more years observed in those populations.

34. Li Bozhong (forthcoming) traces documentation of abortive medicine used as early as in the Han dynasty. Liu Jingzhen (1995b) presents an analysis of infanticide and abortion during the Song dynasty.

35. Hsiung (forthcoming) provides a detailed account of these techniques. Li Bozhong (forthcoming) also documents the use of contraception, sterilization, and abortion techniques in the Lower Yangzi during the Ming and Qing periods. The most popular medical book, *Bencao gangmu,* for example, lists 30 kinds of herbs and medicinal plants that could be used to abort a fetus. See Bray (forthcoming) for a textured discussion of such medical use and esp. Furth (1998) for an innovative history of China's early gynecological tradition.

36. Fei also reported that in the villages he studied in Guangxi and Jiangsu Provinces he observed the deliberate act of child neglect where birth control efforts had failed. In one case, parents left a critically ill child to a minor to take care of, and in another, a toddler was left to walk around without adult supervision and as a result drowned in a ditch (Fei 1947/1998, 108).

37. Mao criticized Western views attributing Chinese revolution to overpopulation, saying in 1949, "it is a great thing that China has so many people. Even if the population increases several-fold we still have a solution, and the solution is production" (Sun Muhan 1987, 66).

38. While several major Chinese leaders actively endorsed population control, Mao's support was more ambivalent. Whereas Liu Shaoqi said openly in December 1954 that the Communist Party of China supported birth control, a position echoed by Zhou Enlai in 1956, Mao would only go so far as to admit in 1957 that "It is both a good thing and a bad thing that China has so many people. The good thing about China is it has many people, and the bad thing about China is also it has many people." Mao did, however, agree that "population needs to grow according to plan" (ibid., 62–68).

39. On March 23, 1958, Mao said: "It is wrong to propagate the pessimistic atmosphere that there are too many people. We should still see that many people is a good thing." Even Liu Shaoqi consequently modified his earlier stand and concurred with Mao that both consumption and production of the population should be considered (ibid., 103).

40. See Chen Pi-chao and Kols (1982), Lavely and Freedman (1990), and Sun

192 · *Notes to Pages 92–97*

Muhan (1987) for detailed accounts of the early development of the Chinese family planning program. In 1975 Mao again endorsed the need for a population policy (Sun Muhan 1987, 165). In 1978 article 53 of the constitution at the Fifth National People's Congress asserted, "the state promotes and implements planned birth." The one-child-per-couple policy was formulated in 1979 (ibid., 185–188).

41. In 1952 the Chinese government allowed abortion and sterilization for women aged 35 or older if continued childbearing was deemed to affect the health of the mother, and if she had already had six children, one of whom had to be age 10 or older (Wang forthcoming).

42. Indeed the contrast with other so-called abortion societies is striking. In 1990 contraceptive use in Russia among married women was 15 percent. In China it was over 90 percent.

43. Total fertility as early as in 1973 was only 2.8 in rural Jilin, 2.82 in rural Jiangsu, 3.46 in rural Zhejiang, and 4.16 in rural Liaoning. By contrast, it was as high as 7.4 in rural Guizhou, 6.48 in rural Gansu, 5.35 in rural Guangdong, and 5.17 in rural Henan (Coale and Chen 1987).

44. According to official Chinese statistics, the annual number of male sterilizations consequently doubled from 649,476 in 1982 to 1,230,967 in 1983, while the annual number of female sterilizations quadrupled, from 3,925,927 in 1982 to 16,398,378 in 1983 (CPIC 1988, 245).

45. The irony is that such coercion is illegal and has been well publicized by the Chinese as well as Western media. Indeed, some of the most celebrated stories of forced family planning "broken" by the Western media were in fact first exposed and criticized by the Chinese government. See the article by Nicholas Kristof, "China's Crackdown on Birth: A Stunning, and Harsh, Success," *New York Times,* April 25, 1993, p. 1. The main tragedy cited, the death on December 30, 1992, of a neonate just nine hours after his seven-month-pregnant mother was forced to induce his birth to meet the birth quotas for that year, was, as Kristof acknowledged, taken from a classified government report.

46. For major changes in Chinese family planning policy in the 1980s, see Greenhalgh (1986); Hardee-Cleaveland and Banister (1988); Zeng (1989); Luther, Feeney, and Zhang (1990); and Feeney and Wang (1993).

47. Greenhalgh (1986, 1993) documents in detail the evolution of one-child policy implementation in rural China, specifically Shaanxi Province. Resistance from peasants and the decline of state power following rural reforms in the 1980s led many rural cadres to delay or defer implementation and to adjust or request adjustments in family planning policy. The central government responded both by formally relaxing the policy and by letting provincial and lower-level governments establish their own conditions under which families are exempted from the one-child policy. Peasant resistance and negotiations resulted in a "peasantization" of the one-child policy.

48. Wang, Lee, and Campbell (1995, 393) compare the number of children ever

born to fathers who survived to age 45 for different periods. With different marriage types controlled for, low-noble fathers had 2.7 fewer births than high-noble fathers in 1681–1720, 2.9 fewer births in 1721–1750, 1 fewer in 1751–1780, and 2.3 fewer in 1781–1820.

49. These restraints were sometimes imposed by the community. In 1947, for example, Fei Xiaotong noted that among the Yao ethnic minority in Guangxi Province, "Each couple can have only two children, regardless of their sex. If they already have two children, they have to abort any additional pregnancies. Those fetuses who are not aborted and are brought to term but not adopted out cannot easily escape a fate of infanticide" (Fei 1947/1998, 248).

50. Lee and Campbell (1997, 99–101). During the two periods of low fertility associated with poor economic conditions, parents in complex households, who were the better off, reduced their female birth rate by 28 percent and 51 percent respectively. But parents in simple households reduced their female birth rates even more, by 42 percent and 71 percent. At the same time, when fertility was high, parents in complex households increased their female birth rate by more than half while parents in simple household raised theirs by only one-fifth.

51. Lavely and Freedman (1990). Poston and Gu (1987) show at the provincial level that a higher level of socioeconomic development was related to lower fertility as of the early 1980s. Similar observations were made by Birdsall and Jamison (1983), Tien (1983), and Peng (1989).

52. A. Wolf and Huang (1980) discuss such familial concerns in some detail, but see too M. Wolf (1968).

7. System

Epigraph: Malthus (1803/1992, 44).

1. "The period of delayed gratification would be passed in saving the earnings which were above the wants of a single man, and in acquiring the habits of sobriety, industry, and economy, which would enable him to enter into the matrimonial contract without fear of its consequences. The operation of the preventive check in this way, by constantly keeping the population within the limits of the food, though constantly following its increase, would give a real value to the rise of wages and to the sums saved by the labourers before marriage" (Malthus 1803/1992, 218; 1826/1986, 475).

2. Ho (1969a, 1969b, 1975, 1977) discusses both the agricultural system that was able to support such a dense population and the system of beliefs that encouraged population growth.

3. We carried out several simulations to compare the relative importance of mortality and fertility on population growth. An increase in female infant mortality by 100 per 1,000 with everything else held constant, for example, would reduce population size by about 25 percent after 300 years. By con-

trast, raising marital fertility to historical English levels with Chinese nuptiality and mortality held unchanged would increase population size by almost 50 times in the same 300-year period. Given universal female marriage, low fertility clearly played a greater role than infanticide in restraining population growth during the last 300 years.

4. There is already a sizable literature on adoption and infant abandonment in late imperial and contemporary China. See esp. A. Wolf and Huang (1980); Johnson, Huang, and Wang (1998); Wang and Lee (1998); and Leung (1997).

5. Larger in part because adoption was illegal in many early modern Western countries and because there are no available statistics on early modern Western fosterage rates. Today, however, adoption rates in the West can rival those in China. In 1986, for example, the ratio of reported adoptions (104,088) to registered live births (3.8 million) was over 2.5 percent in the United States (National Committee for Adoption 1989).

6. See Kurosu and Ochiai (1995) for a similar description of adoption in Tokugawa Japan.

7. In our analysis of adoption among the Qing imperial nobility, among the 1,204 sons adopted, about 30 percent were adopted before age 1, half above age 5, 20 percent above age 20, and 5 percent above age 30. The oldest adoptee was well into his sixties (Wang and Lee 1998). Similarly, if not as extreme, among the Taiwanese peasant populations studied by A. Wolf and Huang (1980), about half of all male adoptions occurred when the boy was 1 year or older, and 15 percent occurred beyond age 5 (table 15.4, p. 212).

8. There are even recorded cases in which a couple with no biological children first adopted a daughter and then adopted their son-in-law as a son.

9. Thus adoption could take place not only when the adopting parents were alive but also after one or both adopting parents were no longer alive. Even an infant who died prematurely could adopt a son of his own, though the actual adoption was arranged by other members of the family.

10. This was clearly the case for the Qing imperial nobility. The imperial court required members of the lineage to adopt from the closest relatives possible. Exceptions were made only in cases in which the applicant could justify the lack of close kin. Adoption required approval both because of the imperial lineage's need to maintain a clear lineage record and because adoption involved changes in entitlement and benefits. Widows who adopted were entitled to subsidies under the name of the adopted son (Wang and Lee 1998).

11. The first term means "to come over as an heir." The second term means "to bring home and to raise up," which is closer to child fosterage.

12. These studies were pioneered by Etienne van de Walle (1976), who was the first to recognize the advantages of such individual-level analysis and to apply some of the lessons of family reconstitution to their analysis. Alter's 1988 study of women in the Belgian city of Verviers expanded on van de Walle's approach and applied techniques from the rapidly developing field of event history analysis. Bengtsson (1989, 1993, 1997) was the first to incorporate

annual series of prices and wages into this analytical framework. His work brings together life-cycle analysis of events within households with the study of short-run fluctuations in economic conditions. This synthesis of two previously separate methodologies, life-event and time-series, is a foundation for much ongoing research.

13. There is one exception to this rule. Some of the differentials according to banner occupation actually widened as prices rose, raising the possibility that those individuals with a fixed state salary may have risen in privilege, at least among their relatives as income from agriculture dropped.

14. The annual population growth rates worldwide, excluding China, were twice as fast—almost 1 per 1,000 (McEvedy and Jones 1978; Biraben 1979).

15. No one has described this process yet in any detail. See Lee (1978, 1982b, 1994) and Lee and Wong (1991) for discussion of the population effects of increased economic opportunity and of increased migration opportunity in particular.

16. The decline in population in the Lower Yangzi during the second half of the nineteenth century was a product of war—the Taiping Rebellion. Bernhardt (1992) and Li Bozhong (1994), however, suggest that even before 1850 population growth rates and population pressure were relatively low.

17. G. Skinner (1986), using data supplied by Lee, has shown that the numbers for Sichuan are suspect. Nevertheless, we can distinguish two periods of growth. The eighteenth and nineteenth centuries were marked by unusually low rates in the Lower Yangzi and unusually high rates in the Upper Yangzi and southwest, and the early twentieth century was marked by exceptionally high rates of growth in the northeast.

18. This will require intensive nominative studies of specific migrant communities, long a staple of American social history. When such studies are done for China, the roots of its population increase will be far better understood.

19. For instance, between 1954, when official registration data become available, and 1960, Shandong Province had an annual out-migration rate of 32.2 to 56.9 per 1,000 and a net in-migration rate of between only −21.4 and 1.7. By contrast, in Jiangsu the annual net in-migration rate fluctuated between −3.1 and 4.4 per 1,000 population.

20. While agricultural products increased from 32.6 billion to 60.4 billion RMB, at 1952 prices, the total industrial value rose from 14 billion to 78.4 billion.

21. Calculated from SSB (1982b, 105). Close to 10 million urban jobs were added in 1949–1952, 8 million more in the subsequent five years, and 13 million more in 1957–1962. The number of urban laborers, in other words, increased almost threefold between 1949 and 1962, from 15.3 million to 45.4 million, while rural labor increased by only 29 percent, from 165 million to 214 million.

22. A comparison of crude death rates from 1959 to 1969 suggests that while the decline in mortality was also important, its contribution to overall population growth during this period was no more than 25 percent.

23. Although the magnitude of this increase may be exaggerated because of possible undercounting of households in the late Republican era, there is no doubt that the number of households increased substantially, a fact corroborated by the decline in mean household size. This was largely a product of land reform. By August 1952 the Chinese state had redistributed over 46 million acres to roughly 300 million rural peasants, removing the economic constraints that had maintained and constrained large households.

24. While communes eventually did charge families for food grain distribution, the price was "at cost." Moreover, the commune often assumed the debts of families who could not pay without halting or taxing their grain entitlements. Among the 28 Guangdong villages surveyed by Parish and Whyte in 1973, for example, only two distributed grain solely on the basis of commune members' work input. The majority distributed food grain either on a per capita basis or on a combination of per capita entitlement and labor contribution (Parish and Whyte 1978, 66).

25. Johnson (1994) discusses the pronatalist legacy of some of these rural institutional arrangements such as farmland allocation and rural social security and health care and argues that changing these pronatalist policies would cause rural fertility to decline even without a birth quota policy (509).

8. Society

Epigraphs: Malthus (1803/1992, 226).

1. David Ricardo, for example, was highly influenced by Malthus and largely agreed with his assessment of the Poor Laws: "The comforts and well-being of the poor cannot be permanently secured without some regard on their part, or some effort on the part of the legislature, to regulate the increase of numbers, and to render less frequent among them early and improvident marriages" (1852, 58).

2. "The whole surface of the empire is, with trifling exceptions, dedicated to the production of food for man alone. There is no meadow, and very little pasture ... There are no commons or lands suffered to lie waste by the neglect, or the caprice, or for the sport of great proprietors. No arable land lies fallow. The soil, under a hot and fertilizing sun, yields annually in most instances double crops, in consequence of adapting the culture to the soil, and of supplying its defects by mixture with other earths, by manure, by irrigation, and by careful and judicious industry of every kind" (Malthus 1826/1986, 128).

3. Because intermediate organizations such as lineages and enterprises were less important than these two extremes, we do not discuss them here.

4. Many scholars have noticed the importance of familial demographic decision making in Chinese society. See, for example, Cohen (1976). Greenhalgh (1988) in particular discusses how a particular demographic outcome, fertility, is an important strategy of Chinese social mobility.

5. Ou-yang Xiu, quoted in Chu T'ung-tsu (1961, 30).

6. Three of these five relationships—father-son, elder brother–younger brother, and husband-wife—deal specifically with the family, and each may be taken as representative of a larger group. Thus the father-son relationship includes all parent-children relationships and by extension the relationship between senior and junior relatives. Elder brother–younger brother may be extended to cover the relationship between older and younger relatives of the same generation. Similarly, the husband-wife relationship represents the ideal hierarchy between the sexes.

7. The role of familial principles in the Qing legal code is discussed in a number of texts. Zhu Yong (1987) is a recent example. See Baker (1976) for a more general formulation.

8. According to Qin law, for example, "A father stealing from his children is not a case of theft; a stepfather stealing from his step-children is a case of theft" (Hulsewe 1985, 125).

9. They could, for example, have their children exiled at will. The surviving Qin code, for example, contains a form entitled "To Banish a Son." This form requires that A, a commoner of X village, should state, "I request to have the feet of my natural son, C, a commoner of the same village, fettered and to have him banished to a border prefecture in Shu, with the injunction that he must not be allowed to leave the place of banishment . . . to the end of his life" (ibid., 195).

10. The surviving Qin code also contains a form for parents to have their children executed. This form, titled "To Denounce a Son," requires that A, a commoner of X village, should state, "My son, C, a commoner of the same village, is unfilial. I request to have him killed." C, after interrogation, must then acknowledge his guilt and state, "I am A's natural son. I have been truly unfilial to A" before the execution can take place. Execution, in other words, required proof of infiliality; banishment did not (ibid., 196).

11. "Beating one's grandparents is punished by tattooing and being made a wall-builder or grain-pounder" (ibid., 141).

12. According to Guy Boulais, the legal definition of unfiliality, one of the ten abominations, specifically refers to parental property rights as well as to parental corporal rights (1924/1966, 29–30).

13. In theory, relatives beyond the immediate family should be reported as uncle (*shu* or *bo*) or aunt (*shen* or *gu*) if senior relatives; male cousin (*xiong* or *di*) or female cousin (*jie* or *mei*) if contemporary relatives; nephews or nieces (*zhi* or *zhinu*) if junior relatives, prefaced by the degree of common descent: *qin* (common parents), *qi* (common grandparents), *xiaogong* (common great-grandparents), *dagong* (common great-great-grandparents), and *sima* (common great-great-great-grandparents). In reality, the terminology occasionally overlaps and is some times obscure, even contradictory. Uncles, for example, are often identified as *qinshu* or *qinbo* rather than *qishu* or *qibo*. See Feng Han-chi (1937) for a summary of these and other kinship terms.

14. Terms such as *wufu* (related outside the five degrees of mourning), *zuren* (lineage member), and *tongxing buzong* (same surname if not same lineage) are quite common.

15. As a result we can identify even very remote family relationships between criminals and victims. Lee (1991) analyzes the patterns of domestic violence during the late imperial period on the basis of reported kin relations for capital crimes for selected years and provinces.

16. Thus according to the Qing code, a son who strikes a parent suffers decapitation irrespective of whether injury resulted, while no penalty applies to parents who beat a son, unless the son dies, in which case the punishment is 100 blows of the heavy bamboo if the beating was provoked by the son's disobedience, and one year of penal servitude plus 60 blows of the heavy bamboo if the beating was done wantonly (Boulais 1924, 616–617).

17. See the discussion on distribution by Hsiao (1979, 109–110).

18. The principle of necessary but light taxation was developed by Mencius and implemented by virtually every Chinese dynasty in the last two millennia. See Zhou (1981, 1984) for a general history and Lee (forthcoming) for a case study from the late imperial period.

19. See Zhang Minru (1982) and Wu Shenyuan (1986) for a general description of these state policies.

20. In the early fifth century B.C., for example, Gou Jian, the king of Yue, ordered that "young men may not marry old women. Old men may not marry young women. If any woman remains unmarried at seventeen, her parents will be considered to have committed a crime. If any man remains unmarried by the age of twenty, his parents will be considered to have committed a crime" (Guo Yu 20.635). Mozi, a major philosopher during the Warring States period (453–221 B.C.), wrote: "What is hard to increase? Only people are hard to increase. But there are policies which can increase population. The former sage kings, for example, required that all men marry by the age of 19 and all women marry by the age of 14. After the kings disappeared, the people did as they pleased. Now those who want to marry early, marry at 20. Those who want to marry late, marry [as late as] 40. The mean age at marriage is 10 years older than under the sage kings. Since it takes about 3 years to suckle a child, we can expect at least two to three more children to survive if we were to reduce the age of marriage by 10 years. Through universal early marriage, we should be able to increase population size" (Sun Yirang 1986, 6.147).

21. Gou Jian also ordered: "All pregnant women are entitled to the care of a state physician. If they give birth to a boy, they will be rewarded with two casks of wine and a boar. If they bear a daughter, they shall be rewarded with two casks of wine and a sow. Women who give birth to triplets will be provided with a wet nurse. Women who give birth to twins will be given special allowances of food" (Guo Yu 20.636).

22. The Tang (618–906 A.D.) code, for example, contains numerous laws on household and individual behavior (W. Johnson 1997, 121–177). Thus article

179.1a declares that "all cases of marriage during the period of mourning for parents or husbands [typically 27 months] is punished by three years of penal servitude" (ibid., 157).

23. See Chapter 4, note 50.

24. Not until the middle of the sixteenth century did population migration become less controlled. Before that time migrants needed permits to travel and to change place of residence. The relaxation of migration control coincided with the beginning of the more rapid increase in population. See Lee (1978).

25. That is, they did not have property rights that took regular precedence over state authority. See Allee (1994), P. Huang and Bernhardt (1994), and P. Huang (1996) on property rights in late imperial China, and Scogin (1990) on property rights in early imperial China.

26. Ho (1968, 18) remains the most succinct and powerful description of the ideal model of Chinese autocracy. R. Huang (1981), an account of one emperor's ineffective reality, is an eloquent counterweight. For other less eloquent but more recent and focused examples see Will (1990) and Will and Wong with Lee (1991).

27. Thus Mencius told King Hui of Liang, "When the people have more grain, more fish and turtles than they can eat, and more timber than they can use . . . This is the first step along the Kingly way" (Mencius 1970, 51).

28. A number of studies document and analyze the content and the impact of these programs. See, for instance, Croll (1981), Andors (1983), K. Johnson (1983), Stacey (1983), and M. Wolf (1992). While some scholars are critical of the overall impact of the Chinese socialist revolution on women's status, almost all agree that initial state programs were fundamental in improving women's status.

29. Not only did urban women receive the same employment guarantees as urban men between the late 1950s and 1970s, but also rural women were first encouraged and later required to participate in the formal labor force. For female labor force participation and compensation, see Parish and Whyte (1978) and M. Whyte and Parish (1984).

30. A number of other institutional arrangements from the 1950s through the 1970s also reinforced the continued importance of the family collective. Thus in the countryside, while rural collectives beginning in the late 1950s recorded each individual member's labor input separately, they distributed income and goods, as well as private land, to families, not to individuals. Similarly, in the cities family connections starting in the 1970s also became increasingly important in getting jobs, food, housing, and other benefits. See Whyte (1995) for a discussion of how some state policies encouraged the role of the family.

31. The current Chinese constitution was originally drafted in 1949 and was revised in 1954, 1975, 1978, 1979, 1980, 1982, etc.

32. For a classic description of the tradition of the "mass line," see Selden (1971). Schurmann (1968) and Soloman (1971) provide detailed analysis of the use of political ideology and mass mobilization in socialist China.

33. Henderson and Cohen (1984) give a vivid description of work and life in an urban unit. Walder (1986) and Bian (1992) provide systematic analysis and description of such units in urban China. Madsen (1984) examines village life in the context of local politics.

34. Until a few years ago most urban Chinese expected their work units to be the main source of their welfare. A recent survey conducted by the Chinese Academy of Social Sciences in 30 Chinese cities reports that 97.5 percent of respondents believe their work units are responsible for their health insurance, 96.6 percent believe that their units are responsible for retirement insurance, 91.8 percent believe that their units are responsible for housing, and 85.9 percent even believe that their work units should mediate family disputes of employees (cited in *Dazhong wenzai*, Popular Digest, August 1997, 15). Moreover, a comparative study of social networks in urban Chinese and Dutch populations reveals that as recently as in the early 1990s the Chinese paradoxically reported far fewer social network ties based on kinship. Whereas 53 percent of Dutch respondents gave names of relatives as sources of emotional, instrumental, and social support, only 38 percent of Chinese did so. The difference is especially sharp in emotional and social support: 74 percent of Dutch but only 40 percent of Chinese turn to relatives when they feel depressed, and 34 percent versus only 10 percent respectively named relatives as the ones to "go out" with for social gatherings. For the Chinese, co-workers play a much larger role (Ruan et al. 1997).

35. Walder (1986) focuses on the importance of political attitude and moral performance in Chinese factories and analyzes these new criteria in light of Chinese tradition as well as Communist ideologies.

36. *Guanxi* reached such importance in the late 1970s and early 1980s that it became the most common term in daily conversation. See M. M. Yang (1994) for an in-depth anthropological study of the meaning, usage, and implications of *guanxi* in contemporary China.

37. Zeng (1996) discusses this new system of responsibility in China's family planning program.

38. See, for example, Fei (1946) for a sociological analysis of the life and function of rural gentry in China. See Henderson and Cohen (1984) and Frolic (1980) for descriptions of such social control in the work place and residential neighborhoods in urban China, and Madsen (1984) on social control in rural China.

39. By contrast, practically every one of the government's other policy initiatives since the 1970s, most notably the economic reforms, have encountered intense opposition from one faction or another within the party or in society at large, and has been implemented only after tortuous negotiations and maneuvering that has in some cases lasted years.

40. Both the Cultural Revolution (1966–1976) and the earlier Antirightists Movement in the late 1950s, for example, targeted intellectuals or officials with dissenting political views.

41. This is, for example, the case of the up-to-the-mountain and down-to-the-village movement during the Cultural Revolution. An estimated 20 million urban youth, equivalent to 10 percent of China's urban population at the time, were sent down to the countryside. Only children from urban families were required to go through such an experience.

42. Just as the more privileged family members in late imperial China had to sacrifice more in bad times, so urban residents, who receive far more state benefits and enjoy much higher living standards, are expected to take the lead in family planning. As a result, whereas rural couples on average have had more than two children over the past two decades, most urban couples have had one.

43. The major exceptions are the national minorities, with whom state attempts at family planning have proceeded more slowly. As a result, the total fertility rate of national minorities was still 4.5 in 1979 compared with 2.8 nationally, and 2.9 in 1989 compared with 2.3 nationally. Some minority populations such as the Tibetans and Uighur continue to have quite high fertility (4.1 and 4.5 respectively), while others such as the Manchus (with a TFR of 1.89) and the Koreans (with a TFR of 1.55) have achieved a fertility decline similar to that of the larger Han population (Yang Shuzhang 1993). Overall, the minority proportions have grown from 6 percent in 1964 to 7 percent in 1982 and to 8 percent in 1990 (Yao and Yin 1994).

44. This does not mean that no attempts have been made by privileged individuals to abuse the system and to evade policy requirements. Most such violations, however, are routinely dealt with through a system of fines for the population at large, and violations by officials are routinely and severely punished. As a result, demographic corruption is much rarer than economic or political corruption.

45. Indeed, most sex education in China today takes place in the context of family planning education. See Honig and Herschatter (1988) and Evans (1995).

46. Most Chinese recognize that government population policy is necessary. In a representative survey conducted in Hebei, Shaanxi, and Shanghai in 1985, women of reproductive age were asked what they believed to be the main reason for the one-child policy. They were provided with five choices: population control, economic development, for both mother's and children's health, other, and don't know. A majority of respondents (50 percent in Shaanxi, 63 percent in Hebei, and nearly 80 percent in Shanghai) reported that the main reason was population control. Between 10 and 20 percent of these women believed it was for women's and children's health, and another 10 percent or so mentioned the need for national economic development (SSB 1986, 1: 98).

47. Public displays of symbols of local achievement have a long history in China. The arches, banners, and inscriptions of the past, however, have generally been replaced by official certificates. Typically the contemporary government awards such certification to families who have a child in the army or model

families or individuals—including, in the late 1970s and early 1980s, when the current family planning program was at its early stage, those couples who pledged to have only one child.

48. One notable feature of China's current economic growth is that most organizations have striven to maintain egalitarianism among their members despite the growing inequality in society as a whole. This "Chinese characteristic" of contemporary society has attracted considerable interest among Chinese, if not Western, social scientists (Xiao et al. 1990).

49. Perdue (1998) describes, for example, how Montesquieu systematically distorted facts to construct his model of "oriental despotism." The contrast with Malthus, who was fastidious in his use of evidence, is testimony to Malthus' scholarship.

9. Demography, Ideology, and Politics

1. Social thinkers, especially political philosophers, have long recognized the existence of such basic dimensions of human behavior and have commented on their implications (Triandis 1995). Not until a few decades ago, however, did social scientists, most notably clinical psychologists, begin to conceptualize and to measure personal traits as individualist or collectivist. Such research has shown that just as individuals from some societies are more likely to demonstrate one inclination over the other, even within the same society substantial differences can also coexist, whether measured by age, birth order, gender, education, ethnicity, occupation, etc.

2. As a result, most studies of Chinese social organization and behavior have tended to focus on descriptions of ideal models (M. C. Yang 1945/1965; Lang 1946; Hu 1948; Freedman 1966; Baker 1976).

3. See the Appendix for a discussion of these archival sources and Thatcher (1998) for instructions on how to access the historical data.

4. These marital fertility rates are calculated from Coale and Treadway (1986, 42–44). The French decline occurred long before 1870. As early as 1831 the French total marital fertility rate was only 6.93, more than 20 percent lower than that in England and Wales two decades later, in 1851.

5. Macfarlane (1978, 1986) spells out this juxtaposition. Just as the market economy ensures that the prices and wages experienced by individuals reflect economic realities, including pressure on resources, the Malthusian marriage system ties population growth rates to economic conditions. As a result, replacing the positive check with the preventive check produces an environment more conducive to the smooth functioning of the market. Individualism, accompanied by a distinct set of legal, political, and social structures, therefore provides the essential framework for market economies and Malthusian marriage systems.

6. See McGovern (1958) for a summary of such traditions. Plato theorized that the state, through its rules or guardians, should regulate in minute details the

moral and economic actions, the literature, the music, and even the thoughts of its citizens. Aristotle argued that the chief function of the state was to promote "the good life" among its citizens—by education, if possible; by force, if necessary. The state, moreover, was to be the sole judge of what was and was not "the good life." Hobbes's theory of sovereignty promoted the idea that the state ought to possess sole ultimate power to control all persons and groups of persons within its territory. Indeed, Hobbes believed that the state had the right to decide not only what was legal or illegal, but also what was moral or immoral. Karl Marx, whose writings have had the strongest resonance in contemporary China, believed that the ultimate stage of social evolution was communism.

7. "It is not the pursuit of individual good but of the common good that makes cities great, and it is beyond doubt that common good is never considered except in republics. The opposite happens where there is a prince, for on most occasions what benefits him is offensive to the city, and what benefits the city is offensive to him" (quoted in Q. Skinner 1997, 62).

8. It is now commonly accepted that there was "scarcely any consciousness of individual liberty as a political ideal in the ancient world . . . the notion of individual rights is absent from the legal conceptions of the Romans and Greeks; this seems to hold equally of the Jewish, Chinese, and all other ancient civilizations that have since come to light" (Berlin 1958, 13).

9. Even as late as the sixteenth century, such thinkers as Wang Ken, Wang Yuan-ming, and Li Zhi extended and elaborated this concept of individual worthiness and went so far as to advocate similar mobility in the absence of formal education (Ho 1964).

10. While this description by Jia Yi, an early second-century B.C. Confucian statesman, is undoubtedly exaggerated, his general description of Qin society seems to have been unchallenged.

11. The major exceptions are in southern Europe. In Italy, for example, divorce was not legalized until 1971 and not liberalized until 1975, when the new family laws also liberalized adoption, foster care, abortion, and contraception. Whereas legal separations increased sixfold from 1965 to 1985 to 12 percent of all marriages celebrated each year, the proportion of Italian couples obtaining divorces rose far more slowly. In 1975 fewer than 2 per 1,000 married women filed for divorce; by 1982 the share was only 4 per 1,000, an order of magnitude lower than in northern Europe (Saraceno 1991).

12. By comparison, in the United Kingdom 4 percent of women marrying for the first time in 1966 cohabited before marriage. In 1993 the comparable figure was 68 percent (Office for National Statistics 1997). We thank Nikki Hart for bringing this source to our attention.

13. Illegitimacy rates, of course, vary dramatically by class and ethnicity. In the United States, for example, the percentage of nonmarital births rose between 1960 and 1992 from less than 5 to over 20 percent for whites and from 25 to 70 percent for blacks (H. Smith, Morgan, and Koropeckyj-Cox 1996).

204 · *Notes to Pages 141–154*

14. Examples include the passing of the Divorce Reform Act in England in 1969, the Family Law Reform of Sweden in 1973, the Divorce Reform Act of France in 1975, the Marriage and Family Law Reform in West Germany in 1976, and the "No-Fault" Movement in the United States between 1969 and 1985. See Glendon (1989) for a detailed survey and analysis of these laws. We thank Judy Treas for bringing this book to our attention.

15. The 1980 marriage law, which is quoted in its entirety in Honig (1984), allowed for divorce on the grounds of incompatibility and removed the previously required civil mediation process before divorce could be granted. While Wu Deqing (1995) provides the only in-depth scholarly analysis of this subject, see Hareven (1987) for a vivid description of the court process.

16. While China's population increased by only 20 percent between 1979 and 1992, the number of divorces in China almost tripled, from 299,932 to 849,611 (Feng Fanghui 1996, 423).

17. The probability of premarital conception also differs by residence and educational level, with urban and more educated youth much more likely to venture into premarital sex. Relaxed state controls and increased individual tolerance have led to such changes and differences. Unlike in the West, however, most of these premarital conceptions have ended as births within marriage.

18. See Pye (1996) for a different analysis of individual and collective in China.

Appendix

1. This appendix is an expansion of Lee and Campbell (1997, 223–237). R. Bin Wong assisted in that composition, and we are grateful for his help.

2. The other two relationships, ruler-minister and friend-friend, though not explicitly familial, are certainly paternalistic.

3. Liu Ts'ui-jung (1978) was perhaps the first contemporary historical demographer to use genealogies to reconstruct the population history of China. See Telford (1986) for a detailed description of the types of data found in Chinese genealogies, and Harrell (1987) and Telford (1990b) for an evaluation of their data quality.

4. A. Wolf and Huang (1980, 16–33) remains the best introduction to the Japanese household registers of Taiwan; Lee and Campbell (1997, 223–237) is the best introduction to the data on Liaoning.

5. See Rozman (1982) for an analysis of this type of population data, and G. W. Skinner (1986) for an important qualification on the completeness and accuracy of these data.

6. Lee, Campbell, and Wang (1993) is the best introduction to the demographic archives of the Qing imperial lineage in English, but see too the essays in Lee and Guo (1994).

7. China's national and provincial-level population figures published in China's Statistical Yearbooks up to 1987 are all based on household registrations.

8. Such an effort began in 1951 with urban population, when the government

issued the decree of Temporary Provisions for Management of Urban Household Registration. A new national household registration system took shape
in the mid-1950s. In 1955 China's State Council issued its Instruction on
Establishing a Regular Household Registration System. In 1958 the National
People's Congress approved the Regulations of Household Registration in the
People's Republic, which established the modern population registration system (Zhang Qingwu and Wang 1997).

9. Compared with results from the 1964 and 1982 censuses, which counted
populations in the preceding year, national population counts based on the
registration system for 1963 and 1981 had an error rate of only 0.8 percent
and 0.1 percent respectively (Zhang Qingwu and Wang 1997, 88). Although
recently increased migration has made timely and complete registration much
more difficult, the quality of household registration remains high. As recently
as 1990, 97.3 percent of census data were identical with household registration data (Sun Jinxin 1997, 6). Moreover, in recent years China has made new
efforts to update and to improve its population registration system. A notable
development is the establishment of the nationwide Computer Management
System for Information of Permanent Residents, which is intended to replace
the manual registration and tabulation system used in the past half-century.
From 1992 through 1996, 10,119 police stations across the country installed
such a system; more than 240 million people's records are now on-line
(Zhang Qingwu and Wang 1997, 91).

10. Perhaps the most ambitious effort to use these demographic data is the 32-
volume series *China's Population,* published mostly in the 1980s (Lavely, Lee,
and Wang 1990).

11. Every household maintains a registration booklet in which each individual
has a one-page form. Initial registration items formulated in 1958 included
relationship with the head of the household, name, date and place of birth,
age at the time of registration or compilation, origin (normally father's place
of birth), ethnicity, religion, class background *(chengfen),* educational attainment, marital status, occupation, location of employment, status of military
conscription, date and origin or destination of migration. In 1981, age, class
background, and conscription status were removed from registration, and in
1985 type of household, conscription status, height, blood type, and reasons
and decisions for applying for a Resident Identification Card were added.

12. The number of items on the census form increased from 6 in 1953 to 21 in
1990. The 1953 census included only household address, name, sex, age,
nationality, and relationship to the household head. The 1964 census added
class status, educational level, and occupation. Many of these added data
were never published. Information on occupation was never even tabulated
because there was no occupational classification scheme. The 1982 census
dropped class background but added household type, number of household
members, number of births in the preceding year in the household, number of
deaths in the preceding year in the household, number of people who have left

place of registration for more than a year, household registration status, industry, occupation, status of nonworking members, marital status, number of children ever born and living, and childbearing status in the preceding year. The 1990 census added questions on place of permanent residence and reasons for population migration.

13. See, for instance Li Chengrui (1986) for documentation and analyses of the 1982 census, SSB (1987) and (1993) for census tabulations from the 1982 and 1990 censuses. Computerized samples of census data have also been made available for individual-level analyses. See Banister (1987) and Coale (1984) for examples in their use.

14. The 1982 survey asked each female respondent aged up to 67 to recall her pregnancy and birth history; the 1988 survey gathered contraceptive histories as well. As a result, the 1988 survey provided data to study not only demographic change in the first half of the 1980s (Coale et al. 1991; Feeney and Wang 1993) but also pregnancy and contraceptive use histories, as well as other sociodemographic issues of contemporary China (Wang and Tuma 1993; Wang and Yang 1996; Wang forthcoming).

15. Coale (1984) presents a demographic baseline construction for China, including time trends of nuptiality and fertility from 1952 to 1982, and of mortality for 1953–1964 and 1964–1982. Lavely (1986) provides marital fertility for China. Coale and Chen (1987) provide age-specific fertility and marital duration fertility data at both national and provincial level, and by urban-rural residence type from 1940 to 1981. Feeney and Yu (1987) calculate fertility by parity for China and by urban-rural residence type.

16. Both Coale, Li, and Han (1988) and Wang and Yang (1996) analyze long birth intervals, while Wang and Tuma (1993) study past marriage behavior. Zhao Zhongwei (1998) demonstrates that even the subpopulation with the highest fertility in Republican China exercised marital fertility control well before the contemporary nationwide fertility decline.

17. Other uses of such multiple sources include Feeney et al. (1989), Coale et al. (1991), and Feeney and Yuan (1994).

References

Aird, John. 1968. "Population Growth." In Eckstein, Galenson, and Liu, 183–328.

——— 1990. *Slaughter of the Innocents: Coercive Birth Control in China.* Washington, D.C.: American Enterprise Institute.

Alexandratos, Nikos. 1996. "China's Projected Cereals Deficits in a World Context." *Agricultural Economics* 15: 1–16.

Alford, William. 1995. *To Steal a Book Is an Elegant Offense: Intellectual Property Law in Chinese Civilization.* Stanford: Stanford University Press.

Allee, Mark. 1994. *Law and Local Society in Late Imperial China: Northern Taiwan in the Nineteenth Century.* Stanford: Stanford University Press.

Allison, P. 1984. *Event History Analysis: Regression for Longitudinal Event Data.* Beverly Hills: Sage Publications.

Alter, George. 1988. *Family and the Female Life Course: The Women of Verviers, Belgium, 1844–1880.* Madison: University of Wisconsin Press.

Anderson, Eugene. 1988. *The Food of China.* New Haven: Yale University Press.

Andors, Phyllis. 1983. *The Unfinished Revolution of China's Women, 1949–1980.* Bloomington: Indiana University Press.

Ashton, Basil, Kenneth Hill, Alan Piazza, and Robin Zeitz. 1984. "Famine in China, 1958–1961." *Population and Development Review* 10: 613–645.

Bai Hewen, Du Fuquan, and Min Zongdian, eds. 1995. *Zhongguo jindai nongye keji shigao* (A draft history of modern Chinese agricultural technology). Beijing: Zhongguo nongye keji chubanshe.

Baker, H. 1976. *Chinese Family and Kinship.* London: Macmillan.

Banister, Judith. 1987. *China's Changing Population.* Stanford: Stanford University Press.

208 · References

Banister, Judith, and Samuel H. Preston. 1981. "Mortality in China." *Population and Development Review* 7: 98–110.

Barclay, George W. 1954. *Colonial Development and Population in Taiwan.* Princeton: Princeton University Press.

Barclay, George W., Ansley J. Coale, Michael A. Stoto, and James Trussell. 1976. "A Reassessment of the Demography of Traditional Rural China." *Population Index* 42: 606–635.

Bardet, Jean-Pierre. 1983. *Rouen aux XVIIe et XVIIIe siècles: Les mutations d'un espace social.* 2 vols. Paris: Société d'Edition d'Enseignment Superieur.

Bardet, Jean-Pierre, and Jacques Dupâquier, eds. 1997. *Histoire des populations de l'Europe.* Vol. 1: *Des origines aux prémices de la Révolution.* Paris: Fayard.

Barrett, Richard E. 1980. "Short-Term Trends in Bastardy in Taiwan." *Journal of Family History* 5: 293–312.

——— 1984. "Chinese Population Processes since the Nineteenth Century." Manuscript.

Basu, Alaka Malwade. 1989. "Is Discrimination in Food Really Necessary for Explaining Sex Differentials in Childhood Mortality?" *Population Studies* 43: 193–210.

Bean, Lee L., and Geraldine P. Mineau. 1986. "The Polygyny-Fertility Hypothesis: A Reevaluation." *Population Studies* 40: 67–81.

Bean, Lee L., Geraldine P. Mineau, and Douglas Anderton. 1990. *Fertility Change on the American Frontier: Adaptation and Innovation.* Berkeley: University of California Press.

Becker, Gary. 1960. "An Economic Analysis of Fertility." In National Bureau of Economic Research, *Demographic and Economic Change in Developed Countries: A Conference of the Universities-National Bureau Committee for Economic Research.* Princeton: Princeton University Press, 209–231.

Benedict, Carol. 1993. "Policing the Sick: Plague and the Origin of State Medicine in Late Imperial China." *Late Imperial China* 14: 60–77.

——— 1995. *Bubonic Plague in Nineteenth-Century China.* Stanford: Stanford University Press.

Bengtsson, Tommy. 1989. *Reallönevariation och vuxendödlighet. Livsförlopp I Västanfors 1750–1849.* Meddelande från Ekonomisk-historiska institutionen, Lunds universitet, no. 60.

——— 1993. "Combined Time-Series and Life-Event Analysis: The Impact of Economic Fluctuations and Air Temperature on Adult Mortality by Sex and Occupation in a Swedish Mining Parish, 1757–1850." In *Old and New Methods in Historical Demography,* ed. David Reher and Roger Schofield. Oxford: Oxford University Press, 239–253.

——— 1995. "Combined Life-Event and Time-Series Analysis: The Impact of Economic Fluctuations and Household Cycles on Mortality in Rural Sweden, 1750–1850." EAP Working Paper Series, no. 5. Kyoto.

——— 1997. "The Vulnerable Child: Economic Insecurity and Child Mortality in

Pre-industrial Sweden: A Case Study of Västanfors, 1750–1850." EAP Working Paper Series, no. 4. Kyoto.

—— Forthcoming. "Inequality in Deaths: Effects of the Agrarian Revolution in Southern Sweden, 1765–1865." In Bengtsson and Saito.

Bengtsson, Tommy, G. Fridlizius, and R. Ohlsson, eds. 1984. *Pre-Industrial Population Change: The Mortality Decline and Short-Term Population Movements.* Stockholm: Almquist and Wiskell International.

Bengtsson, Tommy, and R. Ohlsson. 1985. "Age-Specific Mortality and Short-Term Changes in the Standard of Living: Sweden, 1751–1859." *European Journal of Population* 1: 309–326.

Bengtsson, Tommy, and Osamu Saito, eds. Forthcoming. *Population and Economy: From Hunger to Modern Economic Growth.* Oxford: Oxford University Press.

Berkner, Lutz, and Franklin Mendels. 1978. "Inheritance Systems, Family Structure, and Demographical Patterns in Western Europe, 1700–1900." In *Historical Studies in Changing Fertility,* ed. Charles Tilly. Princeton: Princeton University Press, 209–223.

Berlin, Isaiah. 1958. *Two Concepts of Liberty.* Oxford: Oxford Clarendon Press.

Bernhardt, Kathryn. 1992. *Rents, Taxes, and Peasant Resistance.* Stanford: Stanford University Press.

—— 1995. "The Inheritance Rights of Daughters." *Modern China* 21: 269–309.

Bernstein, Thomas. 1984. "Stalinism, Famine, and Chinese Peasants: Grain Procurement during the Great Leap Forward." *Theory and Society* 13: 339–377.

Bhatia, Shushum. 1983. "Traditional Practices Affecting Female Health and Survival: Evidence from Countries of South Asia." In *Sex Differences in Mortality: Trends, Determinants, and Consequences. Selection of Papers presented at ANU/UN/WHO Meeting,* ed. Alan Lopez and Lado T. Ruzicka. Canberra: Australia National University, Department of Demography, 165–178.

Bian Yanjie. 1992. *Work and Inequality in Urban China.* Albany: State University of New York Press.

Biraben, Jean-Noël. 1979. "Essai sur l'évolution du nombre des hommes." *Population* 1: 13–25.

Birdsall, Nancy, and Dean T. Jamison. 1983. "Income and Other Factors of Fertility in China." *Population and Development Review* 9: 651–675.

Blayo, Yves. 1975. "La mortalité en France de 1740 à 1829." *Population,* special issue, 138–139.

Blayo, Yves, and Louis Henry. 1967. "Données démographiques sur la Bretagne et l'Anjou de 1740 à 1829." *Annales de démographies historiques,* 91–171.

Bledsoe, Caroline H., Alan G. Hill, Umberton D'Alessandro, and Patricia Langerock. 1994. "Constructing Natural Fertility: The Use of Western Contraceptive Technologies in Rural Gambia." *Population and Development Review* 20: 81–113.

Blum, Alain, and Irina Troitskaja. 1996. "La mortalité en Russie aux XVIIIe et

XIXe siècles: Estimations locales à partir des *Revizii.*" *Population* 51: 303–328.

Bond, Michael, ed. 1986. *The Psychology of the Chinese People.* Hong Kong: Oxford University Press.

Bongaarts, John. 1978. "A Framework for Analyzing the Proximate Determinants of Fertility." *Population and Development Review* 4: 105–133.

——— 1996. "Population Pressure and Food Supply in the Developing World." *Population and Development Review* 22: 483–504.

Bongaarts, John, and R. Potter. 1983. *Fertility, Biology, and Behavior: An Analysis of the Proximate Determinants.* New York: Academic Press.

Boserup, Esther. 1965/1996. *Conditions of Agricultural Growth: The Economics of Agrarian Change under Population Pressure.* Chicago: Aldine Publishing.

Boulais, Le P. Guy. 1924/1966. *Manuel du Code Chinois.* Taipei: Ch'eng-wen.

Braudel, Ferdinand. 1981. *Structures of Everyday Life: The Limits of the Possible.* New York: Harper and Row.

Bray, Francesca. 1997. *Technology and Gender: Fabrics of Power in Late Imperial China.* Berkeley: University of California Press.

——— Forthcoming. "Meaning of Motherhood: Reproductive Technologies and Their Uses in Late Imperial China." In Lee and Saito.

Brown, Lester. 1995. *Who Will Feed China? Wake-Up Call for a Small Planet.* New York: W. W. Norton.

Buck, John Lossing, ed. 1937. *Land Utilization in China.* 3 vols. Chicago: University of Chicago Press.

——— 1966. "Food Grain Production in Mainland China before and during the Communist Regime." In *Food and Agriculture in Communist China,* ed. John Lossing Buck, Owen L. Dawson, and Wu Yuan-li. New York: Praeger, 3–72.

Bulatao, R., and Ronald Lee, eds. 1983. *Determinants of Fertility in Developing Countries.* 2 vols. New York: Academic Press.

Burguière, André. 1981. "Réticences théoriques et intégration practique du remariage dans la France d'Ancien Regime, dix-septième–dix-huitième siècles." In Dupâquier et al., 41–48.

——— 1987. "The Formation of the Couple." *Journal of Family History* 12: 39–56.

Buxbaum, David, ed. 1978. *Chinese Family Law and Social Change in Historical and Comparative Perspective.* Seattle: University of Washington Press.

Cain, Mead. 1982. "Perspectives on Family and Fertility in Developing Countries." *Population Studies* 36: 159–175.

Caldwell, John C. 1976. "Toward a Restatement of Demographic Transition Theory." *Population and Development Review* 2: 321–366.

——— 1986. "Routes to Low Mortality in Poor Countries." *Population and Development Review* 12: 171–220.

Caldwell, John C., and Pat Caldwell. 1977. "The Role of Marital Sexual Abstinence in Determining Fertility: A Study of the Yoruba in Nigeria." *Population Studies* 31: 193–213.

Caldwell, Pat, and John C. Caldwell. 1981. "The Function of Child Spacing in Traditional Societies and the Direction of Change." In Page and Lesthaeghe, 73–92.

Campbell, Cameron. 1995. "Chinese Mortality Transitions: The Case of Beijing, 1700–1990." Ph.D. diss., University of Pennsylvania, Departments of Demography and Sociology.

———— 1997. "Public Health Efforts in China before 1949 and Their Effects on Mortality: The Case of Beijing." *Social Science History* 21: 179–218.

———— Forthcoming. "Mortality Change and the Epidemiological Transition in Beijing, 1644–1990." In Liu Ts'ui-jung et al.

Campbell, Cameron, and James Lee. 1996. "A Death in the Family: Household Structure and Mortality in Rural Liaoning, Life-Event and Time-Series Analysis, 1792–1867." *History of the Family* 1: 297–328.

———— Forthcoming. "Price Fluctuations, Family Structure, and Mortality in Two Rural Chinese Populations: A Comparison of Peasants and Serfs in Eighteenth- and Nineteenth-Century Liaoning." In Bengtsson and Saito.

CASS (Chinese Academy of Social Sciences, Population Institute). 1994. *Dangdai zhongguo funu chouyang diaocha ziliao* (Data from the sample survey of women's status in contemporary China). Beijing: Wanguo chubanshe.

Chao Kang. 1986. *Man and Land in China.* Stanford: Stanford University Press.

———— 1990. "The Trend of Real Wages of Farm Workers during the Eighteenth and Nineteenth Centuries." In *China's Market Economy in Transition,* ed. Lee Yung-san and Liu Ts'ui-jung. Taibei: Academia Sinica, Institute of Economics, 154–166.

Chao Kang, Liu Yongcheng, Wu Hui, Zhu Jinfu, Chen Ciyu, and Chen Qiukun. 1995. *Qingdai liangshi muchanliang yanjiu* (Studies of acreage productivity during the Qing). Beijing: Nongye chubanshe.

Chayovan, N., and John Knodel. 1991. *Coital Activity among Married Thai Women: Evidence from the 1987 Thailand Demographic and Health Survey.* Research Report no. 91-221. University of Michigan, Population Studies Center.

Chen, Ann, and James Lee. 1996. "Bigger Is Better: Changes in Chinese Stature, 1890–1990: A Comparison of Mainland China and the Island Province of Taiwan." Manuscript.

Chen Chuansheng. 1992. *Shichang jizhi yu shehui bianqian: 18 shiji Guangdong mijia fenxi* (Market mechanisms and social change: An analysis of rice prices in eighteenth-century Guangdong). Guangzhou: Zhongshan daxue chubanshe.

Chen Guangsheng. 1989. "Songdai shengzi buyu fengsu de shengxing jiqi yuanyin" (The reasons for the rise of infanticide during the Song). *Zhongguo shi yanjiu* 1: 138–143.

Chen, Lincoln, and A. K. M. A. Chowdhury. 1977. "The Dynamics of Contemporary Famine." In *International Population Conference, Mexico.* Vol. 1. Liège: International Union for the Scientific Study of Population, 409–426.

Chen, Lincoln, Emdadul Huq, and Stan D'Souza. 1981. "Sex Bias in the Family Allocation of Food and Health Care in Rural Bangladesh." *Population and Development Review* 7: 55–70.

Chen Pi-chao and Adrienne Kols. 1982. "Population and Birth Planning in the People's Republic of China." *Population Reports,* Series J, no. 25.

Chen Zhenhan. 1955. "Ming mo Qing chu (1620–1720) Zhongguo de nongye laodong shengchanlu, dizu he tudi jizhong" (Labor productivity, land rent, and land concentration in China during the late Ming and early Qing times [1620–1720]. *Jingji yanjiu* (Beijing) 3: 272–294.

Cheng Tiejun and Mark Selden. 1994. "The Origins and Social Consequences of China's Hukou System." *China Quarterly* 139: 644–668.

Cherlin, Andrew. 1994. *Marriage, Divorce, Remarriage.* 2d ed. Cambridge, Mass. Harvard University Press.

China Population Information Center. *See* CPIC.

Chinese Academy of Social Sciences, Population Institute. *See* CASS.

Chinese Anatomical Society Research Group on Human Stature. 1982. *Zhong-guoren tizhi diaocha* (Research on the stature of Chinese). Shanghai: Shanghai kexue jishu chubanshe.

Choe Minja, Hao Hongsheng, and Wang Feng. 1995. "Effects of Gender, Birth Order, and Other Correlates on Childhood Mortality in China." *Social Biology* 42: 50–64.

Choe Minja, and Seung-hyan Han. Forthcoming. "Induced Abortion in the Republic of Korea: 1960–1990." In Lee and Saito.

Chu T'ung-tsu. 1961. *Law and Society in Traditional China.* Leiden: Mouton.

Chuan Hansheng. 1974. "Yapian zhanzheng qian Jiangsu de mian fangzhi ye" (Textile industry in Jiangsu before the Opium War). In *Zhongguo jingji shi luncong* (Essays in Chinese economic history). Hong Kong: Xinya yanjiusuo chubanshe, 625–650.

——— 1976. *Zhongguo jingji shi yanjiu* (Researches in Chinese economic history). 3 vols. Hong Kong: Xinya yanjiusuo chubanshe.

Chuan Hansheng and Richard Kraus. 1975. *Mid-Ch'ing Rice Markets and Trade: An Essay in Price History.* Cambridge, Mass.: Harvard University, East Asian Research Center.

Chuang Ying-chang and Arthur Wolf. 1995. "Marriage in Taiwan, 1881–1905: An Example of Regional Diversity." *Journal of Asian Studies* 54: 781–795.

Coale, Ansley J. 1973. "The Demographic Transition Reconsidered." In *Proceedings of the International Population Conference.* Vol. 1. Liège: International Union for the Scientific Study of Population, 58–71.

——— 1975. "The History of the Human Population." *Scientific American* 231: 31–51.

——— 1984. *Rapid Population Change in China, 1952–1982.* Washington, D.C.: National Academy Press.

———— 1985. "Fertility in Rural China: A Reconfirmation of the Barclay Reassessment." In Hanley and Wolf, 186–195.

———— 1986. "The Decline of Fertility in Europe since the Eighteenth Century as a Chapter in Human Demographic History." In Coale and Watkins, 1–30.

———— 1989. "Marriage and Childbearing in China since 1940." *Social Forces* 67: 833–850.

Coale, Ansley J., and Judith Banister. 1994. "Five Decades of Missing Females in China." *Demography* 31: 459–479.

Coale, Ansley J., and Chen Shengli. 1987. *Basic Data on Fertility in the Provinces of China, 1942–1982.* Honolulu: East-West Center.

Coale, Ansley J., Li Shaomin, and Han Jingqing. 1988. *The Distribution of Interbirth Intervals in Rural China, 1940s to 1970s.* Honolulu: East-West Center.

Coale, Ansley J., and Roy Treadway. 1986. "A Summary of the Changing Distribution of Overall Fertility, Marital Fertility, and the Proportion Married in the Provinces of Europe." In Coale and Watkins, 31–181.

Coale, Ansley J., and James Trussell. 1974. "Modeling Fertility Schedules: Variations in the Structure of Childbearing in Human Populations." *Population Index* 40: 185–258.

———— 1975. Erratum. *Population Index* 41: 572.

———— 1978. "Technical Note: Finding the Two Parameters That Specify a Model Schedule of Marital Fertility." *Population Index* 44: 203–213.

Coale, Ansley J., Wang Feng, Nancy E. Riley, and Lin Fude. 1991. "Recent Trends in Fertility and Nuptiality in China." *Science* 251: 389–393.

Coale, Ansley J., and Susan Watkins, eds. 1986. *The Decline of Fertility in Europe.* Princeton: Princeton University Press.

Cohen, Myron. 1976. *House United, House Divided: The Chinese Family in Taiwan.* New York: Columbia University Press.

Coleman, David, and Roger Schofield. 1986. *The State of Population Theory: Forward from Malthus.* Oxford: Basil Blackwell.

Confucius. 1979. *The Analects,* trans. D. C. Lau. London: Penguin Books.

Cong Hanxiang. 1984. "Lun Mingdai Jiangnan difang de renkou midu jiqi dui jingji fazhan de yingxiang" (Population density in Ming Jiangnan and its influence on economic expansion). *Zhongguo shi yanjiu* 3: 41–53.

CPIC (China Population Information Center). 1988. *Zhongguo renkou ziliao shouce* (Handbook of Chinese population materials). Beijing: Zhongguo renkou qingbao zhongxin.

Croll, Elizabeth. 1981. *The Politics of Marriage in Contemporary China.* Cambridge: Cambridge University Press.

Das Gupta, Monica. 1987. "Selective Discrimination against Female Children in India." *Population and Development Review* 13: 77–100.

———— 1997. "Kinship Systems and Demographic Regimes." In Kertzer and Fricke, 36–52.

Davis, Deborah, and Stevan Harrell, eds. 1993. *Chinese Families in the Post-Mao Era.* Berkeley: University of California Press.

Davis, Kingsley, and Judith Blake. 1956. "Social Structure and Fertility: An Analytic Framework." *Economic Development and Cultural Change* 4: 211–235.

De Bary, Theodore, ed. 1970. *Self and Society in Ming Thought.* New York: Columbia University Press.

Demeny, Paul. 1986. "Population and the Invisible Hand." *Demography* 23: 473–487.

De Vries, Jan. 1975. "Peasant Demand and Economic Development: Friesland, 1550–1750." In *European Peasants and Their Markets,* ed. William Parker and E. L. Jones. Princeton: Princeton University Press, 205–265.

——— 1984. *European Urbanization, 1500–1800.* Cambridge, Mass.: Harvard University Press.

Dibble, Vernon, and Ho Ping-ti. 1961. "The Comparative Study of Social Mobility" (debate). *Comparative Studies in Society and History* 3: 315–327.

Dickeman, Mildred. 1975. "Demographic Consequences of Infanticide in Man." In *Annual Review of Ecology and Systematics,* ed. Richard Johnston, Peter Frank, and Charles Michener. Palo Alto: Annual Reviews.

——— 1979. "Female Infanticide, Reproductive Strategies, and Social Stratification: A Preliminary Model." In *Biology and Human Sexual Behavior: An Anthropological Perspective,* ed. N. A. Chagnon and William Irons. North Scituate, Mass.: Duxbury Press, 321–367.

Ding Yizhuang. 1996. "Assigned Marriage and Eight Banner Registration among the Manchus." Paper presented at the IUSSP Conference on Asian Population History, Taipei, January 4–8.

——— 1999. *Manzu de funü shenghuo yu hunyin zhidu yanjiu* (Research on Manchu women's history and on Manchu marriage). Beijing: Peking University Press.

Drake, Michael. 1981. "The Remarriage Market in Mid-Nineteenth Century Britain." In Dupâquier et al., 287–296.

D'Souza, Stan, and Lincoln C. Chen. 1980. "Sex Differentials in Mortality in Rural Bangladesh." *Population and Development Review* 6: 257–270.

Du Jiaji. 1994. "Qingdai tianhua bing de liuchuan, fangzhi jiqi dui huangzu renkou zhi yingxiang chutan" (The spread and prevention of smallpox by the Qing imperial lineage). In Lee and Guo, 154–169.

Du Halde, Jean Baptiste. 1738–1741. *A Description of the Empire of China and Chinese Tartary.* London: E. Cave.

Dunstan, Helen. 1975. "Late Ming Epidemics: A Preliminary Survey." *Ch'ing-shih wen't-i* 3: 1–59.

Dupâquier, Jacques, et al., eds. 1981. *Marriage and Remarriage in Populations of the Past.* London: Academic Press.

Durand, John. 1974. "Historical Estimates of World Population: An Evaluation." University of Pennsylvania, Population Studies Center.

Easterlin, Richard. 1996. *Growth Triumphant: The Twenty-first Century in Historical Perspective.* Ann Arbor: University of Michigan Press.

Eckstein, Alexander, Walter Galenson, and Liu Ta-chung eds. 1968. *Economic Trends in Communist China*. Chicago: Aldine and Wesley.

Ehrlich, Paul. 1968/1971. *Population Bomb*. New York: Ballantine–Sierra Club.

Ehrlich, Paul, and Anne Ehrlich. 1990. *The Population Explosion*. New York: Simon and Schuster.

Elvin, Mark. 1973. *The Pattern of the Chinese Past*. Stanford: Stanford University Press.

Evans, Harriet. 1995. "Defining Difference: The "Scientific" Construction of Sexuality and Gender in the People's Republic of China." *Signs* 20: 357–394.

Fan Jingjing. 1995. *Zhongguo renkou nianling xingbie jiegou* (China population structure by age and sex). Beijing: Zhongguo renkou chubanshe.

Fang Xing. 1996. "Qingdai Jiangnan nongmin de xiaofei" (On the consumption of peasants in Qing Jiangnan). *Zhongguo jingjishi yanjiu* (Beijing) 3: 91–98.

Faure, David. 1989. *The Rural Economy of Pre-Liberation China: Trade Increase and Peasant Livelihood in Jiangsu and Guangdong, 1870–1937*. Hong Kong: Oxford University Press.

Fauve-Chamoux, Antoinette. 1987. *Evolution agraire et croissance démographique*. Liège: Ordina Editions.

Feeney, Griffith, and Wang Feng. 1993. "Parity Progression and Birth Interval in China: The Influence of Policy in Hastening Fertility Decline." *Population and Development Review* 19: 61–101.

Feeney, Griffith, Wang Feng, Zhou Mingkun, and Xiao Baoyu. 1989. "Recent Fertility Dynamics in China: Results from the 1987 One Percent Population Survey." *Population and Development Review* 15: 297–322.

Feeney, Griffith, and Yu Jingyuan. 1987. "Period Parity Progression Measures of Fertility in China." *Population Studies* 41: 77–102.

Feeney, Griffith, and Yuan Jianhua. 1994. "Below Replacement Fertility in China? A Close Look at Recent Evidence." *Population Studies* 48: 381–394.

Fei Xiaotong. 1939. *Peasant Life in China*. London: Routledge and Kegan Paul.

—— 1946. "Peasantry and Gentry: An Interpretation of Chinese Social Structure and Its Changes." *American Journal of Sociology* 52: 1–17.

—— 1947/1998. *Xiangtu Zhongguo, Shengyu zhidu* (Earthbound China and the system of reproduction). Beijing: Beijing daxue chubanshe.

Feng Erkang. 1986. "Qingdai dc hunyin zhidu yu fuuu de shehui diwei shulun" (The state of women and the Qing marriage system). *Qingshi yanjiu ji* 5: 305–343.

Feng Fanghui. 1996. *Zhongguo hunyin shuju ji* (A collection of marriage data of China). Beijing: Zhongguo renkou chubanshe.

Feng Han-chi. 1937. "The Chinese Kinship System." *Harvard Journal of Asiatic Studies* 2: 142–289.

Field, Robert Michael. 1988. "Trends in the Value of Agricultural Output, 1978–1986." *China Quarterly* 116: 556–591.

Finegan, Michael. 1988. "Inheritance and Family Structure in Qing China: Evidence from Taiwan and Fujian." Manuscript.

Finegan, Michael, and Ted Telford. 1988. "Chinese Archival Holdings at the Genealogical Society of Utah." *Late Imperial China* 9: 86–114.

Finkle, Jason. 1985. "Ideology and Politics in Mexico City: The United States at the 1984 International Conference on Population." *Population and Development Review* 11: 1–28.

Flinn, Michael W. 1981. *The European Demographic System, 1500–1820.* Baltimore: Johns Hopkins University Press.

Floud, Roderick, Kenneth Wachter, and Annabel Gregory. 1990. *Height, Health, and History: Nutritional Status in the United Kingdom, 1750–1980.* Cambridge: Cambridge University Press.

Fogel, Robert. 1986. "Nutrition and the Decline in Mortality since 1700: Some Preliminary Findings." In *Long-Term Factors in American Economic Growth,* ed. Stanley L. Engerman and Robert E. Gallman. Chicago: University of Chicago Press, 439–555.

Freedman, Maurice. 1966. *Chinese Lineage and Society.* London: Athlone.

Freedman, Ronald, Xiao Zhenyu, Li Bohua, and William R. Lavely. 1988. "Local Area Variations in Reproductive Behavior in the People's Republic of China, 1973–1982." *Population Studies* 42: 39–57.

Frolic, Michael B. 1980. *Mao's People.* Cambridge, Mass.: Harvard University Press.

Fu Yiling. 1991. *Ming Qing fengjian tudi suoyouzhi lungang* (An outline about feudal land ownership in Ming and Qing China). Shanghai: Shanghai renmin chubanshe.

Fu Zhufu and Gu Shutang. 1956. "Zhongguo yuanshi ziben jilei fasheng chihuan de yuanyin" (The causes of the slowness of Chinese primitive capital accumulation). *Tianjin ribao,* Dec 7.

Fukayama, Francis. 1992. *The End of History and the Last Man.* New York: Free Press.

Furth, Charlotte. 1994. "Rethinking Van Gulik: Sexuality and Reproduction in Traditional Chinese Medicine." In *Engendering China: Woman, Culture, and State,* ed. Christina Gilmartin et al. Cambridge, Mass.: Harvard University Press, 125–146.

———. 1998. *A Flourishing Yin: Gender in China's Medical History, 960–1665.* Berkeley: University of California Press.

Galloway, Patrick R. 1988. "Basic Patterns in Annual Variation in Fertility, Nuptiality, Mortality, and Prices in Pre-industrial Europe." *Population Studies* 42: 275–303.

——— 1994. "Secular Changes in the Short Term: Preventive, Positive, and Temperature Checks to Population Growth in Europe, 1460 to 1909." *Climate Change* 26: 3–63.

Gamble, Sidney D. 1954. *Ting Hsien: A North China Rural Community.* Stanford: Stanford University Press.

Gautier, Etienne, and Louis Henry. 1958. *La population de Crulai, paroisse Normande: Etude historique.* Paris: Presses Universitaires de France.

Ge Jianxiong, ed. 1997. *Zhungguo yimin shi* (Chinese migration history). Fuzhou: Fujian renmin chubanshe.

Ge Jianxiong, Cao Shuji, and Wu Shengdi. 1993. *Jianming Zhongguo yimin shi* (A short history of Chinese migrations). Fuzhou: Fujian renmin chubanshe.

Gillis, John. 1985. *For Better, for Worse: British Marriages, 1600 to the Present.* Oxford: Oxford University Press.

Gillis, John, Louise Tilly, and David Levine, eds. 1992. *The European Experience of Declining Fertility, 1850–1970: The Quiet Revolution.* Cambridge, Mass.: Blackwell.

Glendon, Mary Ann. 1989. *The Transformation of Family Law: State, Law, and Family in the United States and Western Europe.* Chicago: University of Chicago Press.

Goldscheider, Frances, and Linda J. Waite. 1991. *New Families, No Families? Transformation of the American Home.* Berkeley: University of California Press.

Goldstein, Alice, and Wang Feng, eds. 1996. *China: The Many Facets of Demographic Change.* Boulder: Westview Press.

Goode, William J. 1993. *World Change in Divorce Patterns.* New Haven: Yale University Press.

Goody, Jack. 1983. *The Development of the Family and Marriage in Europe.* Cambridge: Cambridge University Press.

——— 1996. *The East in the West.* Cambridge: Cambridge University Press.

Goubert, Pierre. 1960. *Beauvais et les Beauvaisois de 1600 à 1730.* 2 vols. Paris: SEPVN.

Greenhalgh, Susan. 1986. "Shifts in China's Population Policy, 1984–86: Views from the Central, Provincial, and Local Levels." *Population and Development Review* 12: 491–515.

——— 1988. "Fertility as Mobility: Sinic Transitions." *Population and Development Review* 14: 629–674.

——— 1993. "The Peasantization of the One-Child Policy in Shaanxi." In Davis and Harrell, 219–250.

———, ed. 1995. *Situating Fertility: Anthropological and Demographic Inquiry.* Cambridge: Cambridge University Press.

——— 1996. "The Social Construction of Population Science: An Intellectual, Institutional, and Political History of Twentieth-Century Demography." *Comparative Studies in Society and History* 38: 26–66.

Greenough, Paul R. 1982. *Prosperity and Misery in Modern Bengal: The Famine of 1943–1944.* New York: Oxford University Press.

Grigg, D. B. 1980. *Population Growth and Agrarian Change.* Cambridge: Cambridge University Press.

Gu Baochang and Krishna Roy. 1995. "Sex Ratio at Birth in China, with Reference to Other Areas in East Asia: What We Know." *Asia-Pacific Population Journal* 10.3: 17–42.

Gu Jigang. 1982. "You cheng bao deng hunyin fangshi kan shehui zhidu di bianqian" (Social change and levirate and other marriage forms). *Wenshi* 14: 1–29; 15: 1–25.

Guo Shenyang. 1996. "Determinants of Fertility Decline in Shanghai: Development or Policy?" In Goldstein and Wang, 81–96.

Guo Songyi. 1987. "Qingdai renkou wenti yu hunyin zhuangkuang de kaocha." (An investigation of population and marriage during the Qing dynasty). *Zhongguoshi yanjiu* 3: 123–137.

——— Forthcoming. *Qingdai hunyin jiating guanxi yanjiu* (Marriage and family relations during the Qing). Beijing: Shangwu yinshuguan.

Guo Songyi et al. 1991. *Qingdai quanshi* (The complete history of the Qing dynasty). 6 vols. Shenyang: Liaoning renmin chubanshe.

Guo Wentao. 1988. *Zhongguo nongye keji fazhan shilue* (A short history of the development of Chinese agricultural technology). Beijing: Zhongguo kexue jishu chubanshe.

Guo Zhigang. 1995. *Dangdai Zhongguo renkou fazhan yu jiatinghu de bianqian* (Changes in population and family household in contemporary China). Beijing: Zhongguo renmin daxue chubanshe.

Hajnal, John. 1953. "Age at Marriage and Proportions Marrying." *Population Studies* 7: 111–136.

——— 1965. "European Marriage Patterns in Perspective." In *Population in History: Essays in Historical Demography*, ed. D. V. Glass and D. E. Eversley. Chicago: Aldine Publishing, 101–140.

——— 1982. "Two Kinds of Preindustrial Household Formation System." *Population and Development Review* 8: 449–494.

Hanley, Susan B., and Arthur P. Wolf, eds. 1985. *Family and Population in East-Asian History*. Stanford: Stanford University Press.

Hardee-Cleaveland, Karen, and Judith Banister. 1988. "Fertility Policy and Implementation in China, 1986–88." *Population and Development Review* 14: 245–286.

Hareven, Tamara. 1987. "Divorce Chinese style." *Atlantic Monthly*, April, 70–76.

Harrell, Stevan. 1985. "The Rich Get Children: Segmentation, Stratification, and Population in Three Chekiang Lineages." In Hanley and Wolf, 81–109.

——— 1987. "On the Holes in Chinese Genealogies." *Late Imperial China* 8: 53–79.

———, ed. 1995. *Chinese Historical Microdemography*. Berkeley: University of California Press.

Harrell, Stevan, and Tom Pullum. 1995. "Marriage, Mortality, and the Developmental Cycle in Three Xiaoshan Lineages." In Harrell, 141–162.

Henderson, Gail E., and Myron S. Cohen. 1984. *The Chinese Hospital: A Socialist Work Unit*. New Haven: Yale University Press.

Henry, Louis. 1961. "Some Data on Natural Fertility." *Eugenics Quarterly* 8.2: 81–91.

Hinde, P. R. A. 1985. "The Fertility Transition in Rural England." Ph.D. diss., University of Sheffield.

Ho Ping-ti. 1955. "The Introduction of American Food Plants into China." *American Anthropologist* 57: 191–201.

——— 1956. "Early-Ripening Rice in Chinese History." *Economic History Review* 9: 200–218.

——— 1959. *Studies on the Population of China, 1368–1953.* Cambridge, Mass.: Harvard University Press.

——— 1964. *The Ladder of Success in Imperial China.* New York: Columbia University Press.

——— 1965. "An Historian's View of the Chinese Family System." In *Man and Civilization: The Family's Search for Survival,* ed. Seymour Farber, Piero Mustacchi, and Roger Wilson. New York: McGraw-Hill, 15–30.

——— 1968. "Salient Aspects of China's Heritage." In *China in Crisis,* ed. Ho Ping-ti and Tsou Tang. Chicago: University of Chicago Press, 1–92.

——— 1969a. *Huangtu yu Zhongguo nongye de qiyuan* (The Loess soil of China and the origins of Chinese agriculture). Hong Kong: Chinese University of Hong Kong.

——— 1969b. "The Loess and the Origins of Chinese Agriculture." *American Historical Review* 75: 1–36.

——— 1975. *Cradle of the East.* Hong Kong: Chinese University of Hong Kong Press.

——— 1977. "Chinese Civilization: The Search for the Roots of Its Longevity." *Journal of Asian Studies* 35: 547–554.

——— 1978. "Meizhou zuowu de yinjin juanbo jiqi dui Zhongguo liangshi shengchan de yingxiang" (The introduction and diffusion of American food plants into China and their impact on food production). In *Da Gongbao fukan sanshi zhounian wenji* (A collection of essays in celebration of the thirtieth anniversary of Da Gongbao). Hong Kong: Da Gongbao, 673–731.

——— 1995. *Zhongguo lidai tudi shuzi kaoshi* (An examination of Chinese registered acreage figures). Taibei: Lianjing chubanshe.

Hofsten, E., and H. Lundstrom. 1976. *Swedish Population History: Main Trends from 1750 to 1970.* Stockholm: Statistiska Centralbyrån.

Hong Huanchun. 1989. "Ming Qing shidai Changjiang sanjiaozhou diqu de jingji youshi he tedian" (Economic advantages and characteristic features in the Yangzi delta during the Ming and Qing times). In *Changjiang sanjiaozhou difang shehui jingji shi yanjiu* (Local economic history of the Jiangnan Delta region), ed. Hong Huanchan and Luo Lun. Nanjing: Nanjing daxue chubanshe, 286–365.

Honig, Emily. 1984. "Courtship, Love, and Marriage: The Life and Times of Yu Luojin." *Pacific Affairs* 57: 252–269.

Honig, Emily, and Gail Herschatter. 1988. *Personal Voices: Chinese Women in the 1980s.* Stanford: Stanford University Press.

Hou Yangfang. 1997. "Ming Qing shiqi Jiangnan diqu renkou yu shehui jingji bianqian" (Population and socioeconomic change in the Jiangnan Region during the Ming and Qing). Ph.D. diss., Fudan University.

Hsiao Kung-chuan. 1979. *A History of Chinese Political Thought,* trans. F. W. Mote. Princeton: Princeton University Press.

Hsieh Jih-chang and Chuang Ying-chang, eds. 1985. *The Chinese Family and Its Ritual Behavior.* Taibei: Institute of Ethnology, Academia Sinica.

Hsiung Ping-chen. 1995a. "To Nurse the Young: Breast-feeding and Infant Feeding in Late Imperial China." *Journal of Family History* 20: 217–238.

——— 1995b. *Youyou: Chuantong Zhongguo de chiangbao zhi dao* (Childhood: Traditional Chinese infant care). Taibei: Lianjing.

——— Forthcoming. "More or Less: Cultural and Medical Factors behind Marital Fertility in Late Imperial China." In Lee and Saito.

Hu Hsien-chin. 1948. *The Common Descent Group in China and Its Functions.* New York: Viking Fund.

Huang, Philip. 1985. *The Peasant Economy and Social Change in North China.* Stanford: Stanford University Press.

——— 1990. *The Peasant Family and Rural Development in the Yangzi Delta, 1350–1988.* Stanford: Stanford University Press.

——— 1996. *Civil Justice in China: Representation and Practice in the Qing.* Stanford: Stanford University Press.

Huang, Philip, and Kathryn Bernhardt. 1994. *Civil Law in Qing and Republican China.* Stanford: Stanford University Press.

Huang, Ray. 1981. *1587, A Year of No Significance: The Ming Dynasty in Decline.* New Haven: Yale University Press.

Huang Rongqing and Liu Yan. 1995. *Zhongguo renkou siwang shuju ji* (A collection of mortality data of China's population). Beijing: Zhongguo renkou chubanshe.

Hulsewe, A. F. P. 1985. *Remnants of Ch'in Law.* Leiden: E. J. Brill.

Huntington, Samuel. 1995. *The Clashes of Civilizations.* New York: Simon and Schuster.

INS (Immigration and Naturalization Service Office of Policy and Planning, Statistics Division). 1997. "Estimates of the Unauthorized Immigrant Population Residing in the U.S., October 1, 1996." News release, February 7.

Jain, Anrudh K., T. C. Hsu, Ronald Freedman, and M. C. Chang. 1970. "Demographic Aspects of Lactation and Postpartum Amenorrhea." *Demography* 7: 255–271.

Jain, Anrudh K., Albert Hermalin, and T. H. Sun. 1979. "Lactation and Natural Fertility." In *Natural Fertility: Patterns and Determinants of Natural Fertility,* ed. Henri Leridon and Jane Menken. Liège: Ordina Editions, 149–194.

James, Patricia. 1979. *Population Malthus, His Life and Times.* Boston: Routledge and Kegan Paul.

Jamison, Dean, et al. 1984. *China: The Health Sector.* Washington, D.C.: World Bank.

Jiang Tao. 1993. *Zhongguo jindai renkou shi* (Modern Chinese population history). Hangzhou: Zhejiang renmin chubanshe.

Jiang Zhenhua, Li Shuzuo, and Sun Fubin. 1993. "Zhongguo disici renkou pucha siwang loubao he siwang shuiping yanjiu" (Research on death underreporting and mortality from China's fourth census). In *China's 1990 Population Census*. Beijing: China Statistical Press, 521–528.

Johansson, Sheila. 1994. "Food for Thought: Rhetoric and Reality in Modern Mortality History." *Historical Methods* 27: 101–125.

Johansson, Sten, Zhao Xuan, and Ola Nygren. 1991. "On Intriguing Sex Ratios among Live Births in China in the 1980s." *Journal of Official Statistics* 7: 25–43.

Johnson, D. Gale. 1994. "Effects of Institutions and Policies on Rural Population Growth and Application to China." *Population and Development Review* 20: 503–531.

Johnson, D. Gale, and Ronald D. Lee, eds. 1987. *Population Growth and Economic Development: Issues and Evidence*. Madison: University of Wisconsin Press.

Johnson, Kay Ann. 1983. *Women, the Family, and Peasant Revolution in China*. Chicago: University of Chicago Press.

Johnson, Kay Ann, Huang Banghan, and Wang Liyao. 1998. "Infant Abandonment and Adoption in China." *Population and Development Review* 24: 469–510.

Johnson, Wallace. 1997. *The T'ang Code*. Vol. 2: *Specific Articles*. Princeton: Princeton University Press.

Kertzer, David. 1993. *Sacrificed for Honor: Child Abandonment in Italy*. Boston: Beacon Books.

Kertzer, David, and Tom Fricke. 1997. *Anthropological Demography: Toward a New Synthesis*. Chicago: University of Chicago Press.

Keyfitz, Nathan. 1992. "Seven Ways of Causing the Less Developed Countries' Population Problems to Disappear—in Theory." *European Journal of Population* 8: 149–167.

——— 1996. "Population and the Environment." *Population Studies* 50: 335–359.

Kinney, Anne Behnke, ed. 1995. *Chinese Views of Childhood*. Honolulu: University of Hawaii Press.

Kito, Hiroshi. 1991. "Zen kindai Nihon no shushō-ryoku: Kōshoshushō-ritsu wa jijitsu dattaka" (Fertility in premodern Japan: was fertility truly high?). *Jyōchi keizai ronshū* 36: 83–98.

Knodel, John. 1983. "Natural Fertility: Age Patterns, Levels, and Trends." In Bulatao and Lee, 61–102.

——— 1988. *Demographic Behavior in the Past: A Study of Fourteen German Village Populations in the Eighteenth and Nineteenth Centuries*. Cambridge: Cambridge University Press.

Knodel, John, and Etienne van de Walle. 1986. "Lessons of the Past: Policy Implications of Fertility Studies." In Coale and Watkins, 390–420.

Kolmos, John. 1994. *Stature, Living Standards, and Economic Development.* Chicago: University of Chicago Press.

Kurosu, Satomi, and Emiko Ochiai. 1995. "Adoption as an Heirship Strategy under Demographic Constraints: A Case from Nineteenth-Century Japan." *Journal of Family History* 20: 261–288.

Kwon, T. 1993. "Exploring Socio-cultural Explanations of the Fertility Transition in South Korea." In Leete and Alam, 41–53.

Lach, Donald F., and Edwin J. Van Kley. 1993. *Asia in the Making of Europe.* Vol. 3: *A Century of Advance,* Book 4. Chicago: University of Chicago Press.

LaFleur, William. 1992. *Liquid Life: Abortion and Buddhism in Japan.* Princeton: Princeton University Press.

Landers, John. 1986. "Mortality, Weather, and Prices in London, 1675–1825: A Study of Short-Term Fluctuations." *Journal of Historical Geography* 12: 347–364.

Lang, Olga. 1946. *Chinese Family and Society.* New Haven: Yale University Press.

Langer, William. 1974a. "Further Notes on the History of Infanticide." *History of Childhood Quarterly* 2: 129–134.

——— 1974b. "Infanticide: A Historical Survey." *History of Childhood Quarterly* 1: 553–565.

Laslett, Peter. 1977. *Family Life and Illicit Love in Earlier Generations.* Cambridge: Cambridge University Press.

——— 1983. "Family and Household as Work Group and Kin Group: Areas of Traditional Europe Compared." In Wall and Laslett, 513–564.

Laslett, Peter, and Richard Wall, eds. 1972. *Household and Family in Past Time.* Cambridge: Cambridge University Press.

Lavely, William. 1986. "Age Patterns of Chinese Marital Fertility, 1950–1981." *Demography* 23: 419–434.

——— 1991. "Marriage and Mobility under Rural Collectivism." In Watson and Ebrey, 286–312.

Lavely, William, and Ronald Freedman. 1990. "The Origins of Chinese Fertility Decline." *Demography* 27: 89–116.

Lavely, William, James Lee, and Wang Feng. 1990. "Chinese Demography: The State of the Field." *Journal of Asian Studies* 49: 807–834.

Lavely, William, William M. Mason, and Jiang Hong Li. 1996. "Infant Mortality in a Rural Chinese County." Paper presented at the annual meeting of the Population Association of America, New Orleans, May 9–11.

Lavely, William, and R. Bin Wong. 1998. "Revising the Malthusian Narrative: The Comparative Study of Population Dynamics in Late Imperial China." *Journal of Asian Studies* 57: 714–748.

Lee, Bernice. 1981. "Infanticide in China." In *Women in China,* ed. Richard Guisso and Stanley Johannson. Youngstown, N.J.: Philo Press, 163–177.

Lee, James. 1978. "Migration and Expansion in Chinese History." In *Human Migration: Patterns and Policies,* ed. William H. McNeill and Ruth S. Adams. Bloomington: Indiana University Press, 20–47.

―――― 1982a. "Food Supply and Population Growth in Southwest China, 1250–1850." *Journal of Asian Studies* 41: 709–746. A greatly expanded version was published as "Ming Qing shiqi Zhongguo xinan de jingji fazhan he renkou zengzhang," *Qingshi luncong* 5 (1984): 50–102, 287–288.

―――― 1982b. "The Legacy of Immigration in Southwest China, 1250–1850." *Annales de démographie historique,* 279–304.

―――― 1991. "Homicide et peine capitale en Chine à la fin de l'empire: Analyse statistique préliminaire des données." *Etudes Chinoises* 10: 113–134.

―――― 1994. "Zhongguo renkou zhidu: Qingdai renkou xingwei jiqi yiyi" (The Chinese demographic system: Qing population behaviors and their implications). In Lee and Guo, 8–24.

―――― Forthcoming. *The Political Economy of China's Southwestern Frontier: State Building and Economic Development, 1350–1850.* Cambridge, Mass.: Harvard University Asia Center.

Lee, James, Lawrence Anthony, and Alice Suen. 1988. "Liaoning sheng chengren siwang lu, 1796–1819" (Adult mortality in Liaoning, 1796–1819). In *Qingzhu diyi lishi dang'an guan liushi zhounian lunwen ji* (Proceedings of the symposium on the occasion of the sixtieth anniversary of the First Historical Archives). Vol. 2. Beijing: Zhonghua shuju, 885–898.

Lee, James, and Cameron Campbell. 1997. *Fate and Fortune in Rural China: Social Organization and Population Behavior in Liaoning, 1774–1873.* Cambridge: Cambridge University Press.

Lee, James, Cameron Campbell, and Tan Guofu. 1992. "Infanticide and Family Planning in Late Imperial China: The Price and Population History of Rural Liaoning, 1774–1873." In Rawski and Li, 145–176.

Lee, James, Cameron Campbell, and Wang Feng. 1993. "The Last Emperors: An Introduction to the Demography of the Qing (1644–1911) Imperial Lineage." In *New and Old Methods in Historical Demography,* ed. Roger Schofield and David Reher. Oxford: Oxford University Press, 361–382.

Lee, James, and Guo Songyi, eds. 1994. *Qingdai huangzu renkou xingwei he shehui huanjing* (The Qing imperial lineage: Population behavior and social setting). Peking: Peking University Press.

Lee, James, and Osamu Saito, eds. Forthcoming. *Abortion, Infanticide, and Reproductive Behavior in Asia: Past and Present.* Oxford: Oxford University Press.

Lee, James, and Wang Feng. In press. "Male Nuptiality among the Qing Imperial Lineage: Polygyny or Serial Monogamy." In *Fertility and the Male Life Cycle in the Era of Fertility Decline,* ed. Caroline Bledsoe, Susana Lerner, and Jane Guyer. Oxford: Oxford University Press.

Lee, James, Wang Feng, and Cameron Campbell. 1994. "Infant and Child Mortality among the Late Imperial Chinese Nobility: Implications for Two Kinds of Positive Check." *Population Studies* 48: 395–411.

Lee, James, Wang Feng, and Ruan Danching. In press. "Nuptiality among the Qing Nobility: Implications for Two Types of Marriage Systems." In Liu Ts'ui-jung et al.

Lee, James, and R. Bin Wong. 1991. "Population Movements in Qing China and Their Linguistic Legacy." In *Languages and Dialects of China,* ed. William Wong. Journal of Chinese Linguistics Monograph Series no. 3. Berkeley, 52–77.

Lee, Ronald. 1987. "Population Dynamics of Humans and Other Animals." *Demography* 24: 443–467.

Leete, Richard, and Iqbal Alam. 1993. *The Revolution in Asian Fertility: Dimensions, Causes, and Implications.* Oxford: Clarendon Press.

Leridon, Henri. 1977. *Human Fertility.* Chicago: University of Chicago Press.

Lesthaeghe, Ron, ed. 1989. *Reproduction and Social Organization in Sub-Saharan Africa.* Berkeley: University of California Press.

Leung, Angela. 1987. "Ming Qing yufang tianhua choshi zhi yanbian" (The development of smallpox preventive techniques during the Ming and Qing). In *Guoshi shilun,* 239–253.

——— 1995. "Relief Institutions for Children in Nineteenth-Century China." In Kinney, 251–278.

——— 1997. *Shishan yu jiaohua: Ming Qing de cishan zuzhi* (To do good: The organization of charity during the Ming Qing). Taibei: Lianjing chubanshe.

Levy, Marion J., Jr. 1949. *The Family and Revolution in Modern China.* Cambridge, Mass.: Harvard University Press.

Li Bozhong. 1994. "Kongzhi zengzhang, yibao fuyu: Qingdai qianzhongqi Jiangnan de renkou xingwei" (Controlling population to guarantee wealth: Population behavior in Jiangnan during the Mid-Qing). *Xin shixue* 5: 25–71.

——— 1996a. "Cong 'fufu bing zuo' dao 'nan geng nu zhi'—Ming Qing Jiangnan nongjia funu laodong wenti tantao zhi yi" (From "husband and wife working together" to "men farming and women weaving"—a study of labor of peasant women in Ming-Qing Jiangnan [part 1]). *Zhongguo jingjishi yanjiu* (Beijing) 3: 99–107.

——— 1996b. "'Ren geng shi mu' yu Ming Qing Jiangnan nongmin de jingying guimo" ("A man works on ten mu" and the farm management scale in Ming-Qing Jiangnan). *Zhongguo nongshi* (Nanjing) 1: 1–14.

——— 1996c. "'Renkou yali' yu 'zuidi shenghuo shuizhun' zhiyi" (A query on "population pressure" and "minimum subsistence level of living"). *Zhongguo shehui jingjishi yanjiu* (Xiamen) 3: 31–37.

——— 1997a. "Funu 'banbiantian' juese de xingcheng—Ming Qing Jiangnan nongjia funu laodong wenti tantao zhi er" (The making of the role of "half the sky"—a study of labor of peasant women in Ming-Qing Jiangnan [part 2]). *Zhongguo jingjishi yanjiu* 3: 10–22.

——— 1997b. "You wu shi si shiji de zhuanzhe: Song mo zhi Ming chu Jiangnan renkou, gengdi, jishu yu nongmin jingying fangshi de bianhua" (Was there a "thirteenth- and fourteenth-century turning point": Changes in population, cultivated land, agricultural technology, and farm management in Jiangnan during the period from the late Song to early Ming). Paper presented to the Conference on the Song-Yuan-Ming Transition, Arrowhead, Calif., June 5–11.

—— 1998. *Agricultural Development in Jiangnan, 1620–1850.* New York: St. Martin's Press.

—— 1999. *Fazhan yu zhiyue: Ming Qing Jiangnan shengchan li yanjiu* (Development and its limitation: A study of productive force in Ming-Qing Jiangnan). Taibei: Lienjing Press.

—— Forthcoming. "Duotai, biyun yu jueyu: Song Yuan Ming Qing Jiangzhe diqu de jieyu fangfa jiqi yunyong yu chuanbo" (Abortion, contraception, and sterilization: Birth control methods and their dissemination in Song-Yuan-Ming-Qing Jiangsu and Zhejiang). In *Hunyin yu jiating: Dongxi bijiao shi* (Marriage and family, East-West comparative methods), ed. Ding Yizhuang, Guo Songyi, and James Lee. Peking: Peking University Press.

Li Chengrui, ed. 1986. *A Census of One Billion People.* Beijing: Population Census Office, State Council and Department of Population Statistics, State Statistical Bureau.

Li, Lillian. 1982. "Introduction: Food, Famine, and the Chinese State." *Journal of Asian Studies* 41: 687–707.

—— 1992. "Grain Prices in Zhili Province, 1736–1911." In Rawski and Li, 69–99.

Liang Fangzhong. 1980. *Zhongguo lidai hukou, tiandi, tianfu, tongji* (Chinese population, cultivated acreage, and land-tax statistics through the ages). Shanghai: Shanghai renmin chubanshe.

—— 1984. *Liang Fangzhong jingji shi lunwen ji bubian* (A supplemental collection of essays on economic history by Liang Fangzhong). Zhongzhou: Guji chubanshe.

Liang Jiamian, ed. 1989. *Zhongguo nongye kexue jishu shigao* (A draft history of agrarian science and technology in China). Beijing: Nongye chubanshe.

Liu, Jingzhen. 1994a. "Shazi yu niying: Songren shengyu wenti de xingbie chayi" (Killing sons and drowning daughters: Sex differentials in Song fertility). *Zhongguo lishi xuehui shixue jikan* 26: 99–106.

—— 1994b. "Songren shengzi buyu fengsu shitan: Jingjixing liyou de tansuo" (A preliminary study of the Song practice of infanticide and neglect: The economic rationales). *Dalu zazhi* 88.6: 19–41.

—— 1995a. "Cong huitaide baoying chuanshuo kan Songdai funu de shengyu wenti" (An examination of women's childbearing during the Song dynasty from the stories of punishment for infanticide and abortion). *Dalu zazhi* 90.1: 1–15.

—— 1995b. "Han Sui zhijian de "shengzi buju" wenti: Liuchao shengyu lisu yanjiu zhiyi" (Infanticide and neglect between the Han and Sui dynasties: A study of human fertility during the Six Dynasties). *Bulletin of the Institute of History and Philology* 66: 747–812.

Liu Ta-chung and Yeh Kung-chia. 1965. *The Economy of the Chinese Mainland: National Income and Economic Development, 1933–1959.* Princeton: Princeton University Press.

Liu Ts'ui-jung. 1978. "Chinese Genealogies as a Source for the Study of Historical Demography." In *Studies and Essays in Commemoration of the Golden Jubilee of the Academia Sinica.* Academia Sinica, 849–870.

———— 1981. "The Demographic Dynamics of Some Clans in the Lower Yangtze Area, ca. 1400–1900." *Academia Economica Papers* 9: 115–160.

———— 1983. "Ming Qing renkou zhi zengzhi yu qianyi: Changjiang zhong xiayou diqu zupu ziliao zhi fenxi" (Population growth and migration in the Ming and Qing: Analysis of genealogical materials from the Middle and Lower Yangzi). In *Dierqu Zhongguo shehui jingjishi yanjiuhui lunwen ji* (Papers from the Second Seminar on Chinese Social and Economic History), ed. Hsu Cho-yun, Mao Han-kuang, and Liu Ts'ui-jung. Taibei: Chinese Research Materials and Service Center, 283–316.

———— 1985. "The Demography of Two Chinese Clans in Hsiao-shan, Chekiang, 1650–1850." In Hanley and Wolf, 13–61.

———— 1986. "Agricultural Change and Population Growth: A Brief Survey on the case of China in Historical Perspective." *Academia Economic Papers* 14: 29–68.

———— 1992. *Ming Qing shiqi jiazu renkou yu shehui jingji bianqian* (Lineage population and socioeconomic changes in the Ming and Qing periods). 2 vols. Taibei: Institute of Economics, Academia Sinica.

———— 1995a. "Demographic Constraint and Family Structure in Traditional Chinese Lineages, ca. 1200–1900." In Harrell, 121–140.

———— 1995b. "Historical Demography of South China Lineages." In Harrell, 94–120.

Liu Ts'ui-jung et al., eds. In press. *Asian Historical Demography.* Oxford: Clarendon Press.

Livi-Bacci, Massimo. 1981. "On the Frequency of Remarriage in Nineteenth-Century Italy: Methods and Results." In Dupâquier et al., 347–362.

———— 1986. "Social-Group Forerunners of Fertility Control in Europe." In Coale and Watkins, 182–200.

Lukes, Stephen. 1973. *Individualism.* New York: Harper and Row.

Luo Lun. 1989. "Qingdai Su-Song-Jia-Hu difang nongye jiliang yanjiu de fazhan jiqi tuidong li" (Quantitative analysis of agriculture in the Su-Song-Jia-Hu area during the Qing dynasty). In *Changjiang sanjiaozhou difang shehui jingji shi yanjiu.* (Local economic history of the Jiangnan Delta region), ed. Hong Huanchun and Luo Lun. Nanjing: Nanjing daxue chubanshe.

Luther, Norman Y., Griffith Feeney, and Zhang Weimin. 1990. "One-Child Families or a Baby Boom? Evidence from China's 1987 One-per-Hundred Survey." *Population Studies* 44: 341–357.

Ma Yinchu. 1979. *Xin renkou lun* (A Theory of Population for New China). Beijing: Xinhua shudian.

Macfarlane, Alan. 1978. *The Origins of English Individualism: Family, Property, and Social Transition.* Oxford: Oxford University Press.

——— 1986. *Marriage and Love in England: Modes of Reproduction, 1300–1840.* Oxford: Basil Blackwell.

——— 1987. *The Culture of Capitalism.* Oxford: Oxford University Press, 1987.

——— 1997. *The Savage Wars of Peace: England, Japan, and the Malthusian Trap.* Oxford: Basil Blackwell.

Madsen, Richard. 1984. *Morality and Power in a Chinese Village.* Berkeley: University of California Press.

Mallory, Walter H. 1926. *China: The Land of Famine.* New York: American Geological Society.

Malthus, Thomas R. 1798/1803/1992. *An Essay on the Principle of Population, Second Edition,* ed. Donald Winch. Cambridge: Cambridge University Press.

——— 1826/1986. *The Works of Thomas Robert Malthus,* ed. E. A. Wrigley and David Souden. 7 vols. London: William Pickering.

Mason, Karen Oppenheim. 1997. "Explaining Fertility Transitions." *Demography* 34: 443–454.

Matras, Judah. 1965. "The Social Strategy of Family Formation: Some Variations in Time and Space." *Demography* 2: 349–362.

McAlpin, Michelle. 1983. *Subject to Famine: Food Crises and Economic Change in Western India.* Princeton: Princeton University Press.

McEvedy, Colin, and Richard Jones. 1978. *Atlas of World Population History.* New York: Penguin Books.

McGovern, William M. 1958. "Collectivism and Individualism." In *Essays on Individuality,* ed. Felix Morley. Philadelphia: University of Pennsylvania Press, 339–367.

McNicoll, Geoffrey. 1984. "Institutional Determinants of Fertility Change." *Population and Development Review* 6: 441–461.

——— 1992. "The Agenda of Population Studies: A Commentary and Complaint." *Population and Development Review* 18: 399–420.

Meijer, Marinus. 1978. "Marriage Law and Policy in the People's Republic of China." In Buxbaum, 436–486.

Mencius. 1970. *Mencius,* trans. D. C. Lau. London: Penguin Books.

Menken, Jane, and Cameron Campbell. 1992. "Implications for Long-Term Population Growth of Age Patterns of Famine-Related Mortality Increase." *Health Transition Review* 2: 91–101.

Meuvret, Jean. 1946. "Les crises de subsistence et la démographie de la France d'ancien regime." *Population* 1: 643–650.

Ministry of Public Health of China. 1991. *Selected Edition of Health Statistics of China.* Beijing: Center for Health Statistics Information.

Mitterauer, Michael, and Reinhard Sieder. 1982. *The European Family: Patriar-*

chy to Partnership from the Middle Ages to the Present. Chicago: University of Chicago Press.

Muhuri, Pradip K., and Samuel H. Preston. 1991. "Effects of Family Composition on Mortality Differentials by Sex among Children in Matlab, Bangladesh." *Population and Development Review* 17: 415–434.

Munro, Donald, ed. 1985. *Individualism and Holism: Studies in Confucian and Taoist Values.* Ann Arbor: University of Michigan, Center for Chinese Studies.

Myers, Ramon. 1980. *The Chinese Economy Past and Present.* Belmont: Wadsworth.

Naquin, Susan, and Evelyn Rawski. 1987. *Chinese Society in the Eighteenth Century.* New Haven: Yale University Press.

National Committee for Adoption. 1989. *Adoption Factbook, United States Data, Issues, Regulations, and Resources.* Washington, D.C.

National Research Council. 1986. *Population Growth and Economic Development: Policy Questions.* Washington, D.C.: National Academy Press.

Naughton, Barry. 1995. *Growing Out of the Plan: Chinese Economic Reform, 1978–1993.* Cambridge: Cambridge University Press.

Nee, Victor. 1985. "Peasant Household Individualism." In *Chinese Rural Development: The Great Transformation,* ed. William L. Parish. Armonk: M. E. Sharpe, 164–190.

Needham, Joseph. 1962. *Science and Civilization in China.* Vol. 2. Cambridge: Cambridge University Press.

Notestein, Frank W., and Chiao Chi-ming. 1937. "Population." In Buck 1937, 1: 358–399.

Office for National Statistics. 1997. *Social Focus on Families.* London: Her Majesty's Stationery Office.

Overbeek, Johannes. 1974. *History of Population Theories.* Rotterdam: Rotterdam University Press.

Ozment, Steven. 1983. *When Fathers Ruled: Family Life in Reformation Europe.* Cambridge, Mass.: Harvard University Press.

Page, Hillary, and Ron Lesthaeghe, eds. 1981. *Child Spacing in Tropical Africa: Traditions and Change.* New York: Academic Press.

Pan Ming-te. 1997. "Were They Better Off? Living Standards in the Rural Yangzi Delta, 1650–1800." Paper presented at the Economic History Conference on Rethinking the History of Wages, Prices, and Living Standards, Davis, California.

Parish, William, and Martin K. Whyte. 1978. *Village and Family in Contemporary China.* Chicago: University of Chicago Press.

Park Chai Bin and Nam-Hoon Cho. 1995. "Consequences of Son Preference in a Low-Fertility Society: Imbalance of the Sex Ratio at Birth in Korea." *Population and Development Review* 21: 1–26.

Peng Xizhe. 1987. "Demographic Consequences of the Great Leap Forward." *Population and Development Review* 13: 639–670.

———— 1989. "Major Determinants of China's Fertility Transition." *China Quarterly* 117: 1–37.

Perdue, Peter. 1992. "The Qing State and the Gansu Grain Market, 1739–1864." In Rawski and Li, 100–125.

———— 1998. "Constructing Chinese Property Rights: East and West." Paper presented at the annual meeting of the Association of Asian Studies, Washington, D.C.

Perkins, Dwight. 1969. *Agricultural Development in China, 1368–1968.* Chicago: Aldine Publishing.

Perot, Michelle, ed. 1990. *From the Fires of Revolution to the Great War,* trans. Arthur Goldhammer. Vol. 4 of *A History of Private Life,* ed. Philippe Ariès and Georges Duby. Cambridge, Mass.: The Belknap Press of Harvard University Press.

Perrenoud, Alfred. 1979. *La population de Genève du seizième au début du dix-neuvième siècle, Etude démographique.* Geneve: Julien.

Piazza, Alan. 1986. *Food Consumption and Nutritional Status in the People's Republic of China.* Boulder: Westview Press.

Pomeranz, Kenneth L. Forthcoming. *Economy, Ecology, Comparisons, and Connections: The World in the Age of the Industrial Revolution.* Princeton: Princeton University Press.

Pope, C. 1989. "Adult Mortality before the Twentieth Century: Current Evidence and New Sources." Paper presented to the UCLA Von Gremp Workshop in Economic History.

Population Reference Bureau. 1994. *World Population Data Sheet, 1994.* Washington, D.C.

Poston, Dudley, and Gu Baochang. 1987. "Socioeconomic Differentials and Fertility in Subregions of China." *Demography* 24: 531–552.

Press, Frank, and Raymond Siever. 1994. *Understanding Earth.* New York: W. H. Freeman.

Preston, Samuel T. 1976. *Mortality Patterns in National Populations.* New York: Academic Press.

———— 1980. "Causes and Consequences of Mortality Decline in Less Developed Countries during the Twentieth Century." In *Population and Economic Change in Developing Countries,* ed. Richard A. Easterlin. Chicago: University of Chicago Press, 289–341.

———— 1996a. "The Effect of Population Growth on Environmental Quality." *Population Research and Policy Review* 15: 95–108.

———— 1996b. "Population Studies of Mortality." *Population Studies* 50: 525–536.

Preston, Samuel, and Michael Haines. 1991. *Fatal Years: Child Mortality in Late Nineteenth-Century America.* Princeton: Princeton University Press.

Preston, Samuel, and Etienne van de Walle. 1978. "Urban French Mortality in the Nineteenth Century." *Population Studies* 32: 275–297.

Prost, Antoine, and Gerald Vincent, eds. 1991. *Riddles of Identity in Modern*

Times, trans. Arthur Goldhammer. Vol. 5 of *A History of Private Life,* ed. Philippe Ariès and Georges Duby. Cambridge, Mass.: The Belknap Press of Harvard University Press.

Pye, Lucian. 1996. "The State and the Individual: An Overview Interpretation." In *The Individual and the State in China,* ed. Brian Hook. Oxford: Oxford University Press, 16–42.

Rawski, Thomas. 1979. *Economic Growth and Employment in China.* New York: Oxford University Press

———— 1989. *Economic Growth in Prewar China.* Berkeley: University of California Press.

Rawski, Thomas, and Lillian Li, eds. 1992. *Chinese Economy in Historical Perspective.* Berkeley: University of California Press.

Ricardo, David. 1852. *Works,* ed. J. R. McCulloch. London: Murray.

Rindfuss, Ronald, and Philip Morgan. 1983. "Marriage, Sex, and First Bbirth Interval: The Quiet Revolution in Asia." *Population and Development Review* 9: 259–278.

Riskin, Carl. 1986. *China's Political Economy.* New York: Oxford University Press.

Rogaski, Ruth. 1996. "From Protecting the Body to Defending the Nation: The Emergence of Public Health in Tianjin, 1859–1953." Ph.D. diss., Yale University.

Rong Shoude and Li Guangji. 1986. "Zhongguo renkou siyin diaocha" (A study of mortality causes in China). In *1985 Zhongguo renkou nianjian* (China's population yearbook, 1985). Beijing: China Social Science Press, 1027–68.

Royal Society and National Academy of Sciences. 1991. *Population Growth, Resource Consumption, and a Sustainable World: A Joint Statement.* London: Royal Society.

Rozman, Gilbert. 1982. *Population and Marketing Settlements in Ch'ing China.* New York: Cambridge University Press.

Ruan Danching, Xinyuan Dai, Linton C. Freedman, Yunkang Pan, and Wenhong Zhang. 1997. "Personal Support Networks in China and in the Netherlands." Manuscript.

Saito, Osamu. 1996. "Historical Demography: Achievements and Prospects." *Population Studies* 50: 537–553.

Salaff, Janet. 1973. "Mortality Decline in the Peoples Republic of China and the United States." *Population Studies* 27: 551–576.

Santow, Gigi. 1995. "Coitus Interruptus and the Control of Natural Fertility." *Population Studies* 49: 19–43.

Saraceno, Chiara. 1991. "The Italian Family: Paradoxes of Privacy." In Prost and Vincent, 451–501.

Schofield, Roger. 1983. "The Impact of Scarcity on Population Change in England, 1541–1871." *Journal of Interdisciplinary History* 14: 265–291.

———— 1985. "English Marriage Patterns Revisited." *Journal of Family History* 10: 2–20.

——— 1989. "Family Structure, Demographic Behavior, and Economic Growth." In Walter and Schofield, 279–304.

Schofield, Roger, and David Reher. 1991. "The Decline of Mortality in Europe." In Schofield, Reher, and Bideau, 1–17.

Schofield, Roger, David Reher, and Alain Bideau, eds. 1991. *The Decline of Mortality in Europe*. Oxford: Clarendon Press.

Schran, Peter. 1969. *The Development of Chinese Agriculture, 1950–1959*. Urbana: University of Illinois Press.

——— 1978. "China's Demographic Evolution 1850–1953 Reconsidered." *China Quarterly* 75: 639–646.

Schultz, Theodore. 1983. "Review of John C. Caldwell, *Theory of Fertility Decline*." *Population and Development Review* 9: 161–168.

Schurmann, Franz. 1968. *Ideology and Organization in Communist China*. Berkeley: University of California Press.

Scogin, Hugh. 1990. "Between Heaven and Man: Contract and the State in Han Dynasty China." *Southern California Law Review* 63: 1325–1404.

Selden, Mark. 1971. *The Yenan Way in Revolutionary China*. Cambridge, Mass.: Harvard University Press.

Sen, Amartya. 1992. *Inequality Reexamined*. New York: Russell Sage Foundation; Oxford: Clarendon Press.

Shakai Keizaishi Gakkai. 1978. *Atarashii Edojidai shizo wo motomete* (Toward new perspectives on Tokugawa Japan). Tokyo: Tōyō keizai shinpōsha.

Shepherd, John. 1995. *Marriage and Mandatory Abortion among the 17th-Century Siraya*. Arlington, Va.: American Anthropological Association.

Shiba Yoshinobu. 1991. "Sodai no shohi-seisan suijun shitan" (An inquiry on consumption and production of Song China). *Chugoko Shigaku* 1: 147–172.

Shirokogoroff, S. M. 1924. *Social Organization of the Manchus*. Shanghai: North China Branch of the Royal Asiatic Society.

Skinner, G. William. 1964. "Marketing and Social Structure in Rural China, Part I." *Journal of Asian Studies* 24: 3–43.

——— 1965a. "Marketing and Social Structure in Rural China, Part II." *Journal of Asian Studies* 24: 195–228.

——— 1965b. "Marketing and Social Structure in Rural China, Part III." *Journal of Asian Studies* 24: 363–399.

———, ed. 1977. *The City in Late Imperial China*. Stanford: Stanford University Press.

——— 1985. "The Structure of Chinese History." *Journal of Asian Studies* 44: 271–292.

——— 1986. "The Population of Sichuan in the Nineteenth Century: Lessons from Disaggregated Data." *Late Imperial China* 7.2: 1–79.

——— 1997. "Family Systems and Demographic Processes." In Kertzer and Fricke, 53–95.

Skinner, Quentin. 1997. *Liberty before Liberalism*. Cambridge: Cambridge University Press.

Smedley, Agnes. 1958. *The Great Road: The Life and Times of Chu Teh*. London.
Smil, Vaclav. 1984. *The Bad Earth: Environmental Degradation in China*. Armonk, N.Y.: M. E. Sharpe.
——— 1993. *China's Environmental Crisis: An Inquiry into the Limits of National Development*. Armonk, N.Y.: M. E. Sharpe.
——— 1995. "Who Will Feed China?" *China Quarterly* 143: 801–813.
——— 1996. "Environmental Problems in China: Estimates of Economic Costs." *East-West Center Special Reports* 5: 1–62.
Smith, Adam. 1776/1979. *The Wealth of Nations*, ed. Andrew Skinner. New York: Penguin Books.
Smith, Herbert L., S. Philip Morgan, and Tanya Koropeckyj-Cox. 1996. "A Decomposition of Trends in the Nonmarital Fertility Ratios of Blacks and Whites in the United States, 1960–1992." *Demography* 33: 141–151.
Smith, Peter. *See* Xenos, Peter.
Solinger, Dorothy, J. 1999. *Contesting Citizenship in Urban China: Peasant Migrants, the State, and the Logic of the Market*. Berkeley: University of California Press.
Soloman, Richard H. 1971. *Mao's Revolution and the Chinese Political Culture*. Berkeley: University of California Press.
Song Jian. 1981. "Population Development—Goals and Plans." In *China's Population: Problems and Prospects*. Beijing: New World Press, 25–31.
Song Jian, Chi-hsien Tuan, and Jing-yuan Yu. 1985. *Population Control in China: Theory and Applications*. New York: Praeger.
Spence, Jonathan. 1975. "Opium Smoking in Ch'ing China." In *Conflict and Control in Late Imperial China*, ed. Frederic Wakeman and Carolyn Grant. Berkeley: University of California Press, 143–173.
SSB (State Statistical Bureau). 1982. *Zhongguo tongji nianjian 1981* (China statistical yearbook 1981). Beijing: Zhongguo tongji chubanshe.
———. 1986. *China In-Depth Fertility Survey (Phase I), Principal Report*. 2 vols. Beijing: Department of Population Statistics.
——— 1987. *1982 Population Census of China, One-Percent Household Sampling*. 4 vols. Beijing: Department of Population Statistics.
——— 1993. *Tabulations of the 1990 Population Census of the People's Republic of China*. 4 vols. Beijing: China Statistical Publishing House.
——— 1997. *1995 Quanguo 1% renkou chouyang diaocha ziliao* (Data of 1995 national population sample survey). Beijing: Zhongguo tongji chubanshe.
Stacey, Judith. 1983. *Patriarchy and Socialist Revolution in China*. Berkeley: University of California Press.
Statistika Centralbyrån. 1969. *Historisk statistik för Sverige. Del I. Befolkning. 1720–1967* (Historical statistics of Sweden. Part I: Population, 1720–1967). 2d ed. Stockholm.
Statistisk Sentralbyra. 1980. *Folketeljinga 1801* (Population census, 1801). Oslo: Norges Offisielle Statistikk B 134.

Steckel, Richard, ed. 1997. *Health and Welfare during Industrialization.* Chicago: University of Chicago Press.

Stevenson, Paul. 1926. "Anthropometry in China: An Extended Outline of Research." *Chinese Medical Journal* 40: 95–127.

Sun Jinxin. 1997. "The Characteristics of China's Four Population Censuses." In *Symposium on Demography of China, 23rd IUSSP General Population Conference.* Beijing: China Population Association, 3–14.

Sun Muhan. 1987. *Zhongguo jihua shengyu shigao* (A draft history of Chinese family planning). Beijing: Beifang funu ertong chubanshe.

Sun Yirang, ed. 1986. *Mozi xiangu* (Annotated works of Mozi). Beijing: Zhonghua shuju.

Szreter, S. R. S. 1988. "The Importance of Social Intervention in Britain's Mortality Decline c. 1850–1914: A Re-interpretation of the Role of Public Health." *Social History of Medicine* 1: 1–37.

Tang Qiyu. 1986. *Zhongguo zuowu zaipei shigao* (A draft history of plant cultivation in China). Beijing: Nongye chubanshe.

Tawney, R. H. 1932. *Land and Labor in China.* Boston: Beacon Press.

Telford, Ted A. 1986. "Survey of Social Demographic Data in Chinese Genealogies." *Late Imperial China* 7: 118–148.

———— 1990a. "Mortality and Social Structure in Late Imperial Tongcheng County." Paper presented at the annual meeting of the Association for Asian Studies, Chicago.

———— 1990b. "Patching the Holes in Chinese Genealogies: Mortality in the Lineage Populations of Tongcheng County, 1300–1880." *Late Imperial China* 11: 116–136.

———— 1992a. "Covariates of Men's Age at First Marriage: The Historical Demography of Chinese Lineages." *Population Studies* 46: 19–35.

———— 1992b. "Marital Fertility in the Ming-Qing Transition: Tongcheng County, 1520–1661." Manuscript.

———— 1994. "Family and State in Qing China: Marriage in the Tongcheng Lineages, 1650–1850." In *Jinshi jiazu yu zhengzhi bijiao lishi lunwen ji* (A comparative history of the state and family). Taibei: Academia Sinica, Institute of Modern History, 921—942.

———— 1995. "Fertility and Population Growth in the Lineages of Tongcheng County, 1520–1661." In Harrell, 48–93.

Telford, Ted A., Melvin P. Thatcher, and Basil P. N. Yang. 1983. *Chinese Genealogies at the Genealogical Society of Utah: An Annotated Bibliography.* Taibei: Ch'eng-wen Publishing.

Thatcher, Melvin. 1995. "Local Historical Sources for China at the Genealogical Society of Utah." *Hanxue yanjiu* 3: 419–459.

———— 1998. "Selected Sources for Late Imperial China on Microfilm at the Genealogical Society of Utah." *Late Imperial China* 19: 111–129.

Thornton, Arland. 1988. "Cohabitation and Marriage in the 1980s." *Demography* 25: 497–508.

Tien, H. Yuan. 1983. "China: Demographic Billionaire." *Population Bulletin* 38: 1–42.

Todd, Emmanuel. 1985. *The Explanation of Ideology: Family Structures and Social Systems.* Oxford: Basil Blackwell.

——— 1990. *Invention de l'Europe.* Paris: Seuil.

Touleman, Laurent. 1996. "Cohabitation est ici pour la durée." *Population* 51: 675–715.

Triandis, Harry C. 1995. *Individualism and Collectivism.* Boulder: Westview Press.

Trussell, James, and Charles Westoff. 1980. "Contraceptive Practices and Trends in Coital Frequency." *Family Planning Perspective* 12: 246–249.

United Nations. 1984. *Demographic Yearbook.* New York.

——— 1992. *Demographic Yearbook.* New York.

——— 1993. *World Population Prospect: The 1992 Edition.* New York.

U.S. Bureau of the Census. 1997. *Statistical Abstract of the United States: 1997.* 117th ed. Washington, D.C.: U.S. Government Printing Office, Superintendent of Documents.

Vallin, Jacques. 1991. "Mortality in Europe from 1720 to 1914: Long-Term Trends and Changes in Patterns by Age and Sex." In Schofield, Reher, and Bideau, 38–67.

Vallin, Jacques, and France Meslé. 1988. *Les causes de décès en France de 1925 à 1978.* Paris.

Van de Walle, Etienne. 1976. "Household Dynamics in a Belgian Village, 1847–1866." *Journal of Family History* 1: 80–94.

——— 1992. "Fertility Transition, Conscious Choice, and Numeracy." *Demography* 29: 487–502.

Wachter, Kenneth. 1981. "Graphical Estimation of Military Heights." *Historical Methods* 14: 31–42.

Wachter, Kenneth, and James Trussell. 1982. "Estimating Historical Heights." *Journal of the American Statistical Association* 77: 279–303.

Wakefield, David. 1992. "Household Division in Qing and Republican China: Inheritance, Family Property, and Economic Development." Ph.D. diss., University of California, Los Angeles.

Walder, Andrew G. 1986. *Communist Neo-Traditionalism.* Berkeley: University of California Press.

Walker, Kenneth R. 1988. "Trends in Crop Production, 1978–86." *China Quarterly* 116: 592–633.

Wall, Richard. 1981. "Inferring Differential Neglect of Females from Mortality Data." *Annales de démographie historique,* 119–140.

Wall, Richard, and Peter Laslett, eds. 1983. *Family Forms in Historic Europe.* Cambridge: Cambridge University Press.

Walter, John, and Roger Schofield. 1989. *Famine, Disease, and the Social Order in Early Modern Society.* Cambridge: Cambridge University Press.

Waltner, Ann. 1991. *Getting an Heir: Adoption and the Construction of Kinship in Late Imperial China.* Honolulu: University of Hawaii Press.
—— 1995. "Infanticide and Dowry in Ming and Early Qing China." In Kinney, 193–218.
Wang Feng. 1988. "The Roles of Individual Socioeconomic Characteristics and the Government Family Planning Program in China's Fertility Decline." *Population Research and Policy Review* 7: 255–276.
—— 1996. "A Decade of the One-Child Policy: Achievement and Implications." In Goldstein and Wang, 97–120.
—— Forthcoming. "The Rise of Abortion in Modern China." In Lee and Saito.
Wang Feng and James Lee. 1998. "Adoption among the Qing Nobility and Its Implications for Chinese Demographic Behavior." *History of the Family* 3: 411–427.
Wang Feng, James Lee, and Cameron Campbell. 1995. "Marital Fertility Control among the Late Imperial Chinese Nobility: Implications for Two Types of Preventive Check." *Population Studies* 49: 383–400.
Wang Feng and Nancy Tuma. 1993. "Changes in Chinese Marriage Patterns during the Twentieth Century." In *Proceedings of the IUSSP International Population Conference, Montreal.* Liège: IUSSP, 337–352.
Wang Feng and Yang Quanhe. 1996. "Age at Marriage and the First Birth Interval: The Emerging Change in Sexual Behavior among Young Couples in China." *Population Development Review* 22: 299–320.
Wang Shaowu, ed. 1981. *Zhongguo jin wubai nian hanlao fenbu tuji* (Annual maps of precipitation in China during the last five hundred years). Beijing: Ditu chubanshe.
Wang Tingyuan. 1993. "Lun Ming Qing shiqi Jiangnan mian fangzhi ye de laodong shouyi jiqi jingying xingtai" (On the labor return and management patterns in Ming-Qing Jiangnan cotton industry). In *Zhongguo jingjishi yanjiu* 2: 91–98.
Wang Yeh-chien. 1973. *Land Taxation in Imperial China, 1750–1911.* Cambridge, Mass.: Harvard University Press.
—— 1984. "Spatial and Temporal Patterns of Grain Prices in China, 1740–1910." Paper presented at the Conference on Chinese Economic History, Bellagio, Italy.
—— 1986. "Food Supply in Eighteenth-Century Fukien." *Late Imperial China* 7: 80–117
—— 1992. "Food Supply and Grain Prices in the Yangzi Delta in the Eighteenth Century." In Rawski and Li, 35–68.
Watkins, Susan Cotts, and Jane Menken. 1985. "Famine in Historical Perspective." *Population and Development Review* 11: 647–675.
—— 1988. "On the Roles of Crises in Historical Perspective." *Population and Development Review* 14: 165–170.
Watson, Rubie S., and Patricia Buckley Ebrey, eds. 1991. *Marriage and Inequality in Chinese Society.* Berkeley: University of California Press.

Wei Jinyu. 1983. "Ming Qing shidai nongye zhongdeng jixing guyong laodong xiang fei dengjixing guyong laodong de guodu" (The transition from moderately segmented labor markets to nonsegmented labor markets). In *Ming Qing shidai de nongye ziben zhuyi mengya wenti* (Incipient capitalism during the Ming and Qing periods), ed. Wei Jinyu and Jing Junjian. Beijing: Zhonggguo shehui kexue chubanshe, 318–516.

Weir, David. 1984a. "Life under Pressure: France and England, 1670–1870." *Journal of Economic History* 44: 27–47.

——— 1984b. "Rather Never than Late: Celibacy and Age at Marriage in English Cohort Fertility, 1541–1871." *Journal of Family History* 9: 341–355.

White, Kevin M., and Samuel H. Preston. 1996. "How Many Americans Are Alive Because of Twentieth-Century Improvements in Mortality?" *Population and Development Review* 22: 415–430.

Whyte, Martin King. 1990. "Changes in Mate Choice in Chengdu." In *Chinese Society on the Eve of Tiananmen,* ed. Deborah Davis and Ezra F. Vogel. Cambridge, Mass.: Harvard University Press, 181–214.

——— 1993. "Wedding Behavior and Family Strategies in Chengdu." In Davis and Harrell, 189–218.

——— 1995. "The Social Roots of China's Economic Development." *China Quarterly* 144: 999–1019.

Whyte, Martin King, and William Parish. 1984. *Urban Life in Contemporary China.* Chicago: University of Chicago Press.

Wile, Douglas. 1992. *Art of Bedchamber: The Chinese Sexual Yoga Classics Including Women's Solo Meditation Texts.* Albany: State University of New York Press.

Will, Pierre-Etienne. 1990. *Bureaucracy and Famine in Nineteenth-Century China.* Stanford: Stanford University Press.

Will, Pierre-Etienne, and R. Bin Wong, with James Lee, eds. 1991. *Nourish the People: The State Civilian Granary System in China, 1650–1850.* Ann Arbor: University of Michigan, Center for Chinese Studies.

Wilson, Chris. 1984. "Natural Fertility in Preindustrial England, 1600–1799." *Population Studies* 38: 225–240.

——— 1985. "What Is Natural Fertility? The Modeling of a Concept." *Population Index* 54: 4–20.

Wolf, Arthur. 1981. "Women, Widowhood, and Fertility in Pre-modern China." In Dupâquier et al., 139–150.

——— 1984. "Family Life and the Life Cycle in Rural China." In *Households: Comparative and Historical Studies of the Domestic Group,* ed. Robert McC. Netting, Richard Wilk, and Eric Arnould. Berkeley: University of California Press, 279–298.

——— 1985a. "Chinese Family Size: A Myth Revitalized." In Hsieh and Chuang, 30–49.

——— 1985b. "Fertility in Prerevolutionary Rural China." In Hanley and Wolf, 154–185.

—— 1995. *Sexual Attraction and Childhood Association: A Chinese Brief for Edward Westermark*. Stanford: Stanford University Press.

Wolf, Arthur, and Huang Chieh-shan. 1980. *Marriage and Adoption in China, 1845–1945*. Stanford: Stanford University Press.

Wolf, Margery. 1968. *The House of Lim: A Study of a Chinese Farm Family*. New York: Appleton-Century.

—— 1992. *Revolution Postponed: Women in Contemporary China*. Stanford: Stanford University Press.

Wong, R. Bin. 1992. "Chinese Economic History and Development: A Note on the Myers-Huang Exchange." *Journal of Asian Studies* 51: 600–611.

—— 1997. *China Transformed: Historical Change and the Limits of the European Experience*. Ithaca: Cornell University Press.

Wong, R. Bin, and Peter Perdue. 1992. "Grain Markets and Food Supplies in Eighteenth-Century Hunan." In Rawski and Li, 126–144.

Woods, Robert, P. A. Watterson, and J. H. Woodward. 1988. "The Causes of Rapid Infant Mortality Decline in England and Wales, 1861–1921." *Population Studies* 42: 343–366; 43: 113–132.

Wrigley, E. A. 1978. "Fertility Strategy for the Individual and the Group." In *Historical Studies of Changing Fertility*, ed. Charles Tilly. Princeton: Princeton University Press, 135–154.

—— 1986. "Introduction." In Malthus, 1–39.

Wrigley. E. A., R. S. Davies, J. Oeppen, and R. S. Schofield. 1997. *English Population History from Family Reconstitution, 1580–1837*. Cambridge: Cambridge University Press.

Wrigley, E. A., and R. S. Schofield. 1981. *The Population History of England, 1541–1871*. Cambridge: Cambridge University Press.

Wu Chengming. 1996. "Liyong liangjia biandong yanjiu Qingdai de shichang zhenghe" (Grain price studies of market integration during the Qing). *Zhongguo jingji shi yanjiu* 2: 88–94.

Wu Deqing. 1995. "Dangdai Zhongguo lihun yanjiu" (Research on divorce in contemporary China). Ph.D. diss., Peking University, Institute of Population Research.

Wu Liangkai. 1983. "Qing qianqi nongye gugong de gongjia" (Agricultural wages during the early Qing). *Zhongguo shehui jingji shi yanjiu* 2: 1–16.

Wu Shenyuan. 1986. *Zhongguo renkou sixiang shigao* (A draft history of Chinese demographic thought). Beijing: Zhongguo shehui kexue chubanshe.

Xenos, Peter. 1974. "Asian Marriage Patterns in Transition." *Journal of Family History* 5: 58–96.

Xiao Yanfeng, Wang Hansheng, Shi Xianmin, and Lin Bing. 1990. "Xianjieduan woguo shehui jiegou de fenhua ye zhenghe" (Differentiation and integration of social structure in contemporary China). *Zhongguo shehui kexue* 4: 121–130.

Xie Yu. 1990. "What Is Natural Fertility? The Remodeling of a Concept." *Population Index* 56: 656–663.

Xu Xinwu. 1991. *Jindai Jiangnan sizhi gongye shi* (A history of homespun cloth in modern Jiangnan). Shanghai: Shanghai renmin chubanshe.

Yamaguchi, Kazuo. 1991. *Event History Analysis,* Beverly Hills: Sage Publications.

Yan Ruizhen and Wang Yuan. 1992. *Poverty and Development: A Study of China's Poor Areas.* Beijing: New World Press.

Yan Yunxiang. 1992. "Chuantong Zhongguo shehui de shusao shouji hun" (Levirate in traditional Chinese society). *Jiuzhou xuekan* 5: 91–106.

Yang, C. K. 1959. *Chinese Communist Society: The Family and the Village.* Cambridge, Mass.: Harvard University Press.

Yang, Dali L. 1996. *Calamity and Reform in China: State, Rural Society, and Institutional Change since the Great Leap Famine.* Stanford: Stanford University Press.

Yang Lien-sheng. 1955. "Schedules of Work and Rest in Imperial China." In *Studies in Chinese Institutional History.* Cambridge, Mass.: Harvard Yenching Institute, 38–52.

Yang, Martin C. 1945/1965. *Chinese Village: Taitou, Shantung Province.* New York: Columbia University Press.

Yang, Mayfair Meihui. 1994. *Gifts, Favors, and Banquets: The Art of Social Relationships in China.* Ithaca: Cornell University Press.

Yang Shuzhang. 1993. "Zhongguo shaoshuminzu renkou de zengzhang yu jihuashengyu" (Population growth and family planning among Chinese minority populations). In Population Census Office of the State Council and Department of Population Statistics of the State Statistical Bureau, *Zhongguo 1990 nian renkou pucha guoji taolunhui lunwenji* (China 1990 Population Census—papers for international seminar). Beijing: Zhongguo tongji chubanshe, 313–324.

Yao Xinwu and Yin Hua. 1994. *Zhongguo changyong renkou shuju ji* (A collection of basic data on China's population). Beijing: Zhongguo renkou chubanshe.

Yip Ka-che. 1995. *Health and National Reconstruction in Nationalist China: The Development of Modern Health Services, 1928–1937.* Ann Arbor: Association for Asian Studies.

Yu, Y. C. 1997. "Characteristics and Prospects of the Population Census of China." In *Symposium on Demography of China, 23rd IUSSP General Population Conference.* Beijing: China Population Association, 25–35.

Zeng Yi. 1989. "Is the Chinese Family Planning Program "Tightening Up'?" *Population and Development Review* 15: 333–338.

——— 1996. "Is Fertility in China in 1991–1992 Far below Replacement Level?" *Population Studies* 50: 27–34.

Zeng Yi et al. 1993. "Causes and Implications of the Recent Increase in the Reported Sex Ratio at Birth in China." *Population and Development Review* 19: 283–302, 425, 427.

Zhang Minru. 1982. *Zhongguo renkou sixiang jianshi* (A short history of Chinese demographic thought). Beijing: Zhongguo renmin daxue chubanshe.

Zhang Qingwu and Wang Weizhi. 1997. "Household Registration, Population Statistics, and Computer Management in China." In *Symposium on Demography of China, 23rd IUSSP General Population Conference*. Beijing: China Population Association, 86–94.

Zhang Weimin, Yu Hongwen, and Cui Hongyan. 1997. "Current Changes in China's Population: A Brief Analysis of the Population Data of China's 1995 1% Population Sample Survey." In *Symposium on Demography of China, 23rd IUSSP General Population Conference*. Beijing: China Population Association, 36–71.

Zhao Wenlin and Xie Shujun. 1988. *Zhongguo renkou shi* (Population history of China). Beijing: Beijing Renmin chubanshe.

Zhao Zhongwei. 1994. "Demographic Conditions and Multi-Generation Households in Chinese History: Results from Genealogical Research and Microsimulation." *Population Studies* 48: 412–425.

——— 1997a. "Deliberate Birth Control under a High-Fertility Regime: Reproductive Behavior in China before 1970." *Population and Development Review* 23: 729–768.

——— 1997b. "Long-Term Mortality Patterns in Chinese History: Evidence from a Recorded Clan Population." *Population Studies* 51: 117–128.

——— In press. "Demographic Influences and Multigenerational Household in Chinese History." In Liu Ts'ui-jung et al.

Zhou Boli. 1981. *Zhongguo caizheng shi* (A history of Chinese public finance). Shanghai: Shanghai renmin chubanshe.

——— 1984. *Zhongguo caizheng sixiang shigao* (A draft history of Chinese public finance policy). Xiamen: Fujian renmin chubanshe.

Zhu Kezhen. 1972. "Zhongguo jin wuqiannian lai qihou bianhua de chubu yanjiu" (Preliminary research on climactic change in China during the last 5,000 years). *Kexue tongbao* (Beijing) 1: 95–102.

Zhu Yong. 1987. *Qingdai zongfa yanjiu* (Studies on Qing family law). Changsha: Hunan renmin chubanshe.

Zhuang Yaer. 1995. *Zhongguo renkou qianyi shuju ji* (A collection of human migration data of China). Beijing: Zhongguo renkou chubanshe.

Index

Famine, 4, 7, 12, 16, 23, 29, 32, 35, 36, 44, 45, 119; avoidance of, 41, 56; impact on population growth, 42, 43; relief, 43; Western vs. non-Western, 43; fertility and, 92. *See also* Food

Fang Xing, 40

Fecundity, 83, 91

Feedback loop (economy/population), 37, 40, 41

Fei Xiaotong, 92, 190, 193

Fertility, 15, 62; economic conditions and, 3, 17, 20, 97–98, 119, 121; Western vs. non-Western, 8, 9, 76, 83–84, 86–87, 88–90, 96, 114–115, 138, 141; decision making, 9, 139; control, 10, 37, 41, 84, 92, 94, 96, 114, 115, 133; control within marriage, 12, 41, 83, 84, 86, 90, 98; wage rates and, 15; analysis model, 17; universal marriage and, 19; government policies regulating, 28; unregulated, 40, 83, 88, 90, 114; grain prices and, 51, 97, 110–111; age-specific, 76, 86; male, 76; polygynous, 76; planning, 81; age pattern of ("natural"), 83–84, 88, 90; Malthusian legacy, 83–84, 114; pretransition marital, 83–84, 88; nonmarital, 88, 141; transition, 92–97, 98, 114–115, 138, 150; among nobility, 97; social status as factor in, 97–98; collective and individual strategies, 97–99. *See also* Abortion; Birth(s); Contraception; Family planning

Fertility rates, 156; decline, 3, 4, 8, 9, 11, 13, 17, 21, 22, 61–62, 92, 93–94, 96, 97, 122, 133, 138–139, 155; high, 3, 104, 122; low marital, 8, 23, 41, 84–88, 86, 91, 106–107, 113, 136; replacement level (no. of children per couple), 8, 92, 93; total fertility rate (TFR), 8, 86, 96, 119; total marital fertility rate (TMFR), 8, 86; one-child-per-couple policy, 11, 94, 95–96, 120, 133, 134; variations in, 15; Two-per-Thousand, 57, 155; low, 63, 105, 121; age-specific, 87, 90; adoption and, 109; urban vs. rural, 119–120

Feudalism, 140, 150

Food: demands, 21–22; consumption per capita, 27, 29; population growth/production ratio, 29–32; production per capita, 29; population growth/consump-

tion ratio, 32–35, 40; base, 37; imports, 37; availability, 43, 51; subsidies and rationing, 131, 154. *See also* Famine

France, 48–49, 87, 138, 141, 142, 143, 144, 145

Free market system, 18, 136

Fujian, 118

Gansu, 31, 32, 118

Gender, 10, 39, 64, 79, 98, 130; mortality rates and, 44, 45, 58; in Chinese family system, 124, 125, 132

Germany, 87, 138, 142, 143, 145

Global demographic transition, 44

Goody, Jack, 138

Grain: exports, 22, 36; shortages, 22; production, 30, 31; distribution system, 45, 121, 130; prices, 51, 97, 110–111, 113; commerce in, 115

Great Leap famine, 36, 92, 119

Guangdong, 74, 118, 144

Guangxi, 118

Guizhou, 31, 32, 118

Hajnal, John, 4–5, 17, 138

Han Feizi, 177

Harrell, Stevan, 172, 173

Hayami, Akira, 39

Health: nutritional standards and, 33–34; culture, 44–47, 90–92; child, 91; maternal, 91; reproductive, 91

Health care, 37, 131; government policies and institutions, 4, 36, 44, 52, 53, 55–56; pediatric, 45–46, 49; allocation, 51, 154; policies, 51; preventive techniques, 51

Hebei, 144, 151, 156

Heilongjiang, 118, 151

Ho Ping-ti, 19, 37, 140, 161, 168 169

Hobbes, Thomas, 140

Hong Liangji, 166

Household: formation (independent residence), 17, 125, 140, 150; registration system, 119, 121, 128, 151, 154, 155; size, 121; head, 125, 127, 131; structure, 125–126, 149–151; *baojia,* 151. *See also* Family; Residence

Hsiung Ping-chen, 45

Hua Guofeng, 20

Huang, Philip, 166, 174

Human agency, 9

ventive check, 64. *See also* Population control

Mao Zedong, 20, 92, 191

Market economies, 4, 18, 136

Marriage, 10, 97, 107, 139, 142; delayed, 4, 9, 12, 15, 17, 18, 63, 64, 75, 93, 103, 106, 110, 115, 123; early, 7–8, 9, 16, 17–18, 64, 104, 114; female universal, 7–8, 12, 62, 136; never-married males, 7, 64, 69, 70–71, 106; age at, 8, 12, 20, 64, 65–67, 68, 71–72, 75, 80, 88, 95, 103, 114–115, 128, 130, 136; late, 8, 63–64, 114, 136, 138; never-married females, 8, 65, 67–68, 103, 104; early female, 12, 47, 69, 106; late male, 12, 69; economic conditions and, 15, 18; rates, 16; universal, 16, 17–18, 19, 62, 64, 75, 104; purpose of Western, 18; first, 62, 71–72, 74; late female, 67–68; cost of, 69, 77, 82; purpose of Chinese, 69, 91, 98–99; early male, 71; desire for, 75; universal male, 80; calculus of, 81–82; relations in, 81; among nobility, 86–87; coital frequency, 90–91; delayed consummation, 91; mandatory, 104; probability, 104, 127; restricted, 124; entitlement, 127; permission, 131; individualistic, 138. *See also* Nuptiality; Remarriage

Marriage forms and types: polygyny, 8, 63, 64, 75–76, 86–87, 97, 144; arranged, 9, 10, 81, 82, 91, 109, 130, 138, 144; hypergamy, 47–48, 59–60, 64–65, 79, 80, 81; patrilocal, 47; Malthusian legacy, 63–64; levirate, 65, 75, 77, 78, 82; little-daughter-in-law, 65, 75, 76–78, 82, 107; major marriage, female, 65–68; monogamy, 65, 76, 87, 89, 97; uxorilocal, 65, 75, 78–79, 82, 106, 107, 130, 140; major marriage, male, 68–75; major marriage, 75, 106; serial monogamy, 76; assigned, 81; Western vs. non-Western, 81, 114, 136; concubinage, 138; cohabitation, 141–142

Marriage market, 7–8, 115; gender-differentiated, 64, 79; mortality rates and, 64; social class and, 64, 80–81; hypergamous, 66; availability of females, 74–75, 78, 81–82, 106; economic conditions and, 81–82, 104; population growth and, 106

Marriage patterns and customs: dowries,

48, 60, 61, 65, 81; bride price, 61, 63, 64–65, 77; Western vs. non-Western, 65, 66–70, 71, 72, 138; "stalled convergence," 67–68, 71; bachelorhood, 71, 80, 81; among nobility, 71, 76, 80, 81; collective and individual strategies, 79–82, 121; among commoners, 80; education as factor in, 80–81; income as factor in, 80; residence as factor in, 80; timing, 104, 127; control of, 138

Marx, Karl, 140

Matras, Judah, 114

Medicine, 4, 51, 52, 56, 57. *See also* Health care

Mencius, 75, 90, 150, 184, 199

Middle Yangzi, 47, 78, 118

Migration, 115–119, 129, 130, 153

Misery, 42, 43, 44, 63, 123

Mobility: social, 16, 91, 140, 142; geographic, 115–118, 142

Monogamy. *See* Marriage forms and types

Moral conduct codes, 127, 130, 131

Morbidity, 33–34, 45, 61

Mortality, 4, 14, 40; in Chinese demographic system, 7, 35, 44; decision making, 9, 47, 139; deliberate, 12; causes, 15, 28; population/resource balance and, 19–20, 28–29; population growth and, 35; control, 37, 44–47, 51, 52, 57; crises, 41, 43–45; Malthusian legacy, 42–44; transition, 43–44, 92, sex-selective, 50. *See also* Life expectancy

Mortality rates: decline, 3, 4, 13, 36, 37, 43, 51–52, 122; world, 3; sex-differential, 23, 47–51, 57, 59; infant, 36, 50, 51, 52, 56, 57, 59, 64; age as factor in, 43, 44, 45; class as factor in, 43, 44, 45–47; residence as factor in, 43, 45; gender as factor in, 44, 45, 58; child, 45–47, 48–49, 51, 56, 57, 59, 61, 64, 111, 113, 136; in imperial lineage and nobility, 45, 46, 58, 59; medical intervention as factor in, 46–47; neonatal, 48, 50, 58; Western vs. non-Western, 48; perinatal, 50; among commoners, 51; female infant, 51, 57, 64, 136; male, 51, 57; female, 52, 57; epidemiological transition, 56; birth order and, 58, 59; social status as factor in, 58, 60; sex-selective, 57, 62; marriage market and, 64; high, 104; adoption and, 109; economic conditions

Technology: population growth and, 4; transfers, 21; economic growth and, 29; innovation, 29, 37, 38
Tianjin, 36, 52
Todd, Emmanuel, 139
Total fertility rate (TFR), 8, 86, 96, 119
Total marital fertility rate (TMFR), 8, 86
Trade. *See* Commerce

Ultrasound technology, 61
United Kingdom, 141, 142
United States, 18, 22, 141, 142, 143
Units, in state-controlled society, 131–132, 133
Upper Yangzi, 117, 118
Urban China, 35, 36, 68, 79, 93, 94, 95, 98, 115–116, 119, 120
Urbanization, 116

Vice, 42, 43, 63

Wages, 34, 121; marriage patterns and customs and, 15, 80, 104; low, 19; gender-equal, 39, 130; increase in, 40
War, 35, 43

Wealth. *See* Capital
Western demographic system, 12–13, 15
Western demographic transition: individual decision making in, 16–17; preventive checks in, 17; positive checks in, 44
Western family system, 17–18, 64
Western state system, 139–140, 141–145
Whyte, Martin, 67, 183
Widow, 73, 109, 113
Wolf, Arthur, 75, 184
Women, status of, 130
Wong, R. Bin, 107
World Population Conferences, 18
Wrigley, E. A., 103, 104, 160

Xinjiang, 118

Yangzi: Lower, 31, 34–35, 38–40, 47, 108, 116, 117; Middle, 47, 78, 118; Upper, 117, 118
Yunnan, 31, 32, 118

Zhejiang, 67, 72, 97–98
Zhu De, 180